Social Media Risk and Governance

*This book is dedicated to my loving wife,
Anastasia, and daughter, Adriana.*

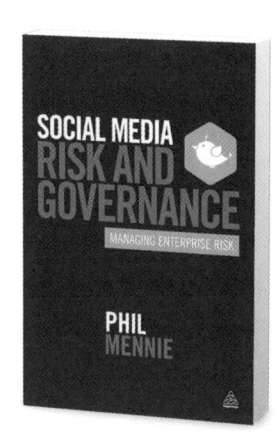

Social Media Risk and Governance
Managing enterprise risk

Phil Mennie

KoganPage

LONDON   PHILADELPHIA   NEW DELHI

Publisher's note

Every possible effort has been made to ensure that the information contained in this book is accurate at the time of going to press, and the publishers and author cannot accept responsibility for any errors or omissions, however caused. No responsibility for loss or damage occasioned to any person acting, or refraining from action, as a result of the material in this publication can be accepted by the editor, the publishers or the author.

First published in Great Britain and the United States in 2015 by Kogan Page Limited

Apart from any fair dealing for the purposes of research or private study, or criticism or review, as permitted under the Copyright, Designs and Patents Act 1988, this publication may only be reproduced, stored or transmitted, in any form or by any means, with the prior permission in writing of the publishers, or in the case of reprographic reproduction in accordance with the terms and licences issued by the CLA. Enquiries concerning reproduction outside these terms should be sent to the publishers at the undermentioned addresses:

2nd Floor, 45 Gee Street	1518 Walnut Street, Suite 1100	4737/23 Ansari Road
London EC1V 3RS	Philadelphia PA 19102	Daryaganj
United Kingdom	USA	New Delhi 110002
www.koganpage.com		India

© Phil Mennie, 2015

The right of Phil Mennie to be identified as the author of this work has been asserted by him in accordance with the Copyright, Designs and Patents Act 1988.

ISBN 978 0 7494 7457 7
E-ISBN 978 0 7494 7458 4

British Library Cataloguing-in-Publication Data

A CIP record for this book is available from the British Library.

Library of Congress Cataloging-in-Publication Data

Mennie, Phil.
 Social media risk and governance : managing enterprise risk / Phil Mennie. – 1st Edition.
   pages cm
   ISBN 978-0-7494-7457-7 (paperback) – ISBN 978-0-7494-7458-4 (E-ISBN) 1. Risk management.
2. Business enterprises–Computer networks.   3. Personnel management–Computer programs.
4. Internet–Security measures.   I. Title.
 HD61.M4596 2015
 659.20285'4678–dc23
                                                                                                                                  2015027327

Typeset by Graphicraft Limited, Hong Kong
Print production managed by Jellyfish
Printed and bound by CPI Group (UK) Ltd, Croydon CR0 4YY

CONTENTS

About the author viii
Preface ix
Acknowledgements x

01 Introduction to social media 1

What is social media? 1
The power of social media 3
Traditional social media vs enterprise social networks 5
Controlling the uncontrollable 8
Why is governance and risk management so important? 9
Chapter overview 10
Summary 12

02 Risk 13

Overview 13
Risk strategy 13
The risk continuum 17
Corporate culture 19
Social media risk maturity model 21
Risk categorization 23
Summary 33

03 Strategy 35

Overview 35
Designing a strategy 35
Getting everyone on the same page 48
Advocates and reverse-mentors 50
Crowdsourcing 56
Aligning your governance to your strategy 62
Summary 64

04 Data privacy and control 65

Overview 65
Data privacy and protection 65
Data management 71
Implementing controls 77
Summary 81

05 Governance 83

Overview 83
Roles and responsibilities 83
Moderation 93
Data quality 99
Monitoring 105
Metrics and performance indicators 109
Operating procedures 115
Summary 122

06 Policy, training and awareness 123

Overview 123
The purpose of a social media policy 123
Creating an effective social media policy 125
The purpose of a privacy policy 130
Creating an effective privacy policy 132
Training and awareness 135
Summary 139

07 Crisis management 140

Overview 140
Planning and preparation 140
Assessing an incident 146
Implementing a crisis response strategy 149
Responding to a crisis 153
Crisis testing and simulation 157
Summary 158

08 Cyber security 160

Overview   160
What is cybercrime?   160
Account management   165
Social engineering   172
Securing your network and data   179
Summary   181

09 Regulation   182

Overview   182
The social media regulatory mix   182
Dealing with character limitations   192
Future of regulation   193
Summary   194

10 The future and its opportunities   196

Overview   196
Social media analytics   196
Farewell, email!   198
Education   203
Democracy 2.0   206
Resilience and the need for trust   211
Summary   213

Further reading   214
Index   215

ABOUT THE AUTHOR

Phil Mennie is PwC's Global Social Media Risk and Governance leader, helping his clients harness the power of social media through good governance and risk management. His expertise stems from experience using web technology to better manage financial and operational data. He has led engagements across a broad range of industries, including banking and finance, where he led the development of a secure web-based payment system and a large-scale customer-facing web application to capture trade data. Phil speaks at a range of social media and technology conferences in the United Kingdom and Europe.

PREFACE

I spend my days helping clients navigate the risk and governance landscape of social media, which is what has led me to write this book. Good governance of social media is a lot more than simply having a social media policy. That's not to say that you don't need a social media policy – you do! But, this book will familiarize you with the other key components and considerations that make up a good social media governance strategy.

The big problem is that social media is used by many different stakeholders across any business. Every person in an organization is impacted by social media and almost every department has a role to play in it. It's difficult to manage social media effectively when there are so many stakeholders, each with their own objectives, agendas and skillsets and experience. Governance is all about how you operate social media and it's about bringing stakeholders together and encouraging them to work towards one common goal – the success of your business.

It became apparent to me while speaking to my clients that there are a number of common themes and problems that often crop up when implementing social media. While you can find books and articles about strategy for what I term 'traditional' social media, such as Facebook, Twitter and LinkedIn, at the time of writing there is very little material that focuses on social media within the enterprise. As such, this book will cover many of the points that need to be considered whether you're looking to harness the power of traditional social media or launch an internal social network within your organization.

I hope you enjoy it!

ACKNOWLEDGEMENTS

I'd like to acknowledge the many people who have supported me in writing this book; and also those who have supported me at other times. Inevitably I may have missed some people, but please rest assured that all your contributions are much appreciated. I'd like to thank all my colleagues at PwC, but especially Paul Smith, Grant Waterfall, Marco Amitrano, Gill Williams, Claire Reid, Simon Perry, Martin Hathaway, James Castro-Edwards, Paula Young, Charles Plunket-Checkemian, Charndeep Gill, Clare Malpass and Amanda Griffiths.

I'd also like to thank the following people:

All my friends for their support, but especially James Villarreal, Omar Budeiri, Yu-San Chan, James Bayliffe and Sandeep Krishan

My friends at the Social Media Leadership Forum, but especially Justin Hunt, Chevy Kelly and Paul Levy

Everyone at Kogan Page but especially Jasmin Naim, Jenny Volich and Megan Mondi

My family: my wife Anastasia, my daughter Adriana and my parents, Liana and Brian

Introduction to social media

01

What is social media?

One of the difficult things about defining social media is that it means different things to different people. Social media is also a relatively new concept and one that is constantly changing, with new platforms and features appearing all the time. The term social media is much broader than many think. Many believe that social media only refers to the social networks, such as Facebook, Twitter, LinkedIn, Pinterest and Reddit, to name just a few. In fact, the term social media can be used to describe any digital systems where people connect with each other. The word 'social' in this context describes the way users on a digital platform share and interact with online content. The content they share could be anything from short status updates to long-form blog posts. It could also include rich media such as images, videos or music. While a simple online radio channel wouldn't be described as a social platform on its own, it would become one if users were able to create profiles, build playlists and share them with others, due to these 'social' interactions.

Many retailers allow the products they sell to be reviewed and rated by customers. By doing this, it turns a simple online shopping site into a site driven by social interactions, where products can trend in popularity. These online retail sites allow users to share their experiences, and even their own photographs of the products, through the online shopping platform. Most people now look at travel review websites such as Tripadvisor before booking a holiday, which is another example of social media. These review sites allow users to create profiles, connect with other holidaymakers and share their experiences, photographs and feedback as well as rate the overall holiday or hotel.

Some push the definition of 'social media' even further and include messaging apps like Whatsapp, and even voice over IP (VOIP) services such as Skype and Viber in the definition of social media. In many ways, these platforms do exhibit many of the qualities associated with social media. New social networks and digital platforms with social features are emerging all the time. The new platforms enter a highly competitive environment where the existing platforms are fighting to keep users away from their competitors. Because of this, some of the most successful new platforms focus either on a specific niche or a unique feature, such as higher levels of security or a promise to never sell user data to third party advertisers. Nowadays, because social media has become so popular all over the world, almost all new online platforms include some form of social features, such as a profile or the ability to rate or 'like' content or products and share them with a user's own network of friends.

Figure 1.1 illustrates that the term social media goes far beyond just the social networks we have grown used to.

FIGURE 1.1 What is social media?

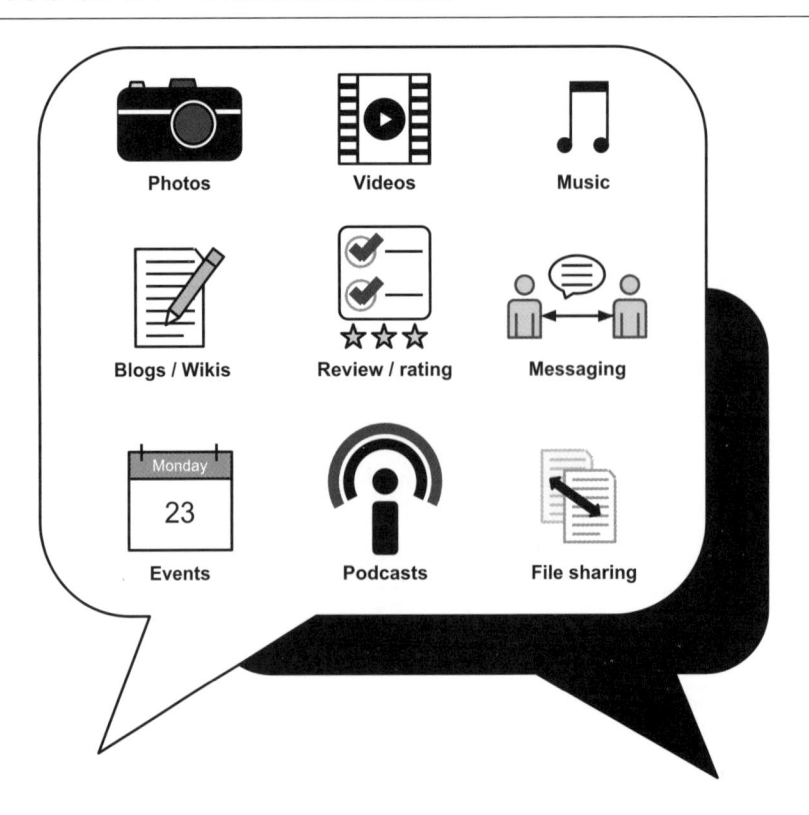

- Photos
- Videos
- Music
- Blogs / Wikis
- Review / rating
- Messaging
- Events
- Podcasts
- File sharing

The power of social media

Social media is a fast-paced, constantly changing landscape. There are hundreds of thousands of conversations taking place all over the world at any given moment and it's highly likely that social media users will be discussing your company, your people and your competitors. This is a valuable opportunity to listen to them and gain intelligence about the opinions of the people that matter most – your customers and your employees. There are a number of products on the market that allow you to listen to social media and analyse the resulting data. This data will allow you to see trends in your industry or in public opinion and can even be used to predict future trends when modelled effectively. But, you must be aware of the constraints that you face when it comes to storing or analysing social media data.

Social media has fundamentally changed the way that people communicate with companies and with each other. We're far more connected now than we ever were. Many people appear to be totally addicted to social media and spend hours on it every day – ignore it at your peril.

Businesses that harness the power of social media gain competitive advantage and stay ahead of change. In fact, there are a whole host of benefits to using social media effectively. Social media shouldn't be used as simply a channel to broadcast company marketing material. Instead, social media allows organizations to connect directly with their customers, their employees and other stakeholders in a deeper, more personal manner. Organizations that harness social media effectively can embed their vision and gain supporters and followers. They can receive real-time feedback faster and more effectively than ever before – if acted upon this can give the board insight into what people think about their company and can influence the future direction of the business.

Successful organizations are open and transparent. They build trust with their stakeholders. Social media can help you do this – it's a fast and extremely effective tool. When someone sends a message to a company on social media, it's there for the whole world to see, and the response will be judged by others. Companies that respond with automated messages or use overly 'corporate' tones face a high risk of receiving complaints en masse from social media users who feel the company isn't relating to them on a personal level. The result can be increased negative sentiment about your company, which could have a snowball effect. What starts as a small issue can be amplified greatly if picked up and shared by social media users.

Creativity and innovation can come from anywhere – it's no longer just the remit of research and development or specially created 'innovation teams'. Social media allows companies to gather ideas from their customers and employees, which it can use to significantly strengthen its competitive advantage. Understanding how to capture these ideas and turn them into reality is important for all forward-thinking organizations.

I often hear 'this doesn't apply to us because we don't do social media...' At this point, I usually have my head in my hands. If any company thinks that social media doesn't apply to them they are seriously mistaken. We're in the digital revolution. Digital technology is fundamentally changing the way that we do business.

Organizations need to know how to respond to the so-called digital disruptors – social media, mobile, data analytics and cloud. You only need to look at examples of former household names such as Blockbuster Video and Kodak to see what happens to companies that fail to keep up with change. Change is inevitable – those companies who embrace it can turn challenges into opportunities and safeguard the future success of their businesses.

CASE STUDY Risk in action: The power of social media campaigns

There have been many successful social media campaigns that have raised awareness about particular issues or which received a large amount of support from users all over the world. Most social media campaigns centre on the use of a hashtag. Three examples of successful campaigns are as follows:

- #BringBackOurGirls – started in April 2014 after the abduction of more than 200 schoolgirls in Nigeria. It was started by a group of campaigners who wanted to exert pressure on the Nigerian authorities to do more to find the girls and bring them back safely. The hashtag was used 3.3 million times. The most shared tweet was a photo of First Lady Michelle Obama holding a piece of paper with the hashtag written on it. The post was retweeted 57,000 times.

- Ice Bucket Challenge – a campaign to raise money and awareness for the Amyotrophic Lateral Sclerosis (ALS) association. People all over the world made videos of themselves pouring a bucket of ice water over their head. The 2014 campaign saw people post their videos on social media and nominate their friends to do the same. The 2014 campaign received

$98.2 million (£64 million), compared with $2.7 million (£1.8 million) during the same period in the previous year.

- #WhyIStayed and #WhyILeft – a campaign that was started in August 2014 in response to a video of an NFL player assaulting his wife. Millions of men and women used the hashtag to organize a conversation about why they stayed with an abusive partner.

These examples illustrate how powerful social media can be when users unite in support of a campaign. But, companies should be very cautious if they want to take part in the conversations around the campaigns. At the time that #WhyIStayed was trending, DiGiorno Pizza tweeted '#WhyIStayed You had pizza'. Unsurprisingly, the company received an immediate backlash from social media users and *Time* published an article with the headline 'DiGiorno used a hashtag about domestic violence to sell pizza'. Companies must understand the context of a hashtag before using it. If a mistake like this happens, apologize profusely, as DiGiorno did.

SOURCES: www.bbc.co.uk/news/blogs-trending-27298696
www.buzzfeed.com/ryanhatesthis/digiorno-whyistayed-you-had-pizza
www.bbc.co.uk/news/magazine-29013707

Traditional social media vs enterprise social networks

It won't come as a shock that the most prominent traditional social media sites are those you're most likely already familiar with, such as Facebook, Twitter, Google+, LinkedIn, Pinterest, Wikipedia and so on. These are the sites millions of us use on a daily basis, often multiple times a day using our mobiles when we're out and about, sometimes even sending messages from unusual places. The first thing that some people do in the morning is open social media, before they've even got out of bed. The key thing to take from this is that 'traditional social media' means the public platforms that we've grown used to over the last 5–10 years and that allow us to interact virtually with our friends and family, or even those we don't even know in person but have a virtual connection with online.

The key characteristics of traditional social media are:

- a profile, usually with a photo, a short biography and some personal information;

- the ability to connect with others, by 'friending', 'following' or 'connecting';
- the ability to share information with a larger network, be that with your group of friends, or a post visible to the general public;
- the ability to comment on information posted to the network by yourself or others;
- tagging or mentioning people, places or businesses in posts or in photos.

There are many social media sites out there that offer other features, however, the points above are common across most social media platforms.

Enterprise social networks, on the other hand, are technology platforms deployed within an organization to allow employees to work collaboratively, taking advantage of features similar to those in traditional social media. It's worth us touching on some of the high-level benefits of enterprise social networks so that we can understand why organizations are implementing them in the first place. There is a rapidly growing trend in industry for organizations, both small and large, to implement platforms that allow their employees to collaborate internally.

You may have already heard these platforms referred to as 'Facebook for the enterprise', or a company's 'internal Facebook'. While this does go a little way in explaining what it is, it falls far short of really defining the benefits of implementing such a system. I would avoid using such terms as it can cause confusion to the end users and give them a false impression of the platform before they've even experienced it.

An enterprise social network allows an organization's employees to connect with each other and to discover other people within their organization across the globe.

Have you ever considered how difficult it can be to find specific people or experts within a large, multinational company? Imagine that you are based in the United Kingdom and you want to find a colleague with a specific skill. Perhaps you're working on an international project involving the use of databases in a foreign country, let's say Russia, and you're stuck on a certain aspect. You want to find someone who understands databases that might be able to help, but they need to have Russian language skills too. My guess is that you would start by leveraging your own personal network, calling your connections and sending a few emails to colleagues. If you work for a large organization this could be like finding a needle in a hay stack...

One of the key features of an enterprise social platform, similar to traditional social media, is a profile. Each user has a profile to which they add their skills, contact information, photos, interests and anything else relevant.

This makes it much easier to find people in your organization by using the in-built search functions. You may think that this sounds like LinkedIn or a glorified internal phone book, however it's far more than that. The internal profiles become much more powerful when you think about the other key feature of Enterprise Social: collaboration.

Enterprise social networks enable collaborative working across the globe. Most platforms allow you to create or join 'groups'. These groups are virtual areas that allow users to connect and post content of interest to members of the group, similar to LinkedIn. So, if you work as a communications professional at a multinational tyre manufacturer, you might want to join a group that focuses on writing, branding or communications. By doing this you'll be able to see other colleagues who also work in communications around the world. Because each user has a profile with details about themselves it's an easy way to find or meet colleagues virtually and build your network. The key features of an enterprise social network are illustrated in Figure 1.2.

Some of the real power of Enterprise Social can be seen in the discussions that are taking place in groups. Using our example from earlier of trying to

FIGURE 1.2 Enterprise social network

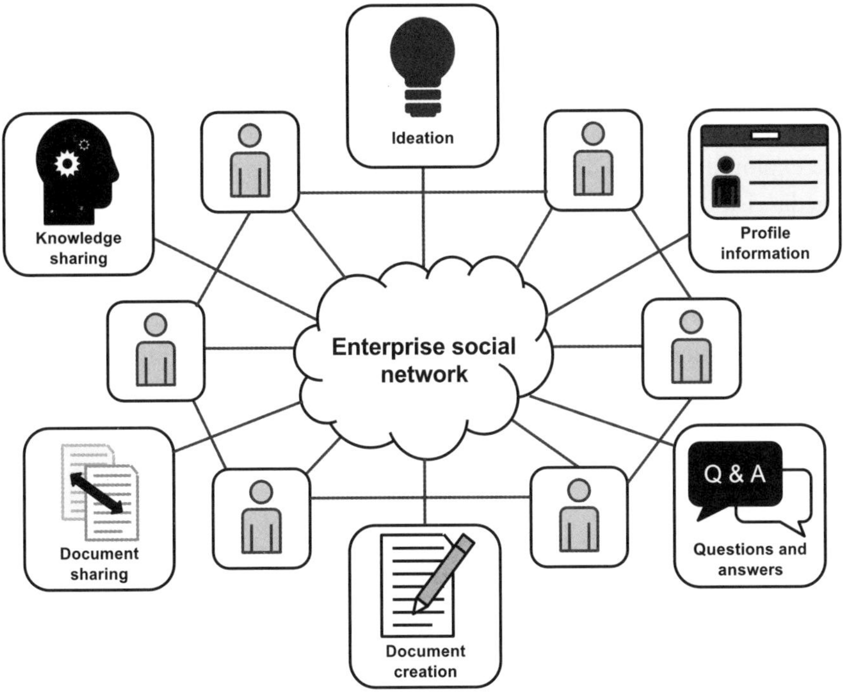

track down a Russian-speaking colleague with experience working with databases, we might enter a search on the platform. By searching, we might discover some groups devoted to discussing the very same issues we're trying to resolve. By reading through the comments and checking out the profiles of the people making the posts we might just find exactly the person we're looking for.

Many of the leading enterprise social networks also integrate into Microsoft Office. This allows two or more people to work on a document at the same time. The document is hosted 'in the cloud' (on the platform itself) and users publish their changes as they go. This reduces effort on versioning as there's no need to keep emailing the latest document around to your team – the latest version, plus all of the previous versions, are neatly organized and stored for reference. This may sound like familiar functionality to some other platforms, such as modern document repositories or file sharing tools, however what's different is the 'social' element that allows users to discover new documents and content.

Controlling the uncontrollable

Social media has grown quickly and organically. Controls weren't designed from the outset. Social media is naturally uncontrollable – people can, within reason, publish whatever they like. Because of this, organizations need to implement good governance to ensure that the risks of social media are managed without putting a stranglehold on it. If too much control is placed around social media, many of its benefits will be lost. This idea will be explored in more detail in the next chapter when we look at the social media risk continuum.

While social media was not created with control in mind, there are a number of things an organization can do to help manage risk. This book covers many of the approaches an organization can take, from designing effective policies, implementing operating procedures and monitoring for compliance. There are also a number of tools on the market that can help you manage traditional social media. We will look at some of these tools, often described as 'social risk and compliance tools', in Chapter 4, Data privacy and control.

Where traditional social media can be somewhat uncontrollable, meaning that you are reliant on the network itself to provide control features such as moderation and privacy settings, enterprise social networks are usually more configurable. As previously discussed, an enterprise social network is an internal social collaboration platform an organization implements to allow its people to connect with each other and work together. Controls must be implemented in and around the enterprise social networks in order to protect the organization. This ranges from security controls to make sure the platform is unlikely to be hacked, to governance frameworks and policies to protect the users and the data within the network.

There are many vendors in the enterprise social network market, each with their own advantages, disadvantages and configuration options. It's important that you understand what controls you need to have in place before you choose a product. If you don't, you could end up paying a lot of money for a product, only to find that it doesn't meet your risk and governance requirements. It could be very costly to implement controls afterwards and, in some cases, the vendors may not offer the protection and control you need, meaning that you might need to consider starting again with another vendor. The key takeaway here is that before making any decisions or commitments, you should carefully plan what you want from your platform, how it will align to your business objectives, and how you will manage the risks. Only then should you think about the technology that will support your goals.

Why is governance and risk management so important?

Good governance is the foundation for success in social media. A good governance strategy will help you understand how you can harness the power of social media to meet your strategic goals. It will help you keep ahead of change and ensure that you can anticipate issues in advance and address them before they turn into a problem.

There are many stakeholders who have an interest in how social media is used in an organization. Typical stakeholders could be marketing, IT, HR, operations, security, sales, and so on. A good governance strategy will bring these different groups together and ensure that everyone is on the same page, working towards a common goal. It will help you understand where you are, where you're going and how you get there, while at the same time satisfying any specific requirements along the way and staying within any constraints to help your company succeed.

It's not unusual to see eyes glaze over when the subject of governance and risk management comes up. There's a perception that governance and risk is a dull, compliance-type topic that you visit only to tick some boxes. But in fact, governance is all about the mechanics of how you operate and it's this that will make your project a success. Furthermore, if you think of all of the social media blunders that are reported in the press almost every day you can begin to understand the importance of good governance and risk management. Many of us, myself included, find some of the social media mistakes organizations make highly entertaining. And the way a company responds to an initial incident can be equally entertaining as they make a bad situation worse! Their mistakes should press home the need to ensure that you don't fall victim to the same thing yourself. This is where good governance and risk management come to the forefront.

All too often I see or hear about companies who have implemented a certain social media strategy only to have it rejected at a later stage by the dreaded risk and compliance department. The reason for this is often because the people running the project had failed to engage them and articulate how the strategy fits into the organization's risk strategy.

Chapter overview

Throughout this book I will introduce you to the key elements that make up good social media governance and risk management. The chapters are broken down into logical themes as follows:

- Chapter 2 covers the fundamentals of risk management, including risk strategy and appetite. We also look at the social media risk maturity model that is used as a way of assessing how mature your organization is in its governance and management of social media risk. Once the fundamentals have been covered, we will look at the five categories of social media risk.

- Chapter 3 is all about strategy. Strategy is an important part of governance because it sets out the direction of your social media programme and in turn dictates what governance you need to implement to support that strategy. In this chapter we will assess the key parts of a good social media strategy, such as the use of content, advocates, ideation and gamification. We will do this with a governance mindset, always thinking about the risks and considering what you need to implement to ensure you achieve your goals.

- Chapter 4 covers data privacy and control. In this chapter we will look at the key principles of data protection and assess how they relate to social media. We will also look at the management of social media data, including storage, classification and archiving. We'll then cover how to practically implement controls to ensure that social media data is managed appropriately.

- Chapter 5 is a deep dive into governance. Governance is all about how to operate social systems at a practical level. We'll look at tactics to bring the key stakeholders in your organization together and how their roles and responsibilities fit into your social media programme. The topics we'll cover in this section include monitoring and moderation, data quality, metrics and operating procedures.

- Chapter 6 covers two important policies: the social media policy and the privacy policy. In this practical chapter we will look at best practice for writing effective policies. We'll also consider ways to ensure that your policies are easily accessible and engaging, and not considered boring compliance paperwork by your employees.

- Chapter 7 provides practical advice about crisis management. We'll look at the crisis lifecycle, and cover how to plan and prepare for crises, how to assess them, how to respond to them and what to do when the crisis has passed and the dust has settled.

- Chapter 8 looks at security in the context of social media and digital systems. In this chapter we look at cybercrime and assess ways that criminals try and hack into your computer systems. We'll cover best practice for account management and look at how phishing attacks can put your social channels at risk.

- Chapter 9 covers the social media regulatory mix. We'll look at the key themes that regulations around the world attempt to control. We'll also look at practical examples of regulatory compliance in social media.

- Chapter 10 looks to the future of social media and digital technologies. In this chapter we'll look at how social media analytics will evolve to a state where accurate predictions about future behaviours can be made based on a user's social media data. We'll also look at The Onion Router (TOR) and the dark web, cryptocurrencies such as Bitcoin, biometric authentication such as retina and fingerprint scanning as well as biochip implants, cyber-bullying and the decline of email. Finally we'll consider our reliance on digital systems and look at how social media is helping safeguard freedom of speech, and how increased security and encryption will lead to a purer form of democracy.

Summary

In this chapter we introduced some of the key topics that we'll explore in depth in the rest of this book. The opportunities that social media offers to business is truly amazing, but it's vital that good governance brings the key stakeholders together and gets them working towards a common goal. An awareness of the risks of social media is vital, as without it, it won't be possible to implement the policies, procedures and controls necessary to manage those risks.

Earlier in the chapter we covered the important difference between traditional social media and enterprise social networks. Simply put, traditional social media refers to the public platforms that anyone can sign up to and use, whereas an enterprise social network is a platform a company operates to allow its employees to collaborate virtually. This understanding will be essential when considering the advice and practical steps in the rest of the book.

Risk

02

Overview

In this chapter I'll outline some of the key risks of social media, help you understand how social media can go wrong and point out where you need to focus extra attention to ensure that the risks are mitigated. I'm not going to use example after example of social media fails to push the point home about where it can all go wrong. Instead, this chapter will help you understand risk and empower you to implement good governance to ensure that you harness the power of social media, manage the risks and avoid embarrassing social media blunders. I will, however, point out good and bad examples from the real world where relevant.

I'll introduce you to some of the basic principles of risk management and explain how they relate to social media. First, a well-defined risk strategy will aid decision making, make the organization more agile and able to respond to change, and allow effective use of resources.

Risk strategy

Organizations need a risk strategy that aligns to their social media strategy and the business's overall objectives. Risk appetite and corporate culture play a big part in a risk strategy, and are essential in achieving the goals of the business through its engagement in social media.

Risk strategy should be established by the board and sets out how an organization's business objectives will be met through risk management. A well-defined risk strategy helps an organization with decision-making and supports the effective allocation of resource and spending by mandating how risks are to be managed.

Your approach to risk

Risk appetite is the amount of risk that an organization is willing to tolerate in order to deliver on its objectives. Having a clearly defined risk appetite will help an organization make decisions about how it will engage with social media to fulfil its goals while keeping the amount of risk that it is willing to tolerate within reasonable limits. The organization can then design processes to avoid exposure to unacceptable levels of risk.

Risk appetite can be categorized as low, moderate or high. A low-risk appetite will require the organization to have robust social media policies and procedures in place, with effective systems and controls to help manage risk. Likewise, an organization with a high-risk appetite may have less robust policies and less control in place because the cost of mitigating the risk may outweigh the impact of the risk occurring. It's worth pointing out that different stakeholders within the organization may view risk very differently. For example, the marketing department may want to gain as many followers or connections on their social media accounts as possible, or to generate and push out as much content as they can. The compliance department, on the other hand, may want assurances around what content the department is posting or who it is connecting with on social media. A good governance strategy will bring these stakeholders together and enable them to work together effectively. We cover this in Chapter 5.

Risk assessment

Social media is fast moving and evolving. This means that the risks it poses are also changing, with new risks emerging and existing risks gaining more or less potential impact. Because of this it's important that risk strategy is documented and that a risk assessment is completed on a regular basis. A risk assessment involves evaluating and documenting the potential risks involved in a project or activity. The risk assessment for a small short-term project will likely only take an hour or so to complete, but a larger project will need more consideration and the risk assessment may take much longer. How often a risk assessment exercise is performed will depend on the organization's risk strategy and risk appetite, but I would suggest that a full social media risk assessment be completed at least annually.

It's important for organizations to be aware of the typical risks of social media. There are five categories of social media risk, which we will look at in turn later in this chapter. I strongly recommend completing a risk assessment in order to understand what risks exist, how they might impact the organization, the likelihood of them happening and a weighting or prioritization of the risks. Doing this will allow senior management to understand where extra resource may be needed or where extra control, policy or process may need to be implemented in order to manage risk. Not all risk will have an adverse effect on the company's objectives; in fact, some risks may not be catastrophic and may represent an opportunity for the company to grow or to increase efficiency. For example, rather than lobby against upcoming social media regulation or facing fines for non-compliance, risk management can help you focus ahead of time and implement programmes to be on the right side of it. This can also result in improved reputation, and being recognized as a company that understands risk and has long-term ambitions.

Measuring risk is a tricky business. It's often difficult to quantify risk but it is possible to think through scenarios to understand how a particular risk event may impact an organization. Likelihood could be expressed using a scale of 'high', 'medium' and 'low', or alternatively a numerical scale could be used such as 1–5 (1 being not likely, 5 being extremely likely). When considering the likelihood of a risk event occurring, it's also useful to think about frequency. Is this risk event likely to happen weekly, monthly or annually?

Figure 2.1 shows a risk matrix which is often used to assess risks based on the likelihood of them occurring, and their potential impact. By deciding the impact and likelihood of a risk impacting, you can plot that risk on the

FIGURE 2.1   Risk matrix

Likelihood	Impact				
	Insignificant	Minor	Moderate	Significant	Severe
Very unlikely	Low 1	Low 2	Medium 3	Medium 4	High 5
Unlikely	Low 2	Medium 4	Medium 6	Medium 8	High 10
Possible	Low 3	Medium 6	Medium 9	High 12	Extreme 15
Likely	Medium 4	Medium 8	High 12	High 16	Extreme 20
Very Likely	Medium 5	High 10	High 15	Extreme 20	Extreme 25

matrix to see what weighting or prioritization a risk might have. As you move through the risk matrix you can see that a risk that is very unlikely to occur and which, if it did occur, would be insignificant, would end up with an overall weighting of low. Using a numerical scale to measure likelihood and impact will help ensure that risks are reported accurately. This will help management to see quickly which risks require their attention. The risk matrix can be tailored to be in line with your risk tolerance. For example, you may decide to change categories slightly by changing a risk that is possible and severe from 'extreme' to 'high'.

When we think about the impact of a certain risk, it's also useful to think about the 'velocity' or 'speed to impact'. By this I mean, how long will a particular risk event take to have a direct impact on the company, and how long will it last? Will it be a one-off event, or will it be a continued event that lasts for, say, a week? In the world of cyber security, a distributed denial of service (DDoS) attack aims to make a company's website unavailable by flooding the web server with thousands of requests. This event could last for a few days, a week, or longer, depending on how the company responds. On the other hand, a natural disaster such as an earthquake may last only a few seconds, but could have a big impact on the organization for months afterwards. We will explore cyber security in Chapter 8.

Risk assessments should be documented and reviewed. Any resulting actions should be tracked to ensure that the risks are managed appropriately, in line with risk strategy and risk appetite. Figure 2.2 shows a suggested form that you could use to assess social media risk. When assessing a risk, it may become clear that new controls need to be implemented, or existing controls changed in some way. When used in conjunction with the risk matrix (Figure 2.1), a risk assessment helps to prioritize tasks or changes and inform decisions and future resourcing needs. Documentation like this is also useful to illustrate that risk management procedures are being adhered to, should a regulator ever challenge the organization over issues relating to social media.

An activity could be something like posting content to corporate Twitter from mobile devices and the risk may be that someone could accidentally mix up the corporate account with their personal account. Controls that you may have in place to safeguard against this might be regular training or a policy dictating that corporate accounts should only be accessed from corporate devices. You may assess the likelihood of this happening to be quite possible (3) because you have a large team, but that the impact would be severe (5) because of the reputational damage that it could bring, and because you operate in a highly regulated environment that could attract fines, for example. The resulting risk rating would be 3 × 5 = 15, 'extreme'. After discussion and consultation, you may decide to implement a social risk and compliance tool, which you assess as having a risk rating of 'low'.

Unfortunately, when dealing with risk there are no absolute right or wrong answers since much depends on the future which, as we all know, is notoriously difficult to predict. However, once serious consideration has been given to the risks it's much easier to prioritize them in a way that senior management or other stakeholders can understand. This means that risk management can be operationalized in a more effective way.

The risk continuum

The risk continuum, shown in Figure 2.3, is an illustration of how risk needs to be actively managed in a balanced way. It shows the fine line between too much control and too little control, both of which would represent a high risk in social media. An environment with too little control is a high-risk strategy that does not adequately protect an organization. Without any control the business is under-protected and any significant risk event could cost the organization dearly.

On the other side, too much control will essentially over-protect the business and will cost a lot to implement. The high cost of implementing these controls and protections outweighs the likelihood of the risk event occurring. An environment that is too highly controlled may suffer from inefficiencies and fail to realize potential benefits. In social media, for example, some activities need to be controlled, but placing too much control may in fact increase risk. Social media is fast moving, and it's important that organizations are agile and able to respond to trends or conversations quickly. If there are too many controls in place around what can be posted, by whom, when and from where, the organization may miss opportunities or be unable to respond to crises in a timely manner.

Effective controls demand resource and sometimes even require external consultants to advise on how they can be created. Too many overcomplicated controls are therefore expensive to implement, and the cost may outweigh the benefit of having them in the first place.

The sweet spot is where an organization has a balance over its risk management activities, where the organization is aware of the risks involved with social media and has implemented a strategy that will allow it to meet its objectives in line with its defined risk appetite.

FIGURE 2.2 Risk assessment form

FIGURE 2.3 Risk Continuum

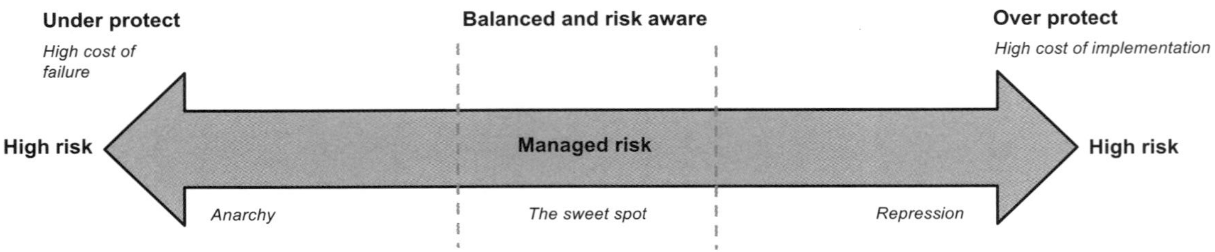

Corporate culture

Culture has a big impact on how an organization uses social media and how much risk they are willing to be exposed to. People are a company's biggest asset, but they are also the biggest risk. If a culture of doing the right thing is well embedded into the organization, it will have a positive effect on how rigorously risk will need to be managed. It is generally accepted that the tone set by those at the top has great impact on the behaviours of the workforce, therefore it is the board that is responsible for defining, communicating and demonstrating its culture in line with its risk appetite and business strategy. The organization's people need to understand what risks they are allowed to take and what is unacceptable. They must also understand the consequences of taking risks beyond tolerable levels.

For all the policies, procedures and controls which an organization implements, if the culture does not naturally reinforce the right behaviours then these risk management devices will prove ineffective. It's all too easy to point the finger at someone who has taken an inappropriate risk, but there are a number of questions that should be considered when this occurs, including:

- Why did they take the risk in the first place?
- Were they driven to it by the corporate culture?
- Did they receive the right training to identify which risks are appropriate, and which are not?

Enterprise social networks can help embed the risk culture because they allow leaders to demonstrate the behaviours that they expect from their people. Having leaders of the organization active on an enterprise social network, perhaps posting regular communications and interacting with people, sets an example to others in the company and it helps set the tone of what is acceptable and what is not.

Figure 2.4 shows the risk culture pyramid, which illustrates how culture is set and demonstrated by leadership. It surrounds everything that a company is and does. The culture, set by leadership, influences the business's goals, its strategy and its mission or purpose. It influences how people within the organization behave and sets boundaries for what is appropriate and what is inappropriate. A company's culture should align with its employees' personal ethics and values, which should in turn set a precedent for how employees behave. Furthermore, messages about corporate culture should be visible within all company communications, whether that be top-down corporate communications or those between individuals.

FIGURE 2.4 Risk culture pyramid

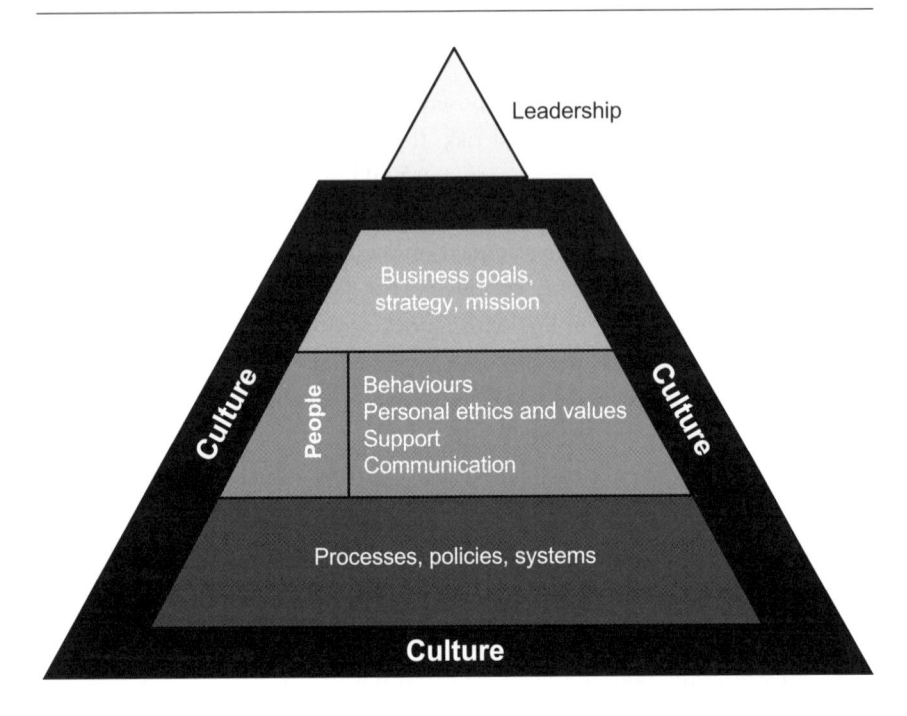

Pyramid layers from top to bottom: Leadership; Business goals, strategy, mission; Behaviours, Personal ethics and values, Support, Communication (with "People" label); Processes, policies, systems. "Culture" labels appear on the left, right, and bottom edges.

Finally, policies and procedures should be aligned to the culture of the organization. If policies undermine company values or ethics, for example by enforcing behaviours or actions that go against the ethics of that company, it will have a negative impact on culture in general.

All of this is particularly important for social media because, as you'll see throughout this book, good ethics are important to ensuring social media success. There are many examples where organizations have used unethical tactics in order to promote their products or encourage users to engage with them but, in almost all cases, unethical behaviour like this results in more significant issues that could have been avoided. Hashtag-hijacking is the most common example of the unethical tactics that some companies have used, by adding trending hashtags to their posts out of context and for the sole purpose of increasing the reach of the post. When a hashtag supporting a social cause is hijacked it often causes the highest level of resentment from users.

Social media risk maturity model

Hopefully it's clear that there is not just one accepted approach to social media risk management, and that the extent to which an organization manages social media risk depends on its culture, risk appetite and overall business strategy. That said, the social media risk maturity model, illustrated in Figure 2.5, can help an organization understand where they are in terms of social media risk management, their 'current maturity', and help them get to where they want to be, their 'aspired maturity'.

The social media risk maturity model shows five levels of maturity, each of which builds on the previous levels. Level 1, 'Initial', is the most basic level of social media risk management. As you can see from the model, an organization at this level will have recognized the risks of social media but has not standardized processes around the management of risk. As you progress through the levels, the amount of risk management, processes, policies and controls increases until you get to level 5, 'Optimized'.

An organization with current maturity at level 2, 'Repeatable', will understand the risks that social media poses and may even have completed risk assessments in relation to it. But there will be no standardized processes or procedures and social media will be managed in an ad-hoc fashion, with little or no formal training available to employees.

At level 3, 'Defined', efforts have been made to implement processes, procedures and policies to govern the use of social media, but there is little control to ensure that they are being followed or adhered to consistently.

When an organization is operating with a maturity at level 4, 'Managed', social media ownership, responsibility and accountability are defined, although there may be a lack of board sponsorship. At this stage, robust processes and policies are defined, documented and controlled, although tools to support or monitor these processes and policies may be lacking. At level 4 you might find that systems to review processes and policies are in place, but that metrics to track social media are basic, or lacking.

Finally, an organization operating at level 5, 'Optimized', understands the impact of social media and it is a board-level agenda. The processes and policies are defined, documented and monitored and a regular review cycle is in place. An organization operating at this level will likely have systems in place to manage social media, such as Social Risk and Compliance tools (see discussion later in this chapter under 'Access controls'), and the tools themselves will be monitored and tested on a regular basis. Incident and

FIGURE 2.5 Social media risk maturity model

Level 1	Level 2	Level 3	Level 4	Level 5
Initial	**Repeatable**	**Defined**	**Managed**	**Optimized**
The organization has recognized the risks of social media, however, there are no standardized processes and any risks are managed on an ad-hoc basis.	Social media has a clear owner, however, it is not being managed through standardized processes. There is no formal training nor procedures being followed.	Social media has a clear owner. Simple processes are defined and documented but are not consistently followed or enforced. Formal training is available and attendance monitored.	Accountability and ownership is clearly defined. Robust processes are defined, documented and monitored. Management tools are used in a limited or fragmented way. Processes are regularly reviewed and improved. Formal training is available and attendance monitored.	Social media and its impact is a board-level agenda which permeates through the organization. Processes and policies are defined, documented, monitored and reviewed regularly. Systems are in place to manage social media and interactions are reviewed and tracked. A comprehensive incident management and escalation process is defined and is regularly tested. Reporting is aligned to business strategy.

crisis management will be well embedded into the organization, including how social media incidents will be addressed or how social media might be used during some other unrelated crisis. Adequate resource, and likely dedicated teams, will be responsible for social media on a day-to-day basis.

It's important to remember that not all organizations aim to be level 5, 'Optimized', and nor should they. It may be that the cost of achieving level 5 maturity could outweigh the benefit of a social media programme in the first place. Still, this model can be used to understand where you are and help you reach your aspired level of maturity.

Risk categorization

There are, broadly speaking, five categories of social media risk, as illustrated in Figure 2.6. Some risks may have an impact on one or more categories.

FIGURE 2.6

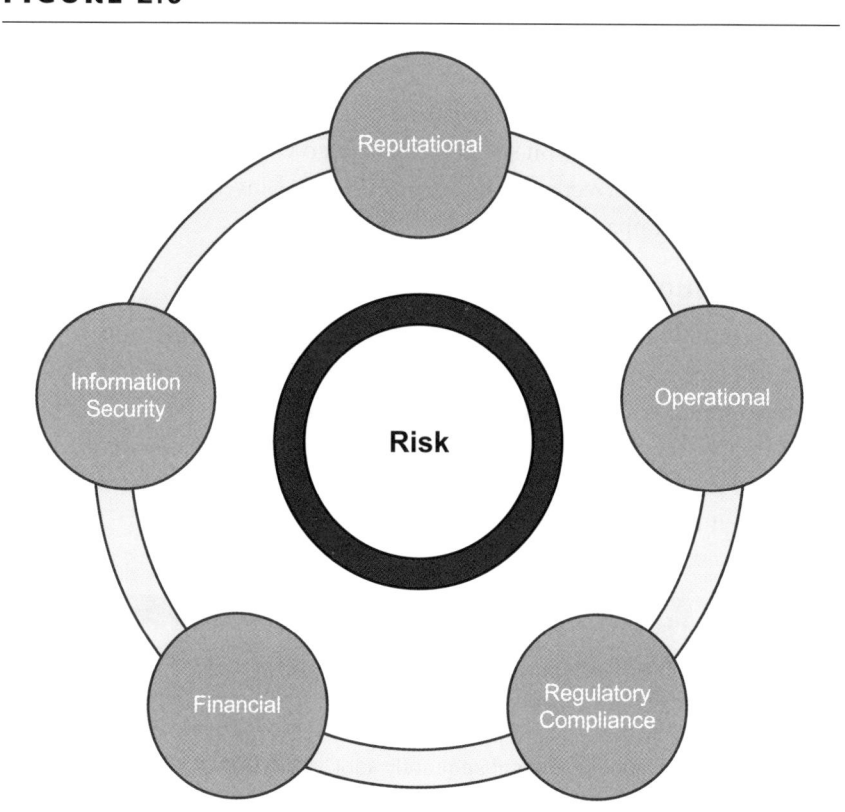

For example, a hacked Twitter account would probably be classified as an information security risk, but if the account was used to post abusive messages it may cause reputational damage. Efforts to regain control of the hacked account would place heavy demand on resource, which is an operational risk. Finally, the hack may lead to an investigation by a regulator, which may enforce financial penalties.

Reputational risks

Reputational risks are most commonly attributed to traditional social media. The risk stems from people posting content online, either deliberately or by accident, which can harm the reputation of an organization. As mentioned previously, a common mistake is when an employee who tweets on behalf of the organization mixes up his or her personal account with the organization's official account. It can be very embarrassing when a rude or inappropriate tweet is sent out from a company's official channel, but unfortunately there are many examples of this.

It's surprising that there are still many executives who don't understand how risky social media can be. For example, Ryan Air boss, Michael O'Leary, hosted a Q&A session on Twitter without regard to how Twitter users might react to some of his comments, such as 'Nice pic. Phwoaaarr!' A company's reputation takes time to build and trust can be lost in the blink of an eye. Seemingly small mistakes on social media can go viral fast. If these incidents are not managed correctly it can lead to a loss of investor confidence and have a negative impact on a company's share price.

Fake accounts

Fake accounts pose a threat to organizations and it's important to have plans in place to deal with this risk. There have been examples in the past where seemingly official, but nonetheless fake, accounts have been set up to act as though they were speaking on a company's behalf. These accounts can attract a lot of followers as well as considerable media attention, which can be a real embarrassment to the company.

CASE STUDY   Risk in action: BP fake Twitter account

In 2010 an oil rig exploded and subsequently sank in the Gulf of Mexico, causing a huge oil spill which is considered to be the largest accidental marine oil spill in the history of the petroleum industry. The rig was operated by British Petroleum (BP) and shortly after the news hit the media, BP faced a barrage of complaints and condemnation from shocked and concerned people all over the world.

What happened next was that a fake and satirical Twitter account was created called @BPGlobalPR which mercilessly posted tweets with dark humour mocking BP, such as 'The good news: Mermaids are real. The bad news: they are now extinct. #bpcares'. In the space of a few months the total number of users following the fake twitter account surpassed those following BP's official Twitter account, gaining over 150,000 followers.

BP's response to the Twitter incident was slow, which you might argue is understandable given that their attention was on fixing the spill in the first place. But this incident does show just how difficult it is for some companies to keep control over their reputation online.

SOURCE: http://blogs.wsj.com/digits/2010/05/24/fake-bp-twitter-account-draws-followers-with-oil-spill-satire/

World events

In order to use social media effectively it's important that companies listen to other users and think before posting. There are many examples of companies using disasters to sell their products. This is clearly a sensitive issue. For example, many would agree it inappropriate for a life insurance company to promote their services in direct connection following some type of catastrophe, such as a plane crash or explosion. Amazingly, though, this is what one life insurance company did shortly after the Malaysian Airlines flight 17 disaster in eastern Ukraine in 2014. When disasters occur it doesn't take long for hashtags or related words to start trending on social media. Companies should carefully consider the impact of posting marketing material linked to disasters as it often attracts high levels of condemnation from social media users. It's often also picked up by the traditional media channels such as TV or the papers, and consequently has an even more damaging effect on the company's image and reputation.

Operational risks

The operational risks of social media also threaten organizations. Far too often I see companies who are worried that their employees are going to be wasting time on social media when they should be working. Often this means that the company has a policy of blocking all social media sites.

But really, is there any point in doing this in this day and age? If you're a fan of social media then the chances are that you're going to have a smartphone to access all of your social media accounts. If an employee can't access Facebook or Twitter at work, they can easily circumvent the block by using an alternative personal device such as a smartphone or tablet. There are other regulatory and compliance issues to consider but we'll cover them in the Regulatory compliance risks section of this chapter.

So, let's think about employee effectiveness and how social media impacts it. I would argue that employees can be motivated by being allowed to use social media for personal use, but what we're ignoring is the business benefit. If you do a quick online search for social media and business you see that there are many articles about how businesses are using social media to gain competitive advantage, recruit top people and even sell products and services. The main risk here is that if a business doesn't embrace social media, it could lose its competitive advantage.

An additional risk relates to culture. The exact definition of 'Generation Y', or 'millennials', is contested, but generally speaking it refers to those people who entered work between 2000 and 2010. These people are 'digital natives' – they have grown up with technology and expect their employers to have embraced it. In 2011 and 2013 PwC, the global network of professional services firms, published 'Millennials at work: Reshaping the workplace' and 'NextGen: A global generational survey 2013' respectively. The reports highlight how millennials approach work and employment. Some millennials admit to breaking policy if it is going to help them complete a task more quickly or efficiently. For example, Drop Box is a cloud-based file sharing service that many organizations block because they are – quite rightly – concerned about what data might be exchanged on the platform. The reason for the concern is because the organization will have no control over what happens to that data once it is uploaded. Yet, many millennials admit to using such systems, even though they know that they are breaking company policy, usually because the company offers no alternative. The solution is to offer a decent alternative that the organization can control. Millenials are used to easy-to-use, always-on, connected services and devices. If you offer them no corporate or approved services to use, they will simply use others without your knowledge.

Furthermore, many millennials expect their employers to be as comfortable with digital technologies as they are themselves. Organizations are constantly fighting a battle to find and employ the best talent, and organizations can appeal more to the younger generation by showing that they are forward-thinking, digitally-aware companies.

Moderation

Another operational risk of social media is the risk that social media is not sufficiently governed. An example of this could be around moderation. In social media, moderation is the activity of removing or censoring posts that appear on your various pages. With a lack of governance and oversight, moderation may be sporadic or could even have serious legal implications for a business. For example, if you run a social media account and users post abusive or threatening messages on it, what should you do? Most would agree that you should remove these posts, but by doing so you are setting a precedent that the post will be moderated. It then becomes your responsibility to continually monitor the posts and determine what is appropriate and what is not. This poses a few risks because, first, it may require considerable resource to monitor and moderate the pages. Second, unless very clear guidance exists about what should be moderated, and in what way, the removal of posts may anger social media users who feel that their voice is being censored.

If you run an enterprise social network that is used to share knowledge, reports and other work-related documents, your organization will be responsible for the content within that network. The risk of not monitoring or moderating the network is high because your users may use it to distribute documents to which they do not have copyright licences, or worse, to distribute illegal materials.

The topic of moderation is covered in more detail in Chapter 5, Governance.

CASE STUDY Risk in action: ChapStick – comment moderation

In 2011, ChapStick, a brand of lip balm manufactured by Pfizer Consumer Healthcare, posted a new advertising image on its Facebook page showing a woman bending over the back of a sofa with her behind in the air and a caption that read 'Where do lost ChapSticks go?' As offensive content goes, this is probably on the less provoking side of the scale, however, some social media users were disgusted by it and complained about it by leaving a comment.

It's what happened next that really caused problems. Comments from users complaining about the image started getting deleted, which only angered users even more and caused them to leave more comments asking why their comments had been removed. People who weren't even fans of ChapStick started to catch on and became angry about comments being deleted, so they joined in, amplifying the outrage at the brand even further.

With so many comments coming in, some were getting through before ChapStick had the chance to delete them. The image was later removed.

This goes to show that moderation should be carefully executed. Social media users do not like to be censored and it can backfire, as it did in this case, by encouraging others to post comments in support of the users whose comments are being deleted. Nobody likes to receive negative comments, but if they are not offensive, threatening, or a breach of the social network's terms and conditions, removing them may look like an act of censorship or a crude and deceptive attempt at improving a brand's image. In this case, ChapStick should have removed the image earlier and apologised for any offence caused.

SOURCE: www.adweek.com/adfreak/chapstick-gets-itself-social-media-death-spiral-136097

Innovation

One of the benefits of social media is its ability to foster innovation. Social media, both traditional and enterprise, allow people to connect with each other and work together virtually. Companies can engage with their customers and get real-time reviews and suggestions about their products or services. This can be vital information for the company as it ponders new services or product lines and allows it to use the ideas of a wider range of people and, in turn, gain competitive advantage. Enterprise social networks provide companies with the full power of their people in a way that was previously extremely difficult. No longer is innovation solely the realm of the research and development teams. Many of the tools allow 'ideation', which is the concept of allowing people to submit ideas online and vote other ideas up and down. This 'crowdsourcing' of ideas with natural peer review (through votes and comments) can be harnessed to drive efficiencies and further encourage innovation. The main operational risk is that if these tools are ignored, or if their implementation is ineffective, there is a chance that a company will lose out on the benefits that could in turn lead to loss of competitiveness, especially if their competitors adopt these technologies. Another point to consider is how easy it might be for someone to cheat the system in some way in order to make their ideas gain more votes, thereby eroding value and making strong ideas less prominent.

Regulatory compliance risks

There are a number of regulatory and compliance risks that affect social media. The risks differ depending on where you are in the world; for example, there are a large number of regulatory bodies in the United States that have issued specific requirements and guidelines around social media. In March 2015 the UK's financial regulator, the Financial Conduct Authority (FCA), published guidance on how to maintain compliance when using social media. Apart from that, however, at time of writing other UK regulators had very little in the way of requirements or guidance around social media specifically. Instead, UK advertising codes cover social media use in advertising.

A particular challenge that companies have experienced when implementing global enterprise social networks is data privacy and protection. Organizations need to be able to prove that they have appropriate controls in place to safeguard data. Much of the data privacy and protection legislation around the world conflicts. For example, in the EU much of the legislation seeks to protect data and stop it being shared without the explicit permission of the owner. In the United States, on the other hand, eDiscovery laws dictate that all information is discoverable when needed for legal proceedings, meaning it can be accessed and held to support a legal case. This often puts the laws head-to-head – on one side, EU data can't leave the EU without permission; on the other side, US data needs to be discoverable. Significant challenges arise when we think about a global system, hosted in, let's say the United Kingdom, but accessed by employees in the United Kingdom, United States and Germany. What happens to the data? Which laws take precedence? This is a complex topic that is covered in more detail in Chapter 4.

The plot thickens on our data privacy journey when we start thinking about data retention and archiving laws. Companies are required to retain certain documents and files for set periods of time. An example of this is the number of years that a company is required to keep its tax returns or accounts before they can, or should, be deleted. If a company breaks these laws it risks heavy fines. Companies also need to keep archives of emails and other communications sent and received so that they can use them if required in a legal case. Now, what about data held on enterprise social platforms or messages posted on external social networks? If email communications need to be retained then it's a safe bet that social networking communications also need to be retained. Some of the strategies for data retention of this kind are covered in more detail in Chapter 4.

Many countries have laws about advertising standards that aim to protect the consumer. It's important to remember that these standards apply to all forms of marketing, and therefore include social media. The regulations may state that advertisements and endorsements need to be clearly marked as such so that social media users understand that that's what they are. Because of this, many companies use the hashtag '#ad' or '#endorsed' to denote posts that are advertisements or endorsements. Another strategy for ensuring regulatory compliance is attaching an image containing terms and conditions to the original post.

You can find out more about how to respond to regulation in Chapter 9, Regulatory response.

Financial risks

Probably one of the most serious financial risks for larger companies is the negative effect social media can have on its share price. Yet, amazingly, many business executives just don't understand this. They understand that reputational issues or a bad article in the press or print media can impact their share price so I'm surprised that a disconnect to social media still exists. After all, there's a giveaway in the word 'media'. There are lots of examples of companies who have suffered declines in their share price following an error. In April 2009 Domino's Pizza suffered a 10 per cent drop in the value of their share price when a video showing two rogue employees committing public health law violations went viral on YouTube and disgusted viewers. The lack of appropriate processes to identify a social media incident and then to respond in a timely manner can lead to investor confidence being lost due to the incident spreading across the globe virally through social media.

Social media can also impact the stock markets more broadly. In April 2013 a hacking group called the Syrian Electronic Army (SEA) hacked the Associated Press Twitter account and posted a tweet with the text 'Breaking: Two Explosions in the White House and Barack Obama is injured'. This caused panic on Wall Street and led to an almost instant drop in the Dow Jones Industrial Average, wiping out $136 billion in value before recovering shortly afterwards.

Remediation efforts are another big financial risk. In 2012 a UK-based bank suffered an IT outage that affected many of its customers. The remediation efforts to fix the problem and provide assurance that it wouldn't happen again were likely sizeable. These risks exist in social media also. If you suffer a social media incident – for example, if your main company account is hacked – you must act quickly to resolve the issue. You'll likely have to pull resource from other projects to provide focus on resolving the issues with your account. This may in turn attract the attention of the regulator, who can impose fines or financial penalties on your organization.

Information security risks

Social media developed organically, meaning that certain security controls that you would expect in corporate systems nowadays weren't implemented very effectively in the early days of social media. Social media has also changed the way that we communicate, which has led to changes in what we share about ourselves online.

Access controls

One of the problems with social networks is the challenge around account management. Twitter, for example, does not allow multiple people to log in to one account. So if you have an account for @MyCompany, you only have one username and password to access that account. This means that if you have a team of people who are tweeting on your company's behalf, they will either be sharing the username and password or using some kind of third party management system. The problem of sharing usernames and passwords is that it increases the risk of the credentials being intercepted by a hacker. For example, if the password for the account is changed you will need to communicate it to the group of people who need access to the account. Although not ideal, most people will send the details by email. This increases the risk that a recipient may be included in error, or that one of the recipients could forward on the message (either intentionally or by mistake). When login credentials are shared via email there is a risk that the email could be intercepted by applications installed on computer networks by hackers which eavesdrop on email traffic. Or, if the login credentials are communicated over the phone, the person receiving the credentials may decide to write them down on a piece of paper and pin it to their screen. The sharing of login credentials also means that it's not possible to see who posted what to the twitter page as everyone is sharing the same username. Whichever way you look at it, sharing login credentials is risky.

The best way to solve this predicament is to implement a system to manage social media interactions. These systems are referred to as social risk and compliance tools. There are many vendors out there and each offer different features such as analytics, sentiment analysis, post scheduling etc. Something that most have in common is that you connect your account to the management system, and each of the users who needs access to that account gets their own login credentials to the management system. This means that they log in to the management system and post updates through it rather than logging in directly to the social media account. This helps reduce the risk of login credentials being stolen. It also means that there is a central management system that is used to create or disable users, for example when someone leaves the company. While this sounds like the ideal solution for managing this risk, it means that you are putting your trust in the vendor to ensure that your account details and other information are secure. If the vendor does not follow good security practices it may be hacked, exposing all of your data or information.

Social risk and compliance tools are covered in more detail in Chapter 4, Data privacy and control.

Careless employees

Unfortunately, people are often the weakest link in the chain when it comes to security. Because of this, company culture and appropriate training are vital. Employees can be duped into sharing information with an attacker. The most common attack of this kind is 'phishing', which is where a user receives an official-looking email asking them to log in to their social media account. Unfortunately for the unsuspecting user, in a phishing attack, they will be logging in to a malicious website that simply looks like the real deal. When they log in, their user credentials can be stolen easily by the attacker.

Careless employees can also be the reason for confidential or sensitive information being shared on social networks when it should not be. Without the appropriate training and awareness, a user may inadvertently announce to the world that your company is about to be acquired, or may share negative views about one of your company's own products. Many of the social media fails are down to users simply making mistakes, for example by accidentally posting something from the company's official account instead of their own personal account. Keeping your confidential information confidential is of the utmost importance to any organization and although often not deliberate, a careless employee can easily make a mistake.

Third parties

Knowing where your data is and how it is protected is vital to the longevity of a business. In an enterprise social network your data may be hosted on data servers that are owned and controlled by the platform vendor. This means that you are reliant on the vendor to ensure that the appropriate information security controls are in place and that the platform itself is resilient, meaning that it won't be unavailable or offline. This risk can be a real headache for many businesses and requires a lot of thought. The process of acquiring an enterprise social network can be long and drawn out. It can involve a long contracting period, security, risk and privacy assessments, external assurance on the vendor's platform and sometimes even security testing, or 'penetration testing', to ensure that the platform sufficiently protects its users' data.

This point is also valid for traditional social media as well as cloud-based services in general. By storing your data in the cloud or on a vendor's servers you are relying on that vendor to keep your data secure. If you use a social risk and compliance tool you are entering a trust relationship with the vendor as they have access to your accounts and some of your data. You should seek assurances that security issues are addressed and that data is being handled appropriately. In the eyes of a regulator, this is the company's responsibility, not the vendor's, and it is the company that is ultimately responsible should a data breach occur.

Regulatory compliance risk rears its head here too. You risk litigation if you do not have the appropriate controls in place to stop information being shared incorrectly cross-territory. For example, you may need to adhere to laws in the EU which dictate where HR data can be accessed from, or in the United States you may be required to provide data to adhere to a data request from a court, but you need to be careful not to break the EU laws at the same time. We will focus on this topic in a lot more detail in Chapter 4, Data privacy and control, where we'll be discussing some of the practical steps that you can take to ensure compliance and protect your data.

Summary

In this chapter you were introduced to the concept of social media risk. You should now feel comfortable with some of the basic concepts of risk management, and understand how risk can be measured and assessed. A company's risk appetite and tolerance to risk should be set by leadership, which influences the culture of the organization and the behaviours of the people working for that organization.

By using the social media risk maturity model (see Figure 2.5), you can assess how mature your organization is in terms of social media risk management and governance. This will inform your decisions about what controls, governance and risk management principles you should incorporate into your operating model.

Finally, we have touched on each of the social media risk categories, which should make you more aware of the risks that social media poses. The following chapters of this book will take you on a journey through the key elements that make up good social media governance. By implementing the suggestions in the following chapters you will go a long way towards achieving your goals of success in social media while managing the associated risks.

Strategy

03

Overview

Strategy is an important element to consider when it comes to thinking about governance and risk management. Governance and risk management are redundant if they have no strategy to support. Likewise, a strategy without supporting governance and an understanding of any potential risks is likely to fail.

'Social media' is far broader than just how a company uses Twitter, Facebook or YouTube. In this chapter, we look at some of the other ways that you might want to use social media as part of your overall social media programme. Throughout the chapter the examples and ideas will be presented with governance in mind so that the concepts can be implemented and their benefits realized.

Whether you're looking at social media inside or outside of your organization, you will need strategies to engage a wide range of stakeholders. These could include company employees, customers and other departments such as HR, IT, Risk and Compliance and so on. This chapter will give you the tools you need to design a strategy with the appropriate governance to support it. It will also give you the confidence to engage other departments effectively in order to foster their support, which is something we will build on further in Chapter 5 and throughout this book.

Designing a strategy

Purpose

It's important to understand what exactly you want to achieve from social media. Once you know this, you can think about the steps you need to take in order to achieve your objectives, and consider what governance you might need to support it. The purpose of your social media programme should align to your organization's objectives as a whole as well as the ethos of the organization. For example, if your organization prides itself on transparency and doing the right thing, then your social media programme should reflect this. Your social media programme should not be a 'bolt-on' that operates independently from the organization.

There are a wide number of reasons that you might want to use social media, often described as 'use-cases', such as:

- *Increasing brand visibility.* Social media is an excellent way to increase brand visibility due to the viral effect of a lot of social media content. If your content touches someone in a positive way, they may be tempted to share that content among their own network. This amplification effect is extremely powerful.
- *Improving customer services.* Many customers now turn to social media as their preferred method of contacting a company because of the speed and openness of the communication. Many organizations are now moving away from the traditional call centre customer service operations and are focusing their support online or through social media support teams. It's important to remember that some customers will find this frustrating, and prefer to speak to a human being. Therefore, it is best to consider your customer base, and establish an appropriate balance accordingly.
- *Promoting products or services.* Clearly, this is a big one that won't need much explanation. I'm sure that we've all seen social media, as well as other marketing channels, used to promote specific products or services. If this is one of your objectives for your social media programme you should ensure that any ethical standards you have for promotion in other channels are replicated within social media. This may seem obvious, but it's astounding how many people see social media as a 'wild west', where anything goes!
- *Driving engagement with your customers, employees or suppliers.* You may want to better connect with your customers, so that you can listen to their needs and provide them with the products and services that they want, when they want them. This is also an excellent way of gaining valuable feedback from your customers as to what they like and dislike about your products or services.
- *Connecting your employees.* Enterprise social networks in particular are great for helping your employees connect with each other. Especially if you are a large organization with disparate or siloed teams operating in different physical locations, helping your

employees connect will allow you to increase employee engagement, satisfaction and efficiency.

- *Knowledge sharing.* Social media can break down silos and enable information and knowledge to be shared throughout your organization more effectively. This allows your people to find the information that they need quickly, and in turn, to work more efficiently.

- *Recruitment.* Social media can be a very effective tool for recruitment. Anyone who's active on LinkedIn will know that it is used actively by recruitment agencies and headhunters to advertise new positions and find potential candidates. Jobs are posted and shared through social media and some networks, such as LinkedIn, offer premium services to help recruitment professionals find and target prospective candidates. Other innovative uses of social media for recruitment that I've seen are where an organization uses social media to tell a story about what it's like to work at that organization. They publish blogs about 'a day in the life of person X' where someone at the company shares information about what it's like to work there on a day-to-day basis. This puts a face to a brand and makes it easier for people to relate to your organization.

As you can see, there are many reasons you might want to embark on a social media programme and the list above is by no means exhaustive. However, it's worth pointing out that you don't need to do everything all at once, and nor should you. How much you can attempt or achieve in social media will depend on the culture of your organization, the maturity of social media use within it, and – of course – your budget! Whatever you decide, the first step to creating a solid strategy is to define and document the purpose of your social media programme.

Listening

Before kicking off any social media programme or campaign it's important to listen and monitor what is happening on social media. If you don't, you are unlikely to achieve your objectives, and may even end up doing more harm than good. Social media is a place for conversations. It's where real people connect with each other, sharing things with their networks and engaging with others on a human level. Your organization can be part of those conversations, but as with face-to-face communication, you wouldn't butt into an existing conversation between a group of people and push your own points while totally disregarding what the others are saying. Well, some might do this, but good etiquette is outside the scope of this book!

It's likely that conversations will be taking place about your company, its products, your competitors or your competitors' products. You have the opportunity to hear what people think about these, and you should take it. Many of your customers and employees will already be active in social media so once you've established the purpose of your social media programme you should complete an exercise to understand what relevant conversations are already taking place, where they're happening and who the influencers are. Once you've completed an exercise to analyse the conversations in social media, don't stop there – you should continue this monitoring constantly. Conversations are fluid and are taking place all the time. Opinions, influencers and topics of discussion will change over time, therefore you need to ensure you have a mechanism to continue listening. Even if your current campaign comes to an end, listening should continue as it is one of the ways that you can be alerted to, or even predict, a crisis. Crisis management is covered in more detail in Chapter 7.

There are many tools that can help you with social media listening and monitoring, and the market appears to be quite saturated in this respect. Whichever platform or tool you choose, ensure that it fits your needs and allows you to identify the social media conversations you want to be part of. The openness and transparency of social media means that you can even listen to conversations between your competitors and their customers, something that can give you a significant competitive advantage if you're able to act on that information. But don't forget that your competitors will also be able to listen to the conversations between you and your customers, so you will need to ensure that you continue to listen, engage appropriately and bring new products and services to market in order to stay competitive.

Content

It's often said that in social media or online, 'content is king'. If you work in marketing, you may have grown to dislike this phrase. It's a term that was splashed around quite a lot in the past. However, I do feel that it's useful for those who haven't worked in marketing. I quite like it because it emphasizes the point that to engage in social media effectively you need to have good content that will engage others. Many times I've been approached by clients or colleagues who tell me that they want to get on social media and promote their products or services. Their next question is usually 'so, how do I monitor and measure the impact of my posts?' When I ask what content they're planning to use in their campaign I usually receive a confused look or a 'we'll cross that bridge later...' This is not the right way to plan a social media programme. You need to create exciting and engaging content, use social media to post that content, and allow your followers or supporters to share that content across their networks.

The content you post also needs to be fit for purpose and suitable for sharing on social media. The vast majority of users access social media through their smartphones and, therefore, you need to ensure that your content is suitable for that medium. If you've ever tried reading a 100-page PDF report on a smartphone, you'll know what I mean. Constantly zooming in and out, scrolling in all directions... it's very frustrating for the user and will mean that much of your content is ignored.

Keep in mind also that attention spans are low online and on social media. People want information or the answer to their question quickly. It's therefore your responsibility as the content provider to give them what they want, in the format that they want. If you don't, you'll probably find that your content has very low engagement metrics. Don't overcomplicate it either, as Einstein said, 'Any intelligent fool can make things bigger and more complex... It takes a touch of genius – and a lot of courage – to move in the opposite direction.'

Also remember the constraints of the social media networks themselves. Posting on Twitter is totally different to posting on Pinterest or YouTube, for example. You need to choose the right content for the network.

Content that works well for social media includes:

- *Blogs*. Blogs are extremely popular on the internet and they give the ability to publish to the masses. Blogs are short-form text, usually around 350 words in length. Blogs can be about anything, literally! If you plan to use blogs in your content strategy, you should consider who is going to be writing, what they're going to be writing about and what the call to action is for the reader. A blog, or any piece of writing, needs a punchy and engaging title or heading that entices people to read the blog. The use of short sentences is advisable in blogs as they make it easier for a reader to quickly scan through the content.
- *Infographics*. These are images that convey statistics, facts or other information in a visually appealing format. Infographics are usually long (vertically) and allow the viewer to scroll down through a story, reading break-out text, quotes and viewing images as they scroll. Infographics are popular online with many being shared on social media networks, but particularly on Pinterest.

- *Pictures/photos.* As the saying goes, 'a picture is worth a thousand words', and as social media users want to consume information quickly and easily, pictures can be an effective way of conveying your messages. Most social networks allow pictures to be embedded directly into posts, and have become a staple of most engaging posts.

- *Video.* If you want to know how to do something, such as install some shelves or cook a new dish for dinner, in the past you may have searched for an article with instructions. Nowadays, however, many users look first for a short video that explains how they can solve their problem. While it may take a little more time and effort to create engaging video content, video content is growing in popularity and many popular social media networks allow video to be embedded directly into posts and shared.

Regardless of the format that you choose to publish your content, you must ensure that you are communicating your messages clearly and effectively, and in most cases you should include a call to action. How do you want your viewers and readers to feel when they read or view your content, and what do you want them to do? Clear calls to action will help make your content more effective, your communication more effective, and in turn drive your engagement metrics. Figure 3.1 illustrates how good content will be shared by social media users which will amplify your key messages.

Don't forget that social media is not a one-way channel for you to broadcast your products, services or content. You will want users to engage with your content in some way. So, for example, if you write a blog, you should consider whether you will allow comments to be left by users. Commenting and user engagement of this type is covered in more detail in Chapter 5, Governance.

Consideration should also be given to who is authoring and publishing your content. Many organizations choose to produce content in advance that can be posted and shared by specific individuals within your organization through their own networks. If your employees are being encouraged to write blogs, you will need to give them the appropriate tools and training to do this effectively, while ensuring that they understand the boundaries, policies and safeguards you have in place. These controls and safeguards are discussed in more detail in the remaining chapters of this book.

Not all content will or should be pushed out repeatedly forever. For example, if you have a social media campaign running during a specific time period, you'll want to ensure that you have plans in place to ensure that the content

FIGURE 3.1 Content is king

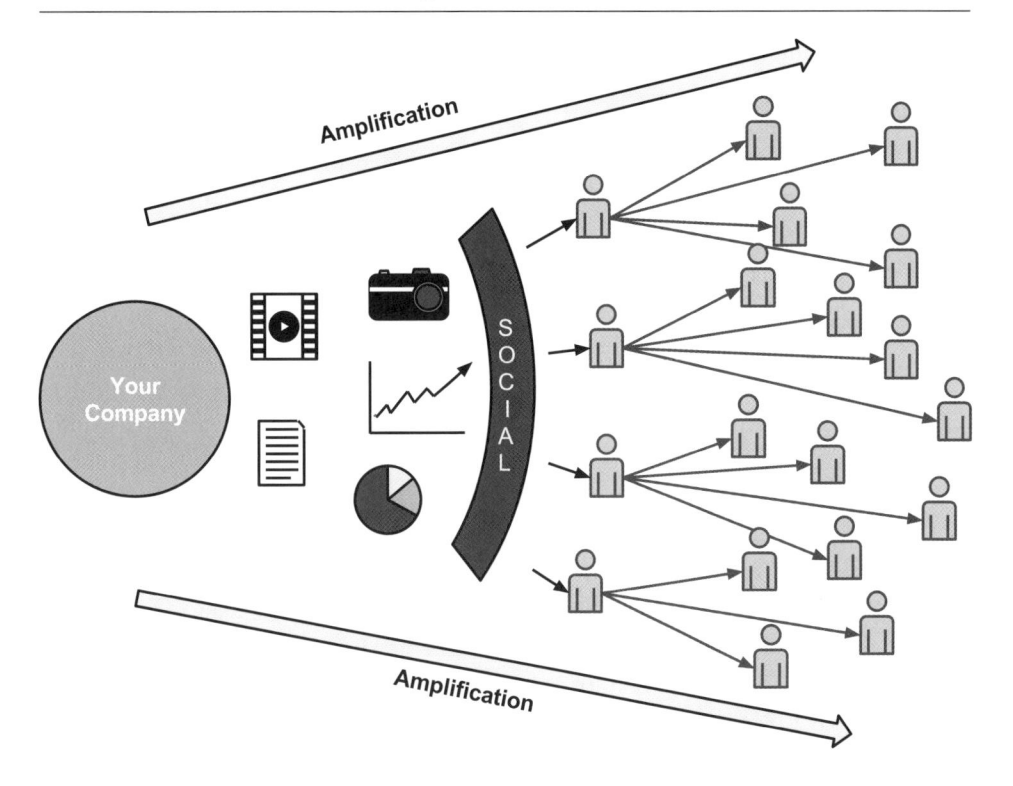

is indeed posted during that period and not afterwards. Content calendars can be an effective tool for planning what content is going to be posted, by whom, how often, and when. Figure 3.2 shows a typical content calendar you could adopt or tailor for your own needs.

FIGURE 3.2

Publish Date	Social Network	Product / Campaign	Owner	Author / from	Post text	Media	Notes
03/09/2015	Twitter	Press release	John Smith	Corporate PR	Read our response to recent complaints about customer service shortURL/1234	N/A	
04/09/2015	Facebook	Widget 2.0	Mary Doe	Marketing	Widget 2.0 is on sale in stores near you from today – take the Widget challenge on our website www.your_company.com	http://url-to/-a-video	Bob to respond to comments
05/09/2015	LinkedIn	Graduate recruitment	Lisa Smith	Recruitment	We're hiring for experienced social media risk advisors. Find out more on our careers site: www.your_company.com/careers	http://url-to/-an-image	

Many companies choose to post content relevant to certain events that are happening in the world and that are trending on social media. If there is a genuine link between something that's happening in the world and your brand, then this can be an effective way of gaining extra exposure, but should be done with caution and tact. There are many examples where companies have posted content related to a specific event only to find that social media users have taken a disliking to it, or it has caused offence in some way. For example, in September 2014 US business tycoon Donald Trump was duped into retweeting a post from a Twitter user that said 'My parents who passed away always said you were big inspiration. Can you pls RT for their memory?' and included a photo of a man and woman. The photo that had been attached was actually a photo of notorious murders Fred and Rose West. After Twitter users pointed out the mistake, Trump deleted the retweet but this just goes to show that you need to be absolutely sure you understand the event that you're posting about.

As a rule of thumb, it's probably worth staying clear of references to natural disasters when promoting products or services, as some fashion retailers in the United States found. American Apparel, a fashion brand, was one such brand guilty of this at the time of Hurricane Sandy, which was a deadly and destructive hurricane that hit the North East of the United States in 2012. American Apparel tweeted 'In case you're bored during the storm. 20% off everything for next 36 hours'. Customers were eligible for the discounts by using the promotional code 'SANDYSALE'. This promotion caused outrage on social media as it was seen to be exploiting a very serious natural disaster in which 285 people died.

In 2014 Catherine, Duchess of Cambridge gave birth to Prince George of Cambridge. The birth of the Royal baby was met with much celebration in the United Kingdom and many companies decided to launch promotions at the same time to celebrate the birth. However, not all got it right. Starbucks Coffee released a photo of three of its coffee cups, each wearing crowns, depicting the royal family, with a small coffee cup at the front. Unfortunately for Starbucks, the post was blasted by social media users who pointed out that babies should not be drinking coffee.

Designing for mobile vs desktop

As previously discussed, people access social media from a variety of different devices, such as smartphones, tablets, desktop/laptop computers and even smartwatches. It's important to bear this in mind when designing the content that you plan to push out on social media. While standard text, images and videos will probably be universally compatible with the main devices, there may be times when you want to encourage people to visit a specific website or application that you have created.

If you plan to launch a specific website or microsite to support a campaign and you plan to publicize it through social media, you had better make sure that the website is compatible with a broad range of devices. You should also consider what software is running on those devices, for example if it's a smartphone or tablet, is it running iOS, Android, Windows or BlackBerry OS? For desktops/laptops you'll need to consider whether it's running Windows, Mac OS or another operating system such as Linux.

To further complicate matters, users have a choice of which internet browser they use. The most popular internet browsers are Internet Explorer, Safari, Firefox, Chrome and Opera. We can take this to another degree of complexity by considering which versions of a browser your website will support. For example, if you wanted to use features of HTML5, a scripting language used for web design, you will need to consider that earlier version of some browsers may not support the functionality.

Clearly, device and browser compatibility is a complex and specialist area, but one that you should be aware of. From experience, I know that if you are not explicit in your conversations with developers regarding compatibility requirements, you may find your new website will only work properly with a small subset of your target audience. If social media users follow your links to your new website and find that it doesn't work, you're likely to feel a backlash.

That said, it's important to know your audience and find a balance. Trying to develop content that will display seamlessly on all devices, all operating systems and all previous versions of web browsers is near impossible. But it is important to consider your requirements in advance. Just because your company is using one of the latest versions of a web browser doesn't mean everyone else is. Many large corporates, for example, have policies in place that stop them from upgrading to the latest version of software until a later date. This is because new software often contains bugs and security holes. Larger organizations wait until these issues have been fixed and the software is more stable before they upgrade.

I was once part of a 'social vote' designed to allow users to vote for the people that they wanted to hear speak at a conference. The votes were captured through Facebook 'likes'. Working at a large organization, our default web browser at the time was Internet Explorer 9 but the latest version available was Internet Explorer 11. To my horror I found that the 'social voting' functionality which had been implemented was not compatible with Internet Explorer 9, meaning that none of my work colleagues were able to vote for me using their work browser. I hoped that perhaps some of my colleagues would be able to vote using their mobile devices, but then discovered that because they were viewing a webpage on their phone, when clicking the 'Like' button, they were prompted to log in to Facebook. This confused many people as they were never normally asked to authenticate themselves when they opened the Facebook app on their phone. It also caused some of my colleagues to become suspicious of the login page and simply close the webpage, thinking that it may be a hoax designed to steal their information. Many developers I speak with are surprised by the fact that many large businesses use older version of internet browsers, so it's worth bearing this in mind when developing new content which you plan to share through social media. If you don't, it could cause a lot of frustration and anger in your social media followers, especially if employees of large organizations are the part of your target audience for your products, services or social media campaign.

'Responsive web design' is the concept whereby websites are developed to provide optimal viewing experiences across multiple devices, as it can be difficult to view websites that have been designed for desktop screens on mobile devices. This is illustrated in Figure 3.3.

FIGURE 3.3 Design for desktop vs mobile

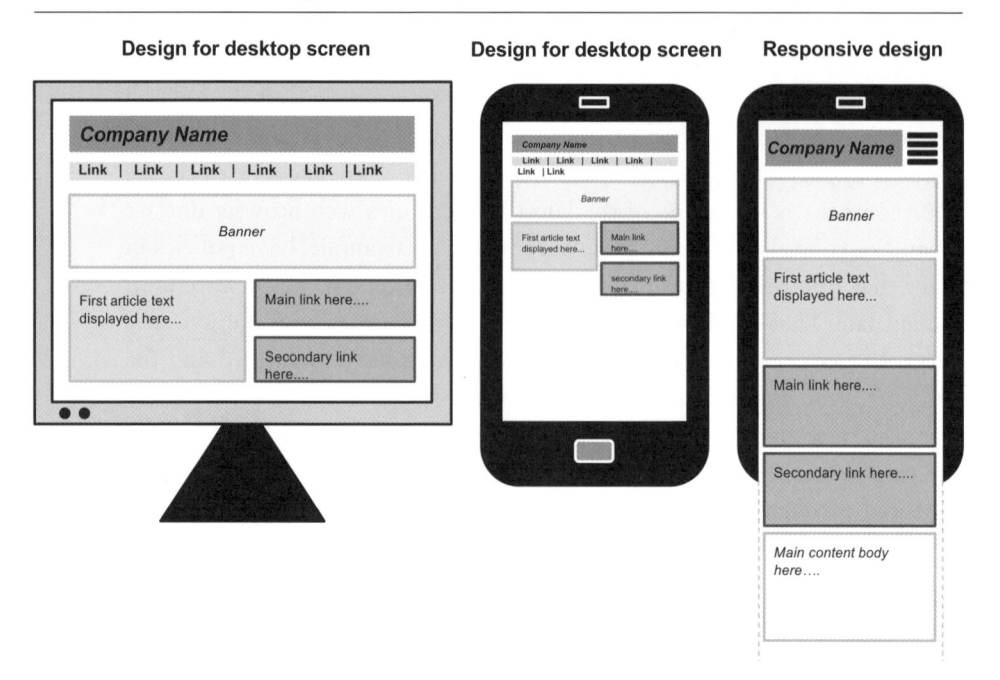

Which networks should you target?

There are certainly a lot of social media networks out there, which can make it difficult to decide where you should focus your efforts. Due to the 'always on' nature of social media conversations, it's not advisable to try to target and maintain a presence on every social network you can think of. By doing this you will be spreading yourself too thinly, and consequently diluting your message. In turn, this increases the likelihood that you will miss something on one of the networks unless you have considerable resource at your disposal. Therefore, as part of your social media listening activities, you should spend time identifying the networks most popular with your target audience. The functionality and purpose of each social network differs, so it's important to know and gain experience using the networks on which you plan to develop a presence.

If your organization operates in countries where English is not the native language you may wish to consider targeting popular networks in those territories. This will, of course, pose challenges related to language as well as time-zone. The multinational organizations which most effectively target non-English social networks have dedicated social media teams located in the country where most of their audience is based. This will allow the local teams to post content that is relevant to the culture of that country, as they will be 'on the ground' and more aware of local issues.

A popular way of demonstrating some of the main differences between the different social networks is by using a doughnut analogy, as depicted in Figure 3.4.

Rome wasn't built in a day

The age-old saying 'Rome wasn't built in a day' is as true in social media as it is elsewhere. While social media is a fast-changing medium where certain posts can go viral, attracting huge numbers of views or shares in the space of minutes or hours, don't expect that you will be able to reach your goals instantly. Building a brand and attracting followers or supporters takes time, perseverance and persistence. It's hard work. Don't be tempted to try to take shortcuts – these more often than not backfire.

One of the typical ways that some people and brands have tried to outsmart the system is by purchasing followers. Many people and brands measure their success by the number of followers/connections they have. In many ways, this is an effective measure; however, it can be manipulated. There are a number of companies that offer social media followers for cash. Unfortunately, though, it's not actually real people who will be following

FIGURE 3.4 Social networks explained through doughnuts

Facebook	I like doughnuts
Twitter	I'm eating a #doughnut
YouTube	Watch me eating a doughnut
flickr	Here's a photo album of doughnuts
Instagram	Here's photo of a doughnut
LinkedIn	My skills include eating doughnuts
Pinterest	Here's a great doughnut recipe
Foursquare	This is where I eat doughnuts
last.fm	I'm listening to 'Doughnuts'
Wordpress	Here's my blog about doughnuts

you or your company. Instead, the companies that offer these services have thousands of fake accounts which they use to follow you. Paying for services like this, aside from being unethical, is usually a breach of the social network's terms and conditions, and therefore increases the risk that your account may be blocked by the network. Social media users will also view your activity as unethical and deceptive, which will cause a breakdown of trust in your faithful followers, who may turn against you. Furthermore, paying for fake followers, likes or retweets will make it much more difficult for you to extract meaningful metrics about your social media engagement.

Often, social media programmes or social media marketing campaigns will run for an extended period of time and will consist of multiple tasks. Some of these tasks may run in tandem, but with different start and end dates. Certain content may need to be created while another part of your project is running, and certain key dates may need to be met in order for other parts of your project to run smoothly. A common way of illustrating project timelines and tasks is to use a Gantt chart, as illustrated in Figure 3.5. Time is displayed horizontally and tasks are listed vertically.

FIGURE 3.5 Project management Gantt chart

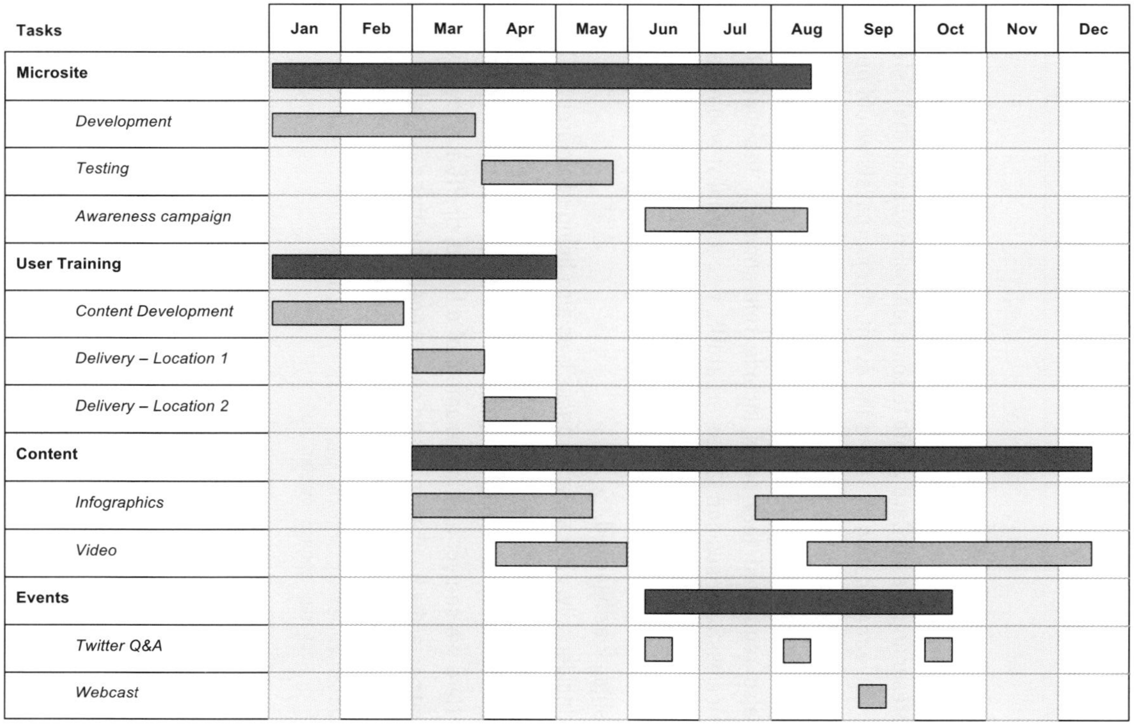

This makes it easy to see what tasks or activities should be running at any given time, and should help you predict any pinch points where extra resource or support might be required.

CASE STUDY   Risk in action: MasterCard #PricelessSurprises

MasterCard was the main sponsor of the 2014 Brit Awards, a glitzy award ceremony recognizing the best artists in British popular music. The PR company representing MasterCard wrote to some journalists saying that before they would provide accreditation to attend the event, the journalists would need to agree to a number of requests.

The email contained a long list of conditions, listing what to tweet and when. It also requested that posts include references to the marketing campaign #PricelessSurprises and @MasterCardUK. One journalist who received the email didn't take kindly to the conditions and posted the email online. Tweets about these requests then started to be shared on Twitter and the #PricelessSurprises hashtag was hijacked.

Incidentally, #PricelessSurprises was also being sponsored by MasterCard at the time. This meant that even more people were stumbling across the posts about this unethical behaviour and began posting even more tweets mocking MasterCard.

Here we see yet another example of a brand, or PR agency, trying to control what social media users can and cannot post, or in this case, what journalists can or cannot post online. These tactics are likely to backfire, as they did in this case.

SOURCE: www.pressgazette.co.uk/journalists-seeking-accreditation-brit-awards-asked-gaurantee-coverage-sponsor-mastercard

---

Getting everyone on the same page

A challenge that many face when starting a social media programme is stakeholder engagement. The chief information officer (CIO) of any given organization will typically be responsible for IT, and the HR department will be responsible for people and people-related issues and policies. When it comes to social media, however, it's often less clear as to who owns it, or who should own it.

Typically, there is some justification to a number of different stakeholders owning social media:

- *Marketing.* In many organizations social media is used as a marketing tool. They may pay for advertising on social media and track who the influencers are so that they can engage them directly. Marketing, therefore, have a valid argument to why they should own it.
- *Communications.* Some organizations use social media primarily, either externally or internally, as a communication tool. They use it to connect with their employees or to communicate press releases externally.
- *Customer services.* The use of social media as a means of providing customer service is quite mature in the United States and is growing in the United Kingdom. Where teams of customer service representatives are using social media regularly to engage with customers there's a valid argument that customer services should be the owners.
- *IT.* Some organizations believe that because social media is accessed through IT equipment, IT should be responsible for and take ownership of social media. Those in IT may also identify social media as a risk, as viruses and other malware could be downloaded to the company's IT equipment and introduced to the corporate network through social media.
- *HR.* As social media is about people connecting with each other, and because social media is seen by some as a 'time wasting activity which employees are engaging in when they should be working', some argue that HR should own social media and its associated policies. The HR department will already have policies and procedures in place to deter bullying or inappropriate behaviour at work and therefore may want to extend this authority to social media too.

So, what's the answer here? Who should be the rightful owner and take responsibility for social media? One answer doesn't fit all, unfortunately, and in many cases there will be a mix of people and departments who have a stake in social media and a role to play. Governance can be used as a way of making the process of identifying an owner and linking up the different stakeholders easier. By engaging each of the groups or communities who have an interest in social media within an organization you can begin to formalize the roles which each will play. I can't stress more firmly the need to ensure that the different stakeholders are brought together to support social media within an organization. Forming working groups and committees that meet regularly to discuss strategy, planned activities and issues is vital to ensuring that the benefits of social media are realized and risks are managed.

How regularly the working group or committee meetings take place will depend on the size and complexity of your organization. As with any working group, an agenda should be circulated beforehand and any actions should be captured, documented and reviewed at the next meeting. This topic is covered in more detail in Chapter 5, Governance.

Engagement in social media will require budget. Even if you do not plan to pay for sponsored posts or other forms of advertising, do not overlook the time commitment. Who holds the budget for social media is often something that many struggle with. As all organizations are structured differently, there isn't a quick answer to finding the budget that you need. You may find that the key stakeholders who have an interest in social media each contribute to the overall social media budget. For example, Marketing may budget an amount for advertising on social media and IT may budget for the necessary tools to monitor and control social media.

Advocates and reverse-mentors

Advocates and reverse-mentors can be instrumental in helping you achieve your goals in social media. An advocate, sometimes called a 'champion', is someone in your organization whose official role is not necessarily related to social media, but who has the energy and enthusiasm to champion your initiative and encourage their colleagues and peers to use social media. Reverse-mentoring is where someone who is more junior in an organization mentors or coaches a more senior colleague. If you want to engage the people within your organization and encourage them to use social media well, then advocates should be one of your secret weapons. When it comes to engaging some of the more senior members, reverse-mentors can be effective in getting them on social media, which in turn should encourage its use further down the organization.

Tone from the top

If you have ambitions to engage the people in your organization and encourage them to use social media to promote the company or to amplify the organization's marketing messages, then you'll need to think about

Strategy 51

how to engage the leaders at the top of the organization. Without buy-in, sponsorship and engagement from the leaders at the top, getting people lower down to engage with social media is likely to be an uphill challenge, to say the least.

Before going to your senior leaders for support you will need to have a clear vision in place for what you want to achieve. You should then try to identify a sponsor, preferably at board level, who will support you. It's likely that you'll need to spend time presenting your plan and vision to the sponsor to gain their support, but once you have it, you'll need to use it. It is important to stress just how important buy-in from senior leaders is to the successful rollout of social media through an organization. Figure 3.6 illustrates how a top-down approach, where your senior leaders lead by example, is more effective than a bottom-up approach, where you encourage people lower down in the organization to adopt social media without support from the top.

Once you have successfully engaged someone to sponsor your initiative you can get to work preparing material to present to the wider leadership team. Everyone fights for time with the senior leadership and everyone believes that whatever it is that they're working on is the most important thing. So, persistence and self-belief will go a long way in helping you achieve your goals. Getting a slot on the agenda may prove difficult, but it's necessary to increase your impact and buy-in across the leadership.

I often find that many senior leaders are supportive of social media initiatives, but are simultaneously cautious because they often haven't had as much exposure to social media as, say, the digital-native generation. I find that a formal programme of reverse-mentoring can be the best way to gain

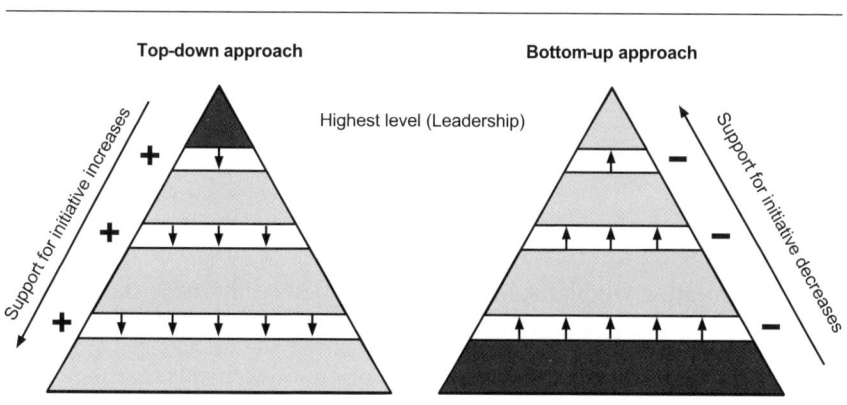

FIGURE 3.6 Tone from the top

further support and help those senior leaders become active on social media. This is hugely rewarding, both for the mentor and the mentee.

Reverse-mentors will need support too, so it's worthwhile creating a short training course for them so that they know what specifically they should be providing coaching on. Courses that include some soft-skills around engaging and dealing with senior leaders may also be necessary, as some people may find it intimidating going to a senior leader and coaching them in something that they see as easy or obvious.

I believe the mentor–mentee relationship should be owned by the two individuals engaged in the coaching, but that the mentor should be offered guidance and supporting material to assist them. A one-off meeting may be effective in the short term, but for the senior leaders to benefit most they should understand the time commitment, engage in the sessions and ensure they happen regularly, for example monthly.

Engaging the rest of the organization

Once the senior leaders in the organization are behind your initiative and are fully bought-in to what you're trying to achieve it will be easier to engage everyone else. Engaging the rest of the people in your organization will not be an easy task, but the use of advocates will greatly increase your chances of success.

Advocates are crucial because they can encourage their colleagues and peers to adopt social media by explaining the benefits to them in a way that is relevant to their part of the business. They're also far more accessible to those who need a bit of support and would rather approach a friendly colleague than a central team.

An effective advocate programme will rely on the successful engagement of advocates throughout the organization at all levels. The advocates are giving up some of their time to support your initiative so it's important to give them the support and materials that they needed to make their job easier.

Some material you may wish to make accessible to the advocate group is:

- Use-cases for social media that explain the benefits of the new way of working.
- Examples of social media success stories.
- Presentation templates and a master deck of ready-made slides that they can pick from and adapt to their needs.
- Ready-made email communications or announcements that they can tailor and send out to their teams.

To engage the advocate community you could run meet-ups or virtual meetings to let them know about important changes or developments before the wider community.

If you are rolling out or already use an enterprise social network, creating a specific group on the platform that can act as a repository for all the resources and materials that an advocate might need is a good idea. Doing this will also give the advocates a platform to allow them to connect with other advocates and bounce ideas around, discuss any challenges and plan the development of new materials.

What makes a good advocate or mentor?

I believe that the most important attribute of an advocate or mentor is passion and energy. They will be playing a challenging role and will probably receive push-back from people at all levels of the organization. People generally don't like change, so it's natural that some will challenge the need to adopt social media or an enterprise social network.

Patience is a virtue, and it's an important attribute for both advocates and mentors to have. Coaching can be tough and the advocates and mentors may find themselves explaining the same, seemingly simple, steps again and again.

Some organizations have a selection process for their advocates. They stipulate a set number of advocates that they are going to be able to accept onto the programme. Other organizations make it completely open and allow anyone to become an advocate if it's of interest to them. What you choose here will depend on the culture within your organization and your operating model. If your organization is large it may work in your favour to allow anyone to become an advocate as it's not always possible to predict who is going to have the required passion, enthusiasm and persistence to really make an impact in the organization.

Motivating advocates and mentors

As previously stated, advocate and mentor roles are usually in addition to an official role. Because of this, it's important to carefully consider how best to engage and motivate your advocate community.

Some ways that you might decide to motivate or reward your advocates are:

- *Advocate of the month award*. A good way of motivating and recognizing their efforts is to run an advocate of the month competition. The prize does not necessarily need to be monetary and instead could simply be having their name in lights as the advocate who made the most impact in that month. Perhaps it could also be something that could lead into their end-of-year performance review.

- *Presenting at advocate meetings.* Some of the advocate community will often be junior members of your organization. Giving them the opportunity to get in the limelight and present some of their success stories, or particular challenges that they have faced and overcome, could be exactly the type of recognition that the advocates will respond to.
- *Badges.* Help your advocates to stand out within your organization by giving them badges that they can wear to help others identify them as advocates of your social media programme.
- *T-shirts.* During any big internal communications campaigns you could provide T-shirts for your advocate team to help others identify them easily.

To coordinate the advocate programme and engage the advocates and mentors is a challenge in itself. It is worth considering whether or not to create a full-time role for an 'Advocate Programme Manager'. Clearly, this will depend on the size of your organization and the ambition of your social media programme. Regardless of whether or not you have budget for this, bear in mind that managing a group of advocates will take considerable time and effort.

Almost all organizations run an annual performance review whereby employees are reviewed against a set of competencies and objectives. It's likely that you could link your social media programme directly to one of the competencies that employees are required to demonstrate. By doing this it gives the advocates and mentors an extra incentive so that, come end-of-year review, they have evidence to show how they have demonstrated one of the competencies through involvement with the social media programme. Many organizations that I have worked with understand the value of communication and knowledge sharing, and therefore include it as one of the competencies that is reviewed at the end of the year. A social media programme, either internal or external, should be able to fit neatly into this category and give the advocates and mentors a big differentiator against their peers as having supported the programme and demonstrated knowledge sharing and communication.

CASE STUDY   Risk in action: PwC – advocate programme

In May 2012 PwC, the global network of professional services firms, launched an enterprise social network that they named Spark. The purpose of the network was to connect their more than 195,000 professionals worldwide on one common platform to enable them to collaborate together and share knowledge more effectively.

PwC's adoption rate was rapid and within months grew to close to 100 per cent in some territories. Key to their success was the use of employee advocates. The advocates' job was to drive adoption within their business units and teams by helping their colleagues get started and understand the benefits of using the platform. The advantage of using advocates was that they were able to articulate the benefits of using Spark in their own business area by using examples they knew would resonate with their colleagues.

PwC employed a full-time advocate manager whose role it was to engage some 1,000 advocates worldwide, giving them the tools and materials they needed. The advocate manager ran update calls and virtual training courses for the advocates to ensure that they were always up-to-date on any new developments or changes.

Anyone could become an advocate, regardless of experience or seniority. This meant that the advocates who put themselves forward were generally those with energy and passion for the new way of working. Some extra motivation was needed, however, so PwC implemented measures to ensure that advocates were recognized for their efforts. One such method was by awarding one advocate every month the title of 'Advocate of the Month' and a special badge in recognition. The advocates were genuinely proud of their achievement and often updated their profile pictures to show them wearing the badge. A year after launch PwC then ran a competition to identify the best advocate from across its global network. The advocate's reward was a trip to a technology conference in Las Vegas where they were able to meet others from the enterprise social network industry and blog about their trip on Spark itself.

PwC also ordered a batch of badges for all advocates, which displayed the text 'Ask me about Spark'. Advocates all over the world wore the badges voluntarily within their offices, which helped to raise awareness of the platform.

The advocate programme made a real buzz within PwC with some teams even creating Spark launch videos for their own territories. Since launch, Spark adoption has continued to grow and is now seen as another tool in people's day-to-day work.

Crowdsourcing

Crowdsourcing is a concept whereby something, such as an idea, is 'sourced' from a larger group of people, 'the crowd'. Crowdsourcing has grown in popularity as people and companies have come to realize that they can use social networks to harness the power, innovation and ideas of large groups of people easily.

The important thing to remember is that 'the crowd' is a wide network of people. You can 'source' anything that you want. Crowdfunding is an offshoot of crowdsourcing and refers to the sourcing of funds, or money. There are a number of crowdfunding websites that enable artists, entrepreneurs, film-makers, scientists or pretty much anyone to harness the power of a wide network to source funding. Typically, someone who has an idea for a project, but needs some funding to get it off the ground, will use a crowdfunding website to raise the funds. Users of the crowdfunding site can 'pledge' money to the project in return for some kind of token gift related to the project. For example, a musician may offer people who pledge money to their project a free song or album in return.

The key here is that social media is usually the enabler because crowdsourcing would not work without a wide network of people who can connect virtually.

What's more, because crowdsourcing relies on social networks, other benefits come to the fore. Users can discuss and appraise projects or ideas within their own networks. Not only does this help drive awareness of a particular project across an even wider network, it also acts as a form of peer review. Projects or ideas are reviewed in public and the idea or project owner receives real-time feedback from a diverse group of users. This information can prove extremely valuable to the project owner as it gives them a chance to test their concepts with a large group of people and make any amendments or changes that might improve their original project.

Ideation

Ideation is the crowdsourcing of ideas. Ideation is enabling organizations to really harness the collective knowledge of their people and foster innovation. Many enterprise social networks have ideation functionality built in, but there are also a number of standalone ideation platforms available.

The huge advantage and opportunity for organizations looking to use ideation is that it gives them the ability to reach out to all of their employees, regardless of their role, location or seniority, and capture ideas about a specific topic or question. For example, an organization might post the question 'How do we grow revenues faster?' or 'How can we improve the way that we share knowledge or communicate?' The employees in the organization can answer the question by submitting ideas. Just imagine the possibilities – ideation can unlock the potential of all of your people to help you innovate and stay competitive.

What's more, ideation functionality or platforms allow ideas that have been submitted to be voted up or down. This acts as a peer review, where the best ideas, as viewed by the users, will rise to the top of the list and the less popular ideas will sink to the bottom. Commenting allows users to critique the ideas and offer guidance or support about how to develop the idea further. Not only is ideation a great way to capture ideas and innovations, it is also a very effective engagement tool. If supported by a good communication campaign and clear leadership support it can quickly become 'the thing everyone's talking about'.

Any ideation project will need appropriate governance to support it. Depending on the solution or platform you choose, you'll need to make a number of decisions about what governance you want to implement. Some things that you can consider are:

- *Moderation.* The good thing about ideation is that ideas are essentially 'peer-moderated'. Ideas are voted up and down by users of the network. However, you may wish to implement an approval step to have ideas reviewed before they are published on the platform to ensure that they don't include any offensive or abusive comments.
- *Review team.* It's important to remember that, as with most things, an oversight or management group will be required to manage the campaign or programme. Particularly if you force all submissions to be reviewed, you will need to define the process for approval or rejection.
- *Ideation stages.* Do you plan to have a number of 'rounds' where the top ideas go through to the next round and the top ideas in that round progress to a third round and so on? If this is the case, you'll need to define the parameters for each round. Some parameters that you might use to dictate which ideas will progress are:
  - minimum number of views;
  - minimum number of positive votes;
  - minimum number of comments; and
  - minimum team size.

- *Management override*. It might be possible for some users to manipulate the platform in some way, for example asking all of their connections to vote for their idea. As a rule, it's best to limit your management intervention so that it doesn't look like everything is being censored and so that it doesn't undermine the whole concept of ideation. However, there may be some particularly strong ideas that are submitted which get missed, perhaps because the idea owner forgot to encourage their network to vote for them. In these cases it may be beneficial to reserve the right to push through particularly good ideas to the next stage if they were not able to reach the required metrics.

You should also note that the functionality available from vendors will differ and some platforms may offer more control over how you govern the platform than others. It's important to complete a review of your requirements and potential vendors before purchasing a platform as getting it wrong could be a costly mistake.

Gamification

Gamification is a term used to describe features and functionality within an online platform that reward users in some way for performing a variety of typical tasks. The simplest example to illustrate this is a points-based system, where users of a platform receive a number of points if they submit or answer questions, upload documents, vote on polls and so on.

The purpose of using gamification techniques is to drive user engagement in a platform. If you are implementing an enterprise social network, for example, and you want to encourage people to post their ideas or share knowledge on the platform, you may find that gamification is one of the mechanisms you could use to encourage these behaviours. It may seem banal at first as you may ask yourself 'why would anyone care that they have more virtual points that another person?', but in fact gamification can result in a large increase in user engagement when effectively implemented.

Caution is needed when considering your gamification strategy as you must ensure you keep a balance between where users are using the platform to add value and when they are simply wasting time. Whether you are trying to drive user engagement inside or outside of your organization, gamification can be very effective as some users get consumed with the 'gaming' nature and can spend long periods of time on the network. Clearly, too much time spent on a social network can have a negative impact on other areas of the users' work or life, so consider functionality carefully. Personally, I would stay clear of immersive games that hook users in for long periods of time. Instead, I'd focus on simple rewards for actions, such as a reward for uploading a document or sharing a post with colleagues.

As previously stated, virtual points are a typical first step into the world of gamification. Users are awarded a variety of points based on a set number of actions, and the number of points that they are awarded will depend on your strategy. For example, if your main objective on a platform is to encourage users to share documents, you might give a user five points for each document uploaded. Comments on a discussion thread may also attract points, but perhaps you would award only one point for every comment that is added to a discussion. It's common to have various 'status levels' based on the total number of points a user has achieved. For example, a user with 0–50 points may have a status level of 'new', 50–100 points may grant the user 'intermediate' status and so on.

Virtual 'badges' are another way of rewarding users for displaying certain behaviours. For example, a user may get awarded points for correctly answering a question. If that user correctly answers a certain number of questions on a certain topic, say 50, they could be awarded a badge, such as 'Subject Matter Expert'. Badges would normally be displayed on the user's profile so that others can see them.

Many companies already offer similar schemes as a way of encouraging brand advocacy and loyalty. On a small scale, many restaurant chains offer loyalty schemes whereby they offer points or free products to loyal customers; for example, a coffee shop may offer its customers the '10th coffee free'. On a larger scale, most hotel chains offer loyalty schemes that reward their customers with 'points' which can be redeemed for things such as a free night's stay or a room upgrade. Most also include different status levels, meaning that those customers who have stayed a predetermined number of times at one of the chain's hotels will get a higher status which will offer them even more benefits. These enticements are similar to the gamification incentives that can be implemented in social media and, from experience, I can confidently say that playing the 'hotel point game' with colleagues can be quite competitive as work colleagues compete to see who can amass the most points.

Hopefully the benefits of implementing some form of gamification as part of a social media programme are clear. Gamification can significantly increase engagement and adoption of a new way of working. However, it's important to consider the governance and controls that might be needed, both to ensure the success of your project and also to ensure that the related risks are managed effectively.

In some parts of the world, enabling gamification functionality can cause a number of legal challenges. Local employment law may disallow certain gamification features if they are seen to feed into an individual's performance review, unless the features were agreed by an authorized group or council. In Germany, for example, 'workers' councils' protect employees and hold power over what an employee is allowed to do in relation to performance appraisals or working conditions. Likewise, trade unions may also have a view on how gamification can be used as a way of measuring an employee's performance. Large organizations will need to ensure that they adhere to the local employment laws of the countries in which they operate. The impact of this may result in a need to implement controls within your enterprise social network or other applications that are specific to certain countries. These specific requirements are important to address, therefore, it's important to seek appropriate legal advice to ensure that you do not face heightened risks in this respect.

Engaging external communities

Many organizations have successfully implemented 'customer advocacy schemes' as a way of engaging with their customers. Customer advocacy is designed to engage a small group of customers of a business in a way that encourages them to support the company or its other customers. Generally, the customers are not paid; instead they are given incentives, such as free access to events, access to the company's professionals or free access to its services. A good example of a strong customer advocacy scheme is Microsoft's 'Most Valuable Professional' programme.

The power of a brand can be truly awesome. You just need to look at the fans of Apple to see it in action. Fans of Apple products sometimes queue for hours outside Apple stores at the release of a new product so that they can be some of the first customers to own one. Many computer games also have fans who support a particular game to such an extent that they will openly defend the game, or the company behind the game, if it faces criticism.

Building a customer advocacy scheme usually means giving customers a platform where they can engage with both the company and its other customers. You'll need to consider:

- How do you want customers to engage?
- What is the outcome you're looking for?
- How will you reward or encourage engagement?
- Do you have the resource capacity to support such a scheme?

A customer advocacy scheme isn't necessarily right for all organizations. One of the best example of customer advocacy in action is in technical help forums. Sometimes, certain customers may be more knowledgeable about a particular software or technical applications than the developers who created it. This may be because those customers have tested the application on a wide range of devices and have identified problems and fixes to problems that they have experienced.

Many technical support sites allow customers to post questions about a particular product. These questions are often answered by other customers who have experienced the same issue. This community of users offering each other advice is an excellent example of customer advocacy. Users of these platforms are often motivated through gamification techniques. Those that answer questions that have been posted by other customers can gain points or badges as a reward. These points and rewards sometimes equate to discounts for other products or services.

An active community like this is a valuable resource for companies. New products or services can be tested by the community, who will then feedback on what they like and dislike and will flag issues or bugs that they identify. This obviously means that when the product or service is released more widely, the company will have had the opportunity to address any issues or problems with it.

The small print

When considering strategies to engage employees or external communities it can be easy to overlook the importance of terms and conditions. For example, if you run an ideation platform for your employees, or even any form of external community, it's important to remember to design terms and conditions that set out the purpose of the platform as well as the ownership of the information within it. I recommend getting independent legal advice to ensure that the terms and conditions provide enough protection for your organization.

Some points to consider are:

- The ownership of any ideas or content submitted on the platform.
- Data privacy.
- Marketing – will you contact them? Will you give their data to third parties/affiliates?

It's important to ensure that the rules of the platform are clearly outlined to the users in your policies and training material. This is both to ensure not only that the platform is used effectively, but also to safeguard the owner of the platform. For example, users may unknowingly break copyright by uploading photos or imagery they do not own. That copyrighted material would then reside on the platform, which may mean that the company providing the platform is breaking copyright.

The key takeaways are:

- seek legal advice regarding the terms and conditions of the platform;
- ensure that users of the platform agree to the terms and conditions before they are able to use the platform; and
- store the user's acceptance of your terms and conditions with the date and time that the terms and conditions were accepted.

Aligning your governance to your strategy

Your strategy should not be held back by governance. Instead, governance is there to help your project succeed. It's designed to help you gain maximum benefit and ensure that any associated risks have been addressed and are managed.

Many people I have worked with get anxious at the thought of approaching the people in risk and compliance. They assume that they might stop the project from going ahead, or might dictate extra requirements, such as the implementation of safeguards, before they can give it their blessing. While this may be true to some extent, it's important to engage all stakeholders early to ensure that you don't find that your project gets shut down at later stage due to some issues that were not addressed.

Trying to implement a social media programme without wider input may mean that you commit to purchasing some tools, only to find that at a later date you need to cancel the contract because of security concerns you had not considered. These mistakes can, of course, be very costly.

Although it may feel like a lot of effort in the short term, designing good governance and solid controls from the outset will help your project succeed in the long term. There will, undoubtedly, be many stakeholders who have an interest in your social media programme. The ideas, concepts and frameworks in this book will help you to engage with those stakeholders more effectively and allow you to address the concerns of each group. You will be able to demonstrate that you have thought about the potential issues and have a plan in place to address them.

The key steps you need to take are:

1 Work out what you want to achieve from your social media programme.
2 Analyse the risks your project may face.
3 Design appropriate governance around it to ensure that the risks are managed according to your risk tolerance.
4 Decide what technology will support your social media programme, and how it will need to be configured to support your governance framework.

This book helps you consider what you want to achieve from your social media programme and makes you aware of the risks that may impact it. The other chapters in this book, and the ideas, frameworks and concepts throughout, will help you decide what governance and control you might want to put in place in order to manage risk.

As demonstrated in Chapter 2, too much governance and control can be expensive to implement and can hamper your project's success by over-protecting it. Therefore, governance and risk management is about achieving a balance, engaging with key stakeholders and working towards a successful outcome for all involved.

Some of the frameworks may need to be tweaked for your specific industry, organizational culture or strategy; however, they should prove to be a solid base for building the governance around your programme.

Documenting your strategy, policies and operational procedures will also go a long way to helping you control risk and achieve success. Should you ever be in a situation where a regulatory is investigating how social media is managed at your organization, one of the first things they will ask for is your documented policies and procedures.

Something that I find many people get mixed up with is when they start thinking of technology first, rather than what they want to achieve. It's often tempting to dive into research about the technologies that might support your goals; however, by taking a step back and documenting what you want to achieve and your requirements, you're more likely to pick the right technology to support your project. Doing this the other way around is likely to impact what you think you are trying to achieve because the various features available can cloud your vision and lead you to try to do too much. Likewise, if you think about how you are going to govern and operate your programme early on, it will allow you to choose the technology provider which meets your needs and discount the ones that offer lots of features, but don't actually meet your needs.

Summary

In this chapter we covered strategy in the context of governance and risk management. We covered how to define the purpose of your social media programme and tactics that you can use to achieve your goals. We also looked at ways of engaging people inside and outside your organization, as well as how to motivate them and encourage them to help you meet your own goals.

You learnt that governance is about how your strategy operates and how being risk-aware while designing a strategy allows you to focus on what you want to achieve and, in turn, what governance you might need to implement in order to support.

In the subsequent chapters we will delve deeper into the risks which you may face while running your social media programme and we'll look at what controls and governance can be implemented to manage those risks.

Any social media programme will involve handling personal data. The next chapter will give an overview of the risks of handling personal data and outline some of the controls you can implement to ensure that it is safeguarded.

Data privacy and control

04

Overview

Data protection is a complex and evolving hot topic that could warrant an entire book on its own. In this chapter, I'm going to draw your attention to some of the common issues that arise in this area and highlight their relevance to social media. I often find that companies are unaware of the importance of data protection and the risk of not getting it right. But, ignorance is not a valid justification for non-compliance. Many countries around the world have their own laws and guidelines related to data protection and this represents a particular challenge for multinational organizations. But even those companies that operate in only one country need to be aware of their local laws and be able to demonstrate compliance to the data regulators.

Data privacy and protection

The law

The law surrounding data protection in the EU is currently being reviewed. The current EU Data Protection Directive 95/46/EC is going to be superseded by the proposed General Data Protection Regulation. At the time of writing, the General Data Protection Regulation is expected to be adopted in 2015 and come into force in 2017. It foresees fines of up to 5 per cent of a company's worldwide revenue for non-compliance. Furthermore, many jurisdictions outside of the EU are implementing similar laws. Enterprise social networks process personal data and are therefore subject to adherence with the law. But, traditional social networks also process personal information so organizations need to understand what data they are capturing, why they're capturing it, what they're going to do with it, and how long they're going to keep it for.

EU legislation prohibits the transfer of data outside of the EU unless certain measures and controls have been put in place. The reason for this is that it is assumed that while the data is in Europe, the rights of its citizens will be protected by EU law, but as soon as the data leaves the EU that may no longer be the case as it is outside of its jurisdiction. For multinational organizations who operate an enterprise social network it is likely that the data within the network will be transferred cross-border. Most enterprise social networks include profiles where employees include information about themselves, often including their skills and experience. I've also seen examples of networks that are configured to capture data such as date of birth or other personal details such as kids' names. Personal data needs extra protection as most data laws or regulations specifically cite how personal data should be handled. In many cases, an organization will engage a third party vendor to operate an enterprise social network. The third party is effectively a data processor and even if they are located outside of the EU, it is the organization that engages them that is ultimately responsible for the protection of the data. Therefore, even if a data breach is the fault of the third party vendor (the data processor) it is the company (the data controller) that bears the responsibility, and it's the data controller that gets their name in the news and faces the heavy fines.

Third party software vendors are not always aware of the legal requirements in each country and often offer their services on a take-it-or-leave-it basis. Any organization purchasing an IT system, such as an enterprise social network, must be clear on how the vendor manages data because in the eyes of the EU and other regulators, claiming that services were offered on a take-it-or-leave-it basis is not an adequate argument.

Before implementing an enterprise social network or embarking on a new social media strategy, a company should complete a data privacy impact assessment. The impact assessment covers things such as:

- What data is going to be collected?
- How long is it going to be stored for?
- Are employee communications going to be monitored?

A privacy impact assessment may take a few days or more to complete, depending on how complex your project or your IT environment is, and may require data protection or legal specialists to complete it properly. As such, it's important that you are aware of the need to perform a privacy impact assessment. How you go about this is beyond the scope of this book; however, if you want to find out more about privacy impact assessments, the

UK's Information Commissioner's Office has released useful guidance that you may wish to read. Further details can be found at: **https://ico.org.uk/ for-organizations/guide-to-data-protection/privacy-by-design/**

The key point is that if there isn't a good reason for collecting certain information, it will increase the risk of incurring a fine or enforcement notice from the data regulator.

CASE STUDY Risk in action: Raytheon develops predictive analytics platform

In February 2013, many media outlets reported stories that multinational defence contractor, Raytheon, had developed a big data analytics platform capable of mining huge amounts of social media data. What's more, the platform, named Rapid Information Overlay Technology (RIOT), was capable of showing trends in user behaviours and predicting where a person might be in the future and at what time.

The *Guardian* newspaper got hold of a video demonstration of the software and published it online.

The platform took feeds from the major social networks and used geo-location data embedded in posts and images to plot a user's movements on a map. This data, plus the timings of the posts, could be plotted on a graph to show the locations that a person spends the most time and at what time they are there. Clearly, this sort of clever predictive analytics would be of real interest to intelligence and security agencies around the world.

While Raytheon maintained that the platform was a proof-of-concept only and that it had not been sold to anyone, it's not surprising that this controversial mining and analysis of social media was met with criticism from human rights groups and privacy activist groups. Some even described it as 'the greatest challenge to civil liberties and digital freedom of our age'.

While most news articles pointed out that the analysis of public information posted online was not illegal and was not a breach of the Data Protection Act, it goes to show that even if your data management strategies aren't breaking the law, any dubious practices may be met with hostility from activist groups.

SOURCE: www.information-age.com/it-management/strategy-and-innovation/2189193/social-analytics-tool-triggers-privacy-backlash

Data protection principles

While the laws governing data protection around the world differ, most of the underlying principles are similar and the laws generally seek to protect data about individuals.

To understand how data protection rules apply to your organization it's useful to gain an understanding of some important definitions:

- *Data subject.* The person who is the subject of the data.
- *Data controller.* The person who determines the purposes or manner in which any personal data is processed.
- *Data processor.* In relation to personal data, the data processor is any person (other than an employee of the data controller) who processes the data on behalf of the data controller.

So, a practical example of this in action would be where an organization (the data controller) intends to store data about their customers (the data subjects) on cloud-based systems that are managed by a third party. In this case, the cloud provider will be the data processor.

Schedule 1 of the UK Data Protection Act (1998) lists a set of eight principles that data controllers must abide by. While this legislation is specific to the United Kingdom, many of the principles are considered best practice for managing and protecting personal data so even if you don't operate in the United Kingdom, it's worth considering them anyway.

The eight principles are:

1 Personal data shall be processed fairly and lawfully and, in particular, shall not be processed unless –
   - at least one of the conditions in Schedule 2 is met, and
   - in the case of sensitive personal data, at least one of the conditions in Schedule 3 is also met.

2 Personal data shall be obtained only for one or more specified and lawful purposes, and shall not be further processed in any manner incompatible with that purpose or those purposes.

3 Personal data shall be adequate, relevant and not excessive in relation to the purpose or purposes for which they are processed.

4 Personal data shall be accurate and, where necessary, kept up to date.

5 Personal data processed for any purpose or purposes shall not be kept for longer than is necessary for that purpose or those purposes.

6 Personal data shall be processed in accordance with the rights of data subjects under this Act.

7 Appropriate technical and organizational measures shall be taken against unauthorized or unlawful processing of personal data and against accidental loss or destruction of, or damage to, personal data.

8 Personal data shall not be transferred to a country or territory outside the European Economic Area unless that country or territory ensures an adequate level of protection for the rights and freedoms of data subjects in relation to the processing of personal data.
(Data Protection Act 1998, c 29, Schedule 1. Contains public sector information licensed under the Open Government Licence v3.0)

These principles are interesting as they pose a number of challenges to organizations. For example, considering the second principle, if you capture data from your customers for a specific purpose but then decide that you could do something else with that data, you may put yourself in a position whereby you might break the principle. Another example that causes organizations a challenge is principle 8 because most large corporate networks rely on data being transferred across international territories, for example through the use of a global enterprise social network. In such cases, you may need to implement extra safeguards to ensure that you don't break the laws of the territories in which you operate.

What is personal data?

When thinking about the data that you plan to capture or analyse, it's worth considering what personal data you might end up handling. Accessing, analysing, storing or generally processing personal data in some way will probably mean that you need to implement extra safeguards to ensure that the personal data is handled appropriately and that you have permission to use it.

The exact legal definitions of personal data differ from country to country, but the best way to think about personal data is data that identifies an individual. This can include information such as individuals' names, their titles, their addresses, their phone numbers and other information.

Sensitive personal data usually includes information about an individual such as their:

- race or ethnic origin;
- political opinions;

- religious beliefs;
- physical or mental health;
- sexual orientation.

Sensitive data needs tighter controls and safeguards around it because the consequences of its exposure will attract the attention of data enforcement bodies, and may also result in direct repercussions to the individuals themselves (for example, racism, abuse etc). If you plan to process personal data you should perform a privacy impact assessment and may need to seek specialist legal advice to ensure that you adhere to the laws governing data privacy within the territories in which you operate.

The role of the data protection officer

Many organizations appoint, or are required to appoint, a data protection officer (DPO). While the appointment of a data protection officer is not mandatory in all jurisdictions, appointing a data protection officer or assigning their responsibilities to a specific individual is considered best practice. The data protection officer's role is to ensure that the organization for which they work complies with all applicable data protection laws and regulations.

Usually, a data protection officer will perform the following roles:

- They must document the type of data being collected and processed.
- They will inform or advise both the data controller and data processors of their responsibilities.
- They are responsible for documentation related to data protection and must record any responses regarding any particular issues or challenges. They will also provide time limits for the deletion of personal data.
- They monitor any data breaches and respond to requests from the enforcing authorities.
- They monitor the implementation and application of data management training and policies.

Data protection officers are independent and report directly to management. Their roles should not be conflicted and they are usually appointed for a minimum term, during which they cannot be dismissed unless there are good grounds to do so.

Clearly, data protection officers must be well versed in the principles of data protection and should have a thorough understanding of the relevant regulations and laws and how to apply them. They will need to understand this at a broad level so as to ensure they can apply the laws and regulations applicable in all of the countries in which their organization operates. There are qualifications that data protection officers can obtain; one of the most common is the Certified Information Protection Professional (CIPP) from The International Association of Privacy Professionals. There are four types of CIPP certificate:

- CIPP/US – US private sector.
- CIPP/C – Canada.
- CIPP/E – Europe.
- CIPP/G – US government.

Due to the large amounts of personal data associated with social media, and the fact that social media is an evolving field, it's worth building a relationship with the data protection officer/s at your organization. This will help you to obtain foresight into any potential data protection issues that might affect your social media programme or strategy and ensure that you can address any concerns early, rather than struggle with them retrospectively.

Data management

Data storage and transfer

Data privacy is important not just because of regulatory compliance requirements but because people and organizations expect that their data will be handled appropriately.

An organization faces two challenges when it comes to data privacy. First, it must safeguard the confidentiality, integrity and availability of the data it holds on its customers, employees or other stakeholders. Second, it must be able to demonstrate to regulators that it is complying with the rules governing the protection of personal information. Data protection is not a new concept, but over the past decade it has become a hot topic in the press and the need to demonstrate compliance with the relevant data protection regulations has had an increased focus around the world.

One of the main issues that has come about in recent years is in relation to the rise in cloud computing. Historically, when an organization implemented any type of IT system, they would purchase the hardware on which their applications would run and install it somewhere within their premises. Increasingly, however, as we have all become more connected to the internet, organizations have started to adopt cloud-based models for their infrastructure and software. In the cloud model, instead of an organization buying the required infrastructure and installing it in their premises, they rent the infrastructure or storage from a cloud provider. The infrastructure or applications are then accessed over the internet. This is great for organizations as it means their IT hardware is far more scalable, meaning that if an organization needs more space, they simply pay the cloud provider more to get access to more space. In theory, it also means that they spend less time and money maintaining these services, although in practice, most CIOs have said that the expected cost savings are low or non-existent.

The problem with cloud services is that applications and data are 'hosted' (or stored) on a server, or collection of servers, in a specific physical location. This is a simplistic explanation of cloud computing, but it should suffice in the context of data protection. If your cloud provider hosts your data in a specific jurisdiction, you will probably need to comply with the data protection legislation within that specific country. But, because the data will be accessed by people in your organization who are physically sitting in other parts of the world, other data protection legislations come into play as well. Essentially, by accessing data from one jurisdiction that is hosted on a server in another jurisdiction, the data being accessed is being transferred cross-territory, as depicted in Figure 4.1. These sorts of international data transfers often cause some of the biggest challenges for organizations who are implementing cloud-based global IT systems. It's therefore very important to carefully consider where the data will be physically stored and from which jurisdictions the data will be accessed. There are specific actions you can take to enable inter-territory data transfers, such as through the use of so-called 'Binding Corporate Rules (BCRs)' or through compliance with US–EU Safe Harbor, however these are outside the scope of this book and become technical topics in their own right which usually require specialist legal advice.

The ongoing public debate around data privacy has also led some countries to consider implementing laws that aim to protect their citizens' data by requiring that it be physically stored on servers situated within that particular country. In today's world, where most of us rely on the technology giants who provide access to their services, such as the social networks, the countries that are considering implementing such legislation are trying to stop their citizens' data from being transferred out or being intercepted by foreign

FIGURE 4.1 Cloud storage: Cross-border data transfer

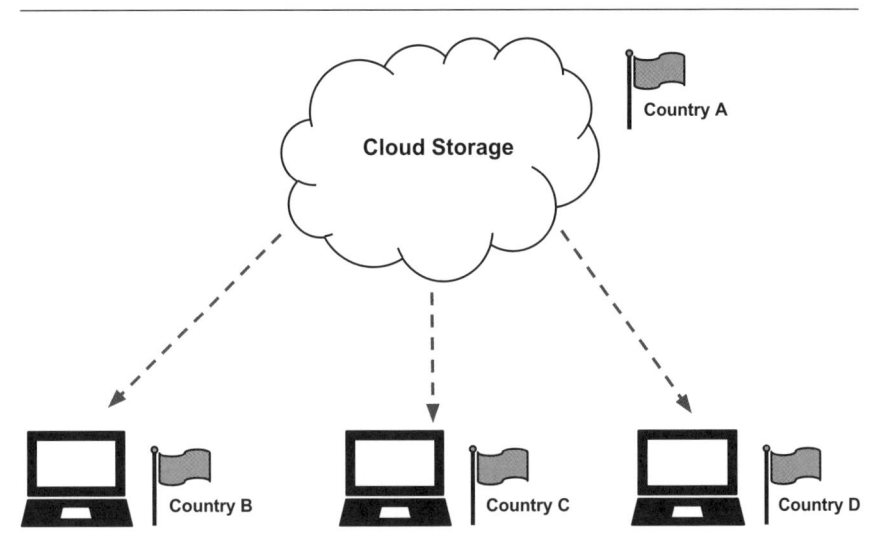

governments. Russia is one such example of a country that in 2014 announced that it would require personal data about its citizens to be stored within Russia. This is another example of the fast-changing data privacy environment that poses a challenge to organizations and data protection officers.

Data classification

It is good practice to have a data classification framework implemented at your organization. Data classification is important when thinking about social media governance because you need to understand what data you are storing and sharing across your network. You need to do this to ensure that you don't break the law (such as through copyright infringement) or share information that should be handled in a different way. Your social media policy, which we cover in Chapter 6, should reference your data classification policy.

Data classification aims to define and classify any particular data in order to help guide a user on how they can use or transfer that particular piece of data. Typically, most organizations adopt four or five classifications of data. Figure 4.2 shows the classifications of data in a pyramid.

The pyramid in Figure 4.2 demonstrates that the more confidential the data, the less of it there is. As you go down the pyramid from top to bottom the amount of control around the data decreases, but the amount of data increases. So, as data becomes more sensitive, control must increase but the amount of data in that classification will decrease.

FIGURE 4.2   Data classification pyramid

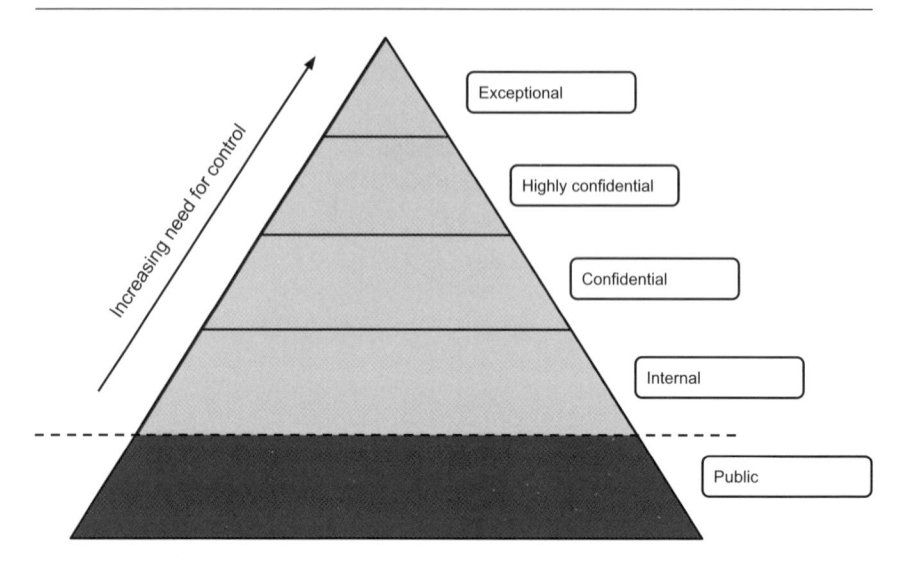

Pyramid showing data classification levels from bottom to top: Public, Internal, Confidential, Highly confidential, Exceptional. An arrow along the left side indicates "Increasing need for control".

The data classifications are defined as follows:

- *Public.* Public data is anything in the public domain and can, therefore, be treated as such. It's important to note, however, that a lot of data that is publicly available may be subject to copyright and you may not be able to copy or store that data on your own systems. Take, for example, a report from a research organization. You may have a licence that permits you to use the report but the copyright may prohibit you from making a copy available on your own system.

- *Internal.* Internal data is, surprise surprise, data that is internal to the company and is not therefore in the public domain. It should be shared internally only. Typical guidance for internal data is that it should not be shared outside of the company unless an authorized person has approved its use. An example of an internal document could be one that includes examples of client work, with client names explicitly cited. It would likely be in the company's interest to keep this out of the public domain as they wouldn't want their competitors to get hold of such information. It could also cause offence to the clients themselves if the data was leaked publicly, particularly if a non-disclosure agreement had been signed.

- *Confidential.* Data in this category is usually company or client data that is not freely available to all employees of the organization and is protected by the organization itself. This could be intellectual property, information about company deals, data from some internal company systems. Confidential data should never be transmitted or stored on traditional social networks, but an organization may allow the data to be shared on their enterprise social network, provided adequate controls around the data are implemented. The controls are important to ensure that the confidential data can be shared in the company only among those who are authorized to view it. The next section of this chapter, 'Implementing controls', delves into the types of controls that can be implemented on an enterprise social network to ensure security of the data.

- *Highly confidential.* For data classified at this level it is essential that it is highly protected. Probably only a small amount of data will fit into this category and it will usually relate to data that could move markets or government data where there is a specific requirement or obligation to maintain its confidentiality. An organization should have specific requirements around how highly confidential data should be handled, such as requirements around minimum levels of encryption, how long the data can be held and how it can be transmitted. I recommend that highly confidential data should never be stored on nor transmitted over a traditional social media network, and serious consideration needs to be given as to whether this data will be permitted on an enterprise social network. Most organizations I have come across do not allow highly confidential data to be stored on enterprise social networks and there is often a specific requirement from the client or organization, whose data it is, which stipulates where the data can and cannot be stored. Other data that may be classed as highly confidential could be HR data that includes sensitive personal data or the intellectual property or other sensitive data held on behalf of an organization's client or customers.

- *Exceptional.* Some organizations may not even have an exceptional category as they may not handle data of this type. Data of this type tends to be government protectively marked data (such as Top Secret) or where a client has specifically stipulated exceptional security requirements.

It's important to think about data classification, in line with your risk appetite (covered earlier in Chapter 2), when considering what you want your employees to share on either traditional social media or your enterprise social network. By setting clear criteria for defining data you can provide guidance to your employees and help them understand what they can and cannot share. On enterprise social networks you may want to think carefully about what types of data you allow your users to share. If you decide to allow highly confidential information to be shared, are you confident enough in the security and control over your chosen platform? Are you confident that you have implemented the right controls within the application to stop unauthorized persons within your own company from accessing that highly confidential information? These are all decisions that will be easier to make when you have set out your criteria for data classification.

Data archiving

While the issue of data archiving is mainly a regulatory and compliance one, it's important to recognize that it also applies to data on social networks – especially enterprise social networks. You are probably aware that organizations are required to retain certain pieces of data for some time depending on the type of data and the country in which the company operates. Many companies choose to retain and archive some of their data even if they are not required to do so by a regulator as it means that the data can be referred to at a later date if needed, for example in a court case. However, companies should be cautious about archiving all data because there can be separate regulatory requirements around it with regard to personal data and the requirements about how long that personal data can stored.

Data on traditional social networks can be a little tricky to archive, but there are tools available that will archive your social media posts for a fee. For enterprise social media, most of the vendors will be able to advise on their own options to support your archiving requirements and it's well worth investigating the options available early in order to get the right one for your organization.

In most countries, data subjects and law enforcement authorities have the right to request data about themselves or about a particular individual or entity, respectively. Because of this you'll also need to consider how quickly you can get access to your archived data, should you need it, and build this into your strategy.

Figure 4.3 illustrates, at a high level, how data archiving tends to be implemented. An online system can be accessed and used in real time and, usually on a periodic basis, data from the online (also known as 'live') system will be copied or moved to an offline data store. Accessing the data

FIGURE 4.3 Data archiving

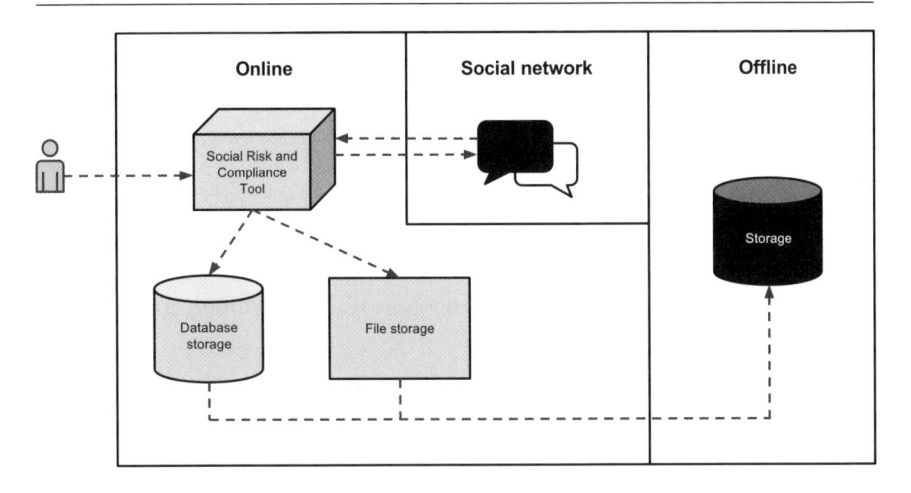

on the online systems is quick and easy, however accessing data on offline data stores is usually considerably more time consuming and expensive. In some ways, social networks sit in between these because they are third-party networks that have their own data archiving procedures. For example, some networks hold social media posts for only short periods of time before they are deleted, which means that your organization needs to implement an archiving solution to ensure that you can retrieve any conversations from social media should you be required to do so.

Implementing controls

There are two main types of control: policy controls and technical controls. In social media, policy controls are the rules that users or employees must follow. This also includes the procedures that users should follow, such as the approval process for the creation of a new group within an enterprise social network or the creation of a new account on a traditional social network.

Technical controls are those controls that physically limit an employee from doing something. For example, a policy may say that passwords should be changed every 30 days. Without a technical control, it is hard to ensure that this policy is adhered to, so a technical control such as a social risk and compliance tool may be implemented and configured to force the user to regularly change their password, in line with the policy. An accompanying procedure will also dictate how a user should go about allowing others to use a specific account, for example. Policy is covered in detail in Chapter 6. This section focuses on some of the technical controls that you can implement to control access to your social media accounts or to protect data within an enterprise social network.

Social risk and compliance tools

As discussed in Chapter 2, there is a significant information security risk related to the sharing of login credentials for traditional social media networks.

If you're creating an account on Twitter, for example, you may have 10 people in your communications and marketing teams who all need access to the account in order to make posts on your company's behalf. Unfortunately, without a tool to manage the accounts it means that the users will need to share the login credentials between each other. This represents a number of issues:

- It increases the risk that the credentials could be intercepted by a malicious attacker if they are sent over email. For example, a user may receive a phishing email containing a bogus link. The user clicks the link and enters their login details. At this point, the attacker would have captured the password and could then change the password for the social media account, meaning that nobody can log in until they have regained access to the account (which could take some time).
- If an employee who has access to the account leaves the company, you will need to have a process in place to change the login credentials. Again, the credentials will need to be communicated to the whole team.
- If the account credentials are changed too regularly users are more likely to start writing the credentials down, such as on a note attached to their computer screen. This obviously increases the risk that someone may spot the credentials and use them for malicious intent.

In the example above, one method of allowing multiple people to use the same account would be to implement a social risk and compliance tool, or a social media management system. These tools allow users to log into them with their own username and password and, once authenticated, can post content to the company social media account through the tool itself. This means that only the administrator of the tool would need the login credentials for the corporate social media account. The password would be configured in the tool, so there would be no need for users to log into the corporate social media account directly.

There are other advantages too – many of these tools can be configured with rules around what can be posted. For example, you may decide to include a dictionary of certain words within the tool and set rules around them as to what the tool should allow and what it should stop. It's possible to configure these tools to allow certain words, to block others, or to push certain posts through an approval process before being posted. This is clearly an attractive approach for those worried about the risks of social media. However, if all posts were forced through an approval process it can have a detrimental impact on the effectiveness of the posts since social media is inherently a fast-moving environment.

Figure 4.4 shows the difference between how employees access a social media account directly and how they would access a social media account

FIGURE 4.4 Social risk and compliance tool

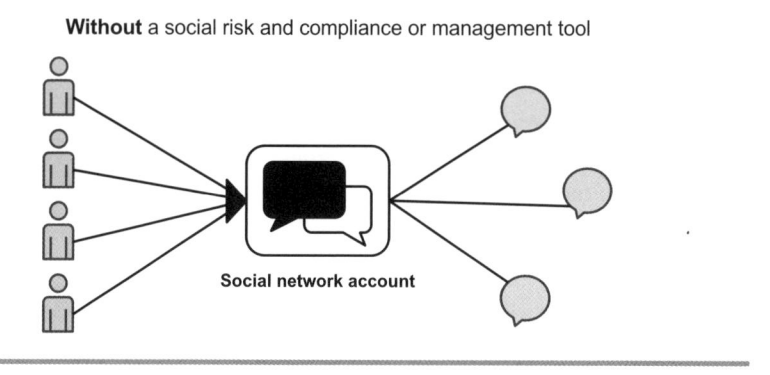

Without a social risk and compliance or management tool

Social network account

With a social risk and compliance or management tool

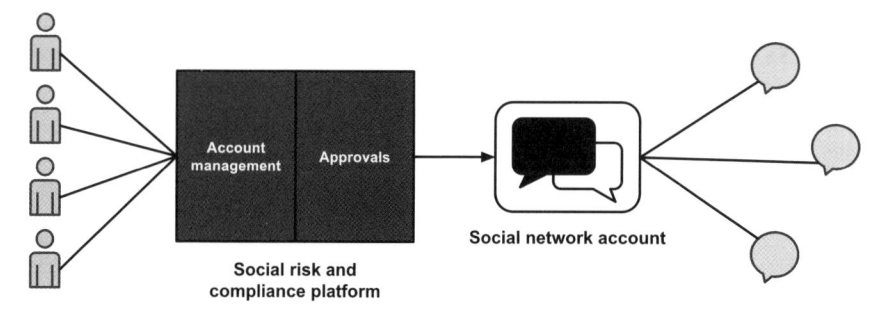

Account management | Approvals

Social risk and compliance platform

Social network account

when a social risk and compliance tools has been implemented. It illustrates that a social risk and compliance tool is an extra level of protection between your users and your social media account.

Another feature commonly included in social risk and compliance tools is archiving. Earlier in this chapter we covered the importance of archiving. Because all social media interactions take place through a social risk and compliance tool it means that it can easily capture and archive what was posted, to whom and when. By using such a tool you may be able to satisfy your data archiving requirements more easily.

CASE STUDY   Risk in action: UBS

In 2010 Swiss investment bank UBS implemented Jive, an Enterprise Social Network. In 2012, however, the bank was hit with a rogue trader scandal after one of its employees ran up a $2 billion loss on the bank's derivative desk.

The bank's legal department were worried that that they did not have enough control over what their employees could and could not comment on, thus the Jive platform was closed and their global head of online media and IT was quoted as having had to implement 'millions of controls' to satisfy legal.

This example shows how important it is to understand the risk management impact that the implementation of an internal social system can have. Engaging stakeholders in risk, compliance and legal early is more likely to yield long-term results than trying to push digital changes through an organization without their support.

SOURCE: www.computerworlduk.com/news/it-business/3472104/ubs-relaunches-internal-social-network-after-rogue-trader-scandal-forced-temporary-shutdown/

Access control within an enterprise social network

Once you have completed a data classification exercise, as detailed earlier in this chapter, you can decide what types of data you want to allow in your enterprise social network. You may want a mix of data, which means that you'll need different controls and procedures to handle each type of data. Let's say that you want to allow internal data (presentations, marketing material etc) to be shared openly on your platform. Let's say that you also want to allow your employees to gain the maximum benefit of an enterprise social and that you are going to encourage them to collaborate in teams on projects that might involve confidential data. It's at this point that you need to implement appropriate controls to ensure that only those within the project team are able to view the confidential content. Almost all enterprise social networks allow 'Groups' or 'Spaces' to be created within them. These are virtual areas that can be segregated from the wider network. You should define a policy and accompanying procedures for setting up such a project group, including appropriate approval procedures. Once a group has been created, you should make someone a group owner – it will be their responsibility to manage the users within the group and monitor the content being posted within the group. By doing this you can get comfort that the group owner will manage the group effectively and that confidential or sensitive data being shared within the group is only visible by those who are valid members of the project. Of course, the group owner needs to be aware of their responsibilities and should therefore be trained on how to manage the group, its members and its content appropriately. Training and awareness is covered in more detail in Chapter 6.

When implementing an enterprise social network it's also important to note that you can't rely solely on the controls within the network itself. It's important to ensure that outsiders aren't able to gain access to the platform, and that internal users cannot impersonate another user in some way to gain access to their data or the groups which they have access to. Security is covered in more detail in Chapter 8.

Summary

In this chapter I introduced the topic of data protection and familiarized you with some of the fundamental principles. While we didn't go into specific legislation in detail, we looked at data protection more generally and assessed some of the considerations that you need to make when implementing a global IT system, such as an Enterprise Social Network.

You now know what is important when it comes to data protection and you should now be more familiar with the issues and challenges that will be on the mind of your data protection officer. This knowledge will enable you to engage the data protection officer more effectively and, in turn, ensure the overall success of your social media programmes.

Finally, we looked at some of the practical steps that you can take to ensure the data within your systems is controlled and protected appropriately.

In the next chapter we will consider the different governance models and frameworks. Good governance will enable you to effectively engage with the other social media stakeholders in your organization and implement the required policies and procedures needed to ensure that social media risk is managed and that your social media programme is a success.

Governance

05

Overview

Governance is all about how you manage and operate social media within your organization. It's about connecting differing stakeholder groups and getting them to work together and pursue a common strategy and goal. Everyone has a role to play in social media. Governance sets out what those roles are and establishes mechanisms that enable stakeholders to work together and achieve success while managing risk and monitoring progress.

Measurement of social media success is an important part of governance because it will inform decision making. In this chapter, we will cover some of the key performance indicators that can be used to track your social media programme. We will also discuss some of the more controversial ways that organizations have attempted to control social media risk.

Roles and responsibilities

Why are they important to define?

Managing social media can be complex because of the wide range of stakeholders who have an interest in it. Defining clear roles and responsibilities makes it easier to visualize your social media landscape and to understand what drives different stakeholder groups. If roles and responsibilities are not clearly defined it increases the risk that the business's strategy will not be well executed and will increase the risk of something going wrong.

I like to define the stakeholders within three groups: those working for the organization; those external parties who are outside of the day-to-day operation of the company; and those that are transient and sit somewhere in the blurred line between inside and outside the company. Within the company there will be, undoubtedly, a number of departments or stakeholder groups who have an interest in social media use. The marketing department is probably the most obvious group who use social media but there are others who also have an important role to play, such as those in IT, Risk and Compliance, Recruitment etc.

Companies are structured and operate differently and sometimes you may find one person who plays a number of roles, while in others you may find whole teams of people responsible for one particular area with little crossover to other areas.

It's important to remember that it's not just those who have a formally defined role related to social media within a company who have a role to play; there are those outside the company too. Perhaps you have engaged an external PR company or social media agency to manage some or all of your accounts. Your suppliers may be using social media and may wish to engage with you on it. Don't forget that your competitors and their customers have a role to play too. Conversations and interactions on social media are often open to the public, which can be an opportunity for you to keep abreast of developments elsewhere in your industry. Keeping an eye on what your competitors are doing in social media and how their own customers are interacting with them can give you real insights into the competitive landscape and alert you to issues sooner. For example, if you know that both you and one of your competitors have a supplier in common and you begin to notice customers of your competitor complaining about an issue related to that supplier, it can act as a warning that can be flagged to your senior management, allowing you to plan for potential issues.

I like to describe employees and the connections and friends of employees as those in the 'transient' layer. They are obviously part of the organization but will probably not have a formal role to play in how it is managed. The reason that I describe them as 'transient' is because, while they may follow a company's social media accounts and occasionally share some of its content or post links to new products or services, they will have other personal interests that they share on social media.

Figure 5.1 illustrates the different stakeholders inside and outside an organization. The list below details the different groups of stakeholders within an organization and includes commentary about what their roles and responsibilities might be.

Internal stakeholders
Marketing
Marketing is often the owner of social media because social media is traditionally seen as a medium that can be used to market products and services and connect a business with its consumers. Marketing will be interested in improving brand loyalty and driving sales and will focus on hitting its social media targets.

Communications

Communications professionals will want to use social media to post information to the public or to their customers but not necessarily with the goal of driving sales. Instead, they will be more focused on informing them of something. Communications professionals will use traditional social media to broadcast information publicly or announce press releases. They will use an enterprise social network to broadcast messages or news internally.

Human resources

Human resources (HR) professionals will be the guardians of the policies that employees must follow, including social media. HR will want to ensure that employees are not spending excessive amounts of time on social media when they should be working, and that they are not using social media inappropriately, by engaging in cyberbullying or leaking company information.

IT

The IT department are the technical owner of an enterprise social network and are responsible for its accessibility and how it is used. IT will control how employees can access an enterprise social network, as well as whether or not employees can access traditional social networks and for how long each day.

Customer services

Nowadays, many people find it easier to simply send a tweet to a company instead of calling customer services to discuss some kind of issue or complaint. Many companies, particularly in the United States, have realized this and have trained up their customer services agents to use social media to engage with and respond to customers.

Recruitment

Many recruitment agencies already use LinkedIn aggressively to headhunt candidates for the jobs they are trying to fill. Employees of a company may also use social media to advertise positions that are open at the company. Recruitment managers are using social networks to do extra research into potential candidates, and many now feel that a candidate's LinkedIn profile can be a fairer reflection of a candidate because it has not been tweaked for a particular position, as CVs are.

Sales

The concept of social selling has emerged and we're now seeing sales people turning to social media to makes sales. Social media cuts down the amount of travel and face-time that has historically been required to sell a product. Sales professionals now use social networks to identify their targets, engage with them and build relationships online as a pre-sales activity.

Knowledge workers
The job of the knowledge worker is to ensure that information can be found by those who need it, and is a role that is common in knowledge-centric businesses such as consulting, engineering or law. Knowledge workers historically relied on archaic knowledge databases or repositories, however the rise of enterprise social networks has meant that they have turned their attention to encouraging knowledge sharing through these networks because it can be far more effective.

Risk, compliance and legal
The risk and compliance professionals within any organization will, more likely than not, have an opinion on how social media can, or should, be used. These people have a thorough understanding of any regulatory requirements that affect your business, and it's their job to ensure that these requirements are met. Risk and compliance professionals wield a lot of power when it comes to what can and cannot be done in the course of business and it's important, therefore, to engage them early in any plans to implement an enterprise social network to ensure that any specific requirements are included.

Internal audit
Organizations are waking up to the fact that social media poses a risk to business. Social media is now being listed on the risk register and internal auditors have begun including it within the scope of internal audits. They review the policies, procedures and other documentation related to social media in order to obtain reassurance that social media is being managed appropriately.

External stakeholders
Public relations or social media agency
Many organizations outsource the management of their social media presence to external agencies instead of employing in-house teams. In many cases, the external agency has complete control over the organization's social media accounts. This means that the organization will need to provide clear guidance about what the external agency can and cannot do in social media.

Competitors
Your competitors may be active in social media, perhaps more active than you are. They will be monitoring your posts and may even be analysing your own social media engagement to see if they can convert some of your followers to their own brand. You need to be aware of what your competitors are doing so that you can defend yourself if needed, or to exploit any potential opportunities.

Investors
Your investors and shareholders may have an interest in what your organization is doing on social media due to the impact that social media can have on your reputation and your share price. There are often strict legal or regulatory rules that govern how certain information can be released to investors or the public, so it's important that you are cautious about how you use social media to publish investor information.

Suppliers
By monitoring your suppliers' social media feeds you may be able to spot any issues in advance and implement any necessary contingency plans. Social media is the most effective way to detect any widespread negative sentiment about one of your suppliers. It may also make you aware of any potential ethical issues that your suppliers are facing and that go against the values of your own company.

Customers
Your customers play an important role in social media. Your customers may be reviewing your products or services online and will be able to influence other customers when it comes to the decision to buy your product.

Media/press
Media or news organizations might be following your company to report on any newsworthy events. This also means that if you make any embarrassing mistakes in social media, they will hit the mainstream news faster than you expect.

Regulator
Your regulator plays an important role in social media as they set out the rules with which you must comply, some of which will have an impact on how you use social media.

FIGURE 5.1 Social media stakeholders

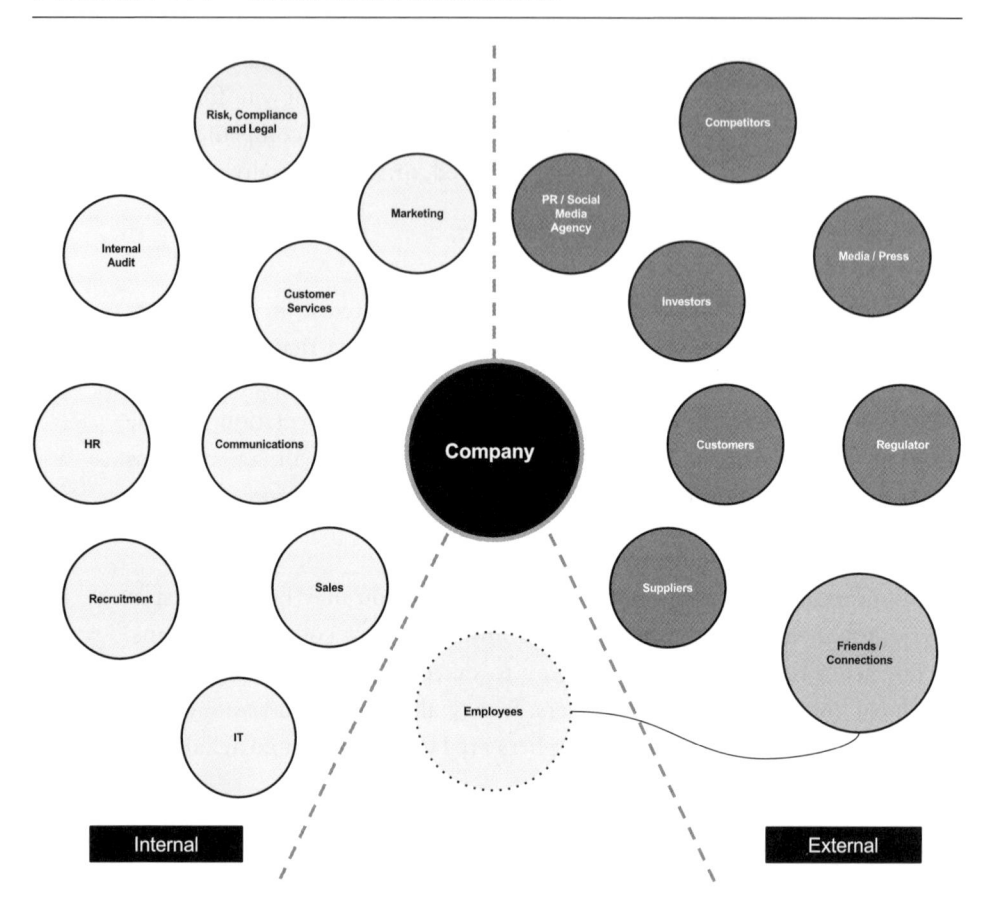

Ownership and sponsorship

Social media needs a clear owner who takes responsibility for, and is accountable for, social media. This is important because of the wide range of stakeholders who have an interest in social media at any given organization. It is also important because in times of crisis or when decisions need to be made quickly, having someone with authority will greatly improve the speed in which any issues can be resolved. It will depend on your organization as to who exactly takes ownership of social media, but the key thing is for someone to take this responsibility and be held accountable for its use.

Social media sponsorship is when someone in a senior position at a company, preferably on the board of directors, pledges support, or 'sponsorship', for a social media programme. The sponsor will provide support, funding and champion the programme at the senior levels of the company. Having a social media sponsor will give more weight to how social media is perceived and how it is operated. Social media is a board-level issue, and the board should be aware of it and have comfort that it is being managed appropriately. As we have seen, social media spans multiple departments, which can make it difficult to agree which department should take the hit to their budget for any investments that are needed. Having a board sponsor will also make it easier when it comes to budgets and investments, because the sponsor may be able to approve investments in social media, which will benefit multiple departments.

Figure 5.2 illustrates a typical structure of how social media might be governed in an organization.

Working groups and oversight

When it comes to managing social media on an operational basis, it's good to regularly arrange working groups where key representatives of each stakeholder group can meet to discuss what's happening in social media and give some oversight to any potential issues. The purpose of the meetings is to flag any new developments such as new accounts, new product launches, major events, press releases or risks that the organization may face and which may permeate social media.

Having a community that meets regularly like this will make it far easier to manage social media effectively, and the representation from other stakeholder groups will allow issues to be raised and debated collectively to ensure that appropriate actions, in line with the business strategy and risk appetite, are taken. Creating an email distribution list for all attendees or stakeholders is worthwhile in case there are absences from a meeting or in case certain people are out of the office at the time of the meeting. Any communications can also act as an audit trail to show that issues were raised and addressed, should there be a need to do so. A virtual private group within an enterprise social network can also be an effective way of both cutting down on email traffic and allowing better collaboration and communication around specific issues.

Regular meetings like this are also an opportunity for metrics to be tracked and assessed so that performance can be measured and any performance issues or risks can be addressed early to allow remediation plans to be implemented. The use of a RAG (Red, Amber, Green) status is a common way of assessing progress against objectives or the potential impact of any given risk. There will be a lot happening at any given time and the use of a RAG status is something that, when used correctly, can help focus attention on the

FIGURE 5.2 Social media governance framework

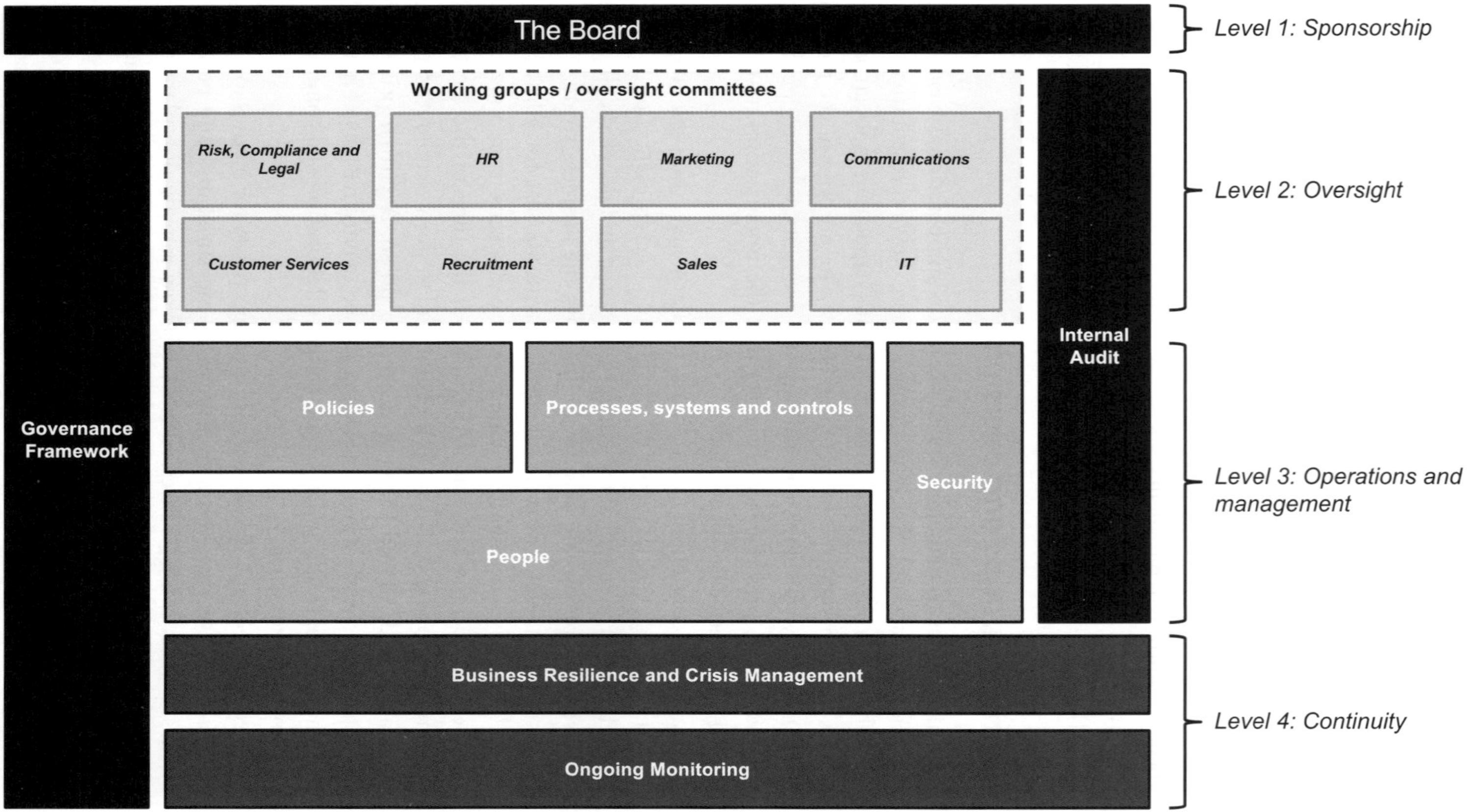

things that matter most. Be warned, however, that RAG statuses should be used honestly. I've seen progress dashboards in the past that have shown 'Green' for weeks when, in fact, there have been problems and an 'Amber' rating would have been more appropriate, but some people have a tendency to manipulate the status to hide those issues. I recommend that if a status is challenged during one of the working groups and the consensus is that it should be changed, that the dashboard be updated and retained as an audit trail.

A good way of keeping the board sponsor engaged in what's happening in social media is to present a monthly dashboard to them. This will ensure that social media continues to get the oversight it needs, and will give the board sponsor the opportunity to comment on any issues or developments that need their attention.

Figure 5.3 shows a suggested template for a working group dashboard that you can use and adapt to your own needs. You'll notice that it includes a section on risk and issues, which is a practical implementation of some of the risk management principles we looked at in Chapter 2.

Approvals and processes

Any organization that takes social media seriously should have well thought-out and documented processes, and should understand what sorts of activities need approval. What will need approval will depend on the nature of your business and its culture. For example, if you operate in a highly regulated industry, such as banking and finance, you will probably have more stringent approval processes around what content you post on social media and how you engage with people on social media than a business operating in a less regulated industry.

Seeking approval can take time, and in the fast-moving world of social media, being forced to obtain approval for social media posts can hamper how effectively an organization engages in social media. This may cause a risk that a response to any particular incident could be slowed considerably, causing the incident to gain prominence. I think the best balance is to allow a specific team or group of individuals the ability to post to social media without having to go through an approval process. These individuals, of course, should be well trained and experienced in understanding the impact that posts can have. They should also attend the working groups and have regular contact with other key teams within the organization to ensure that they are aware of any major developments or potential risks.

Many social media risk and compliance platforms can be configured to support your approval processes. You can grant permissions to a subset of

FIGURE 5.3 Social media working group dashboard

Social media working group dashboard

Period from: to: Overall RAG:

Progress tracking

Achievements this period:	Next steps:

Risk and issues

Description of risk	Description of impact	Likelihood (1 - 5)	Impact (1 - 5)	Risk Rating (likelihood x impact)	Owner	Comments

Milestones

Ref	Description	Planned Start Original	Planned Start Revised	Planned End Original	Planned End Revised	RAG	Status	Owner	Comments

users so that their posts do not need to be approved by another user. Many platforms also allow you to configure rules so that, for example, any use of a specific term forces the post to go into an approval queue.

Having resilient processes with agreed timescales is a good idea. It's worth always thinking of the 'what if' so that you can understand where there might be a breakdown in the process if, for example, one of the approvers is unavailable, sick or in a meeting when they're needed.

One of the tasks of the working group should be to design and document the process for the approval of content. Because the working group has representation from the key stakeholders, it should own the process and, once finalized, the documentation can be distributed to the wider social media stakeholders for reference. I recommend that a document repository is created where all of the documentation related to social media processes and policies can be stored. The repository could be as simple as a shared network drive or as complex as a document sharing platform such as Microsoft Sharepoint. It could also be stored within a private virtual group on an enterprise social network, which would allow comments and suggestions to be posted. What's more, most enterprise social networks keep a version history, making it easy to look back at previous changes.

Moderation

What is moderation?

In social media, moderation is the activity of removing or censoring posts that appear on your various pages. This could be moderation of the comments that appear on your videos on YouTube for example, or moderation of the content within your own enterprise social network. Moderation is an interesting topic because there are a number of different viewpoints and it can be difficult to agree on what should be moderated and what shouldn't. On one hand, the comments that some social media users post can be abusive, threatening or contain many unsavoury uses of language so you could argue that this content should be removed as it may offend other users. On the other hand, the removal of posts or comments can be fiercely opposed by some people who see it as censorship and an infringement of free speech.

It's understandable why it can be tempting to moderate posts if they contain false accusations or information, or if they reflect badly on your organization or its brand. Likewise, if inappropriate information or comments are posted on your enterprise social network then you will have a responsibility to respond to it and may be required to remove it. The most transparent way to moderate social media is to publish guidelines on what is acceptable and what is not, and moderate strictly according to these guidelines. Another effective way of performing moderation is through peer moderation, which we will cover in the next section.

Peer moderation

Peer moderation is performed by the users of a social network. You rely on the users to moderate posted content by giving them an option to mark certain posts as inappropriate or abusive. It's an effective method of moderation as it means that you, as moderator, only need to review those comments that are flagged by other users as abusive. You can review and then make a decision on what action to take, which could be to allow the comments, censor them in some way such as by replacing swear words with asterisks, or to remove the comment altogether.

When rolling out an enterprise social network it can be advantageous to implement peer moderation as it means that content does not need to be approved before it is posted. Configuring your system to instantly remove content that is flagged as inappropriate until someone has reviewed it is a sensible way of moderating content. You will need to consider who will receive alerts, and should consider global time zones and public holidays if your organization is global because the content may have been marked in error and your users will expect a quick turnaround.

If you have engaged an external PR or social media agency you should consider what timescales you want the agency to respond to content which has been marked as inappropriate. Ensuring that these terms are written into your contract should give you some comfort that the accounts are being managed appropriately.

Figure 5.4 shows an example of the process that you might set up to handle the moderation and how you might document it.

Automatic moderation with dictionaries

A common way of automatically moderating content is to use a dictionary of terms that the application will look up to ensure that none of the users' input contains any disallowed terms. This is a nice way of catching swear words or other offensive language, which you may want to keep off your enterprise social network and indeed most networks allow a dictionary to be configured. Some dictionaries of offensive terms are available online and

FIGURE 5.4 Moderation process flow

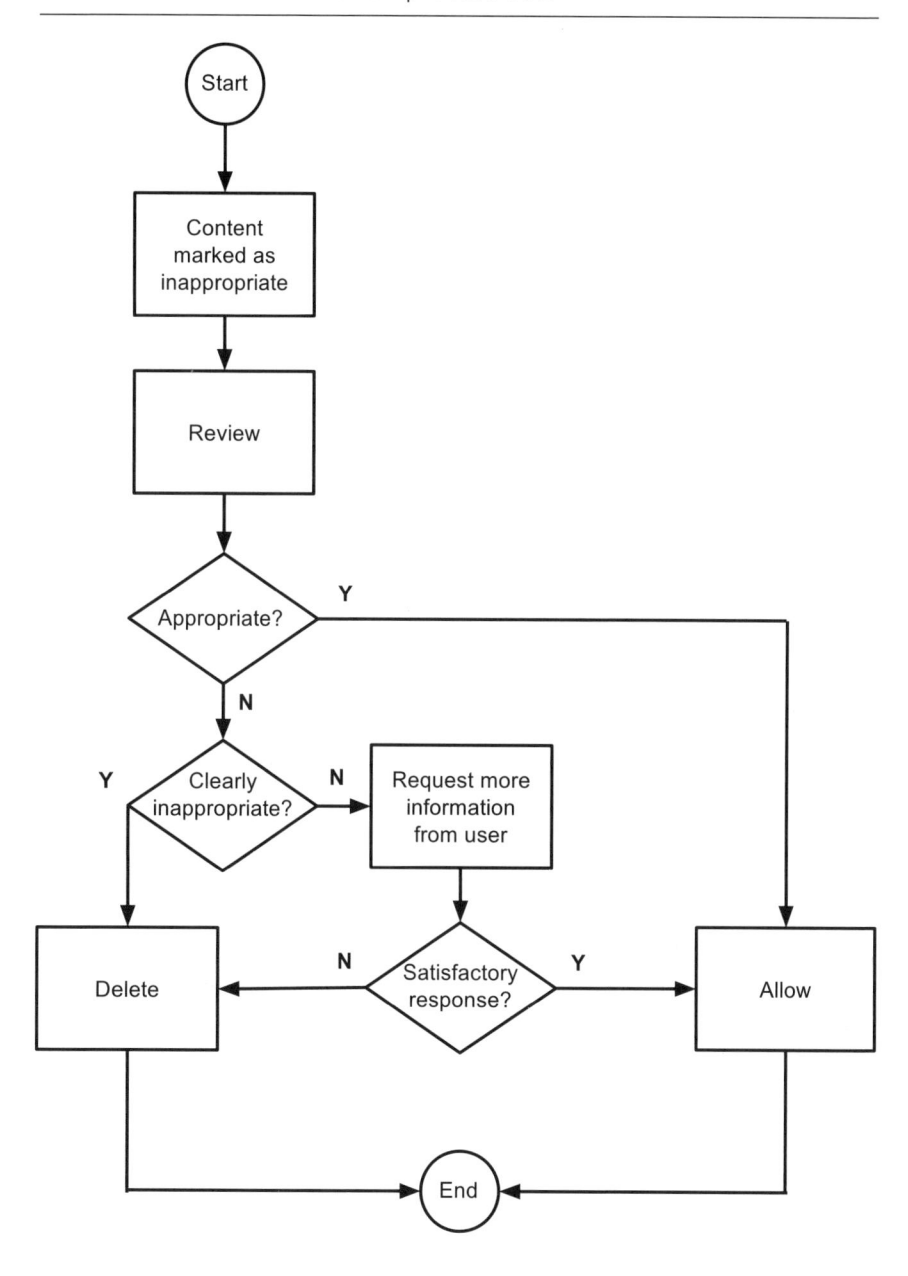

some come pre-bundled with the application or network you purchase. Some social risk and governance tools can also be configured to look up posts against a dictionary of terms. It's often possible to configure the tool so that certain words will be automatically blocked, or for certain words to force the post through a review process.

While dictionaries are useful to identify and remove offensive language, they also have other uses. For example, if you are going through a sensitive deal such as a merger or acquisition, and you do not want your employees to discuss or speculate on the deal, you could add the name of the other party or terms related to the deal to your dictionary as a way of stopping posts related to the deal going onto your network. You may have made a policy decision not to allow clients to be discussed on your enterprise social network, so adding your clients into the dictionary of terms would be another neat way of controlling their use. Some industries are obviously more regulated than others and the regulator may have specific requirements around how certain work can be carried out. Adding keywords into a dictionary to stop certain topics from being discussed, such as employee bonuses or other HR issues, can be effective at managing these risks. Be careful not to add common words, however, so that you don't end up inadvertently discouraging people from using the network. And don't forget that if you have implemented peer moderation (by the use of an 'inappropriate' button, for example) you are already on your way to managing the risks of the content posts by your users.

A word on censorship

Being in control of the content posted about your company on social media or within your enterprise social network is clearly important as it can expose you to a wide variety of risks if not monitored and managed effectively. That said, it's wise to think very carefully before deleting any content. The saying goes, 'think before you post', but 'think before you delete' is equally as relevant. When it comes to censorship, many organizations have learnt about the wrath of social media users the hard way. Many people fiercely oppose any type of censorship and indeed the question of online freedom continues to be hotly debated all over the world. There are many, many examples of companies trying to control what is said about them online, only to find the strategy backfires spectacularly. From the small bed and breakfast that issued fines to its guests who wrote negative feedback on TripAdvisor to huge multinational companies who try to hide information from the public, censorship in any form can be dangerous and can cause a somewhat small anecdote of bad service into a full-blown national news story.

CASE STUDY   Risk in action: hotel fines for negative reviews

Many people use travel review sites, such as TripAdvisor and Yelp, to research hotels before making bookings for upcoming journeys. This allows them to peruse reviews left by other guests, and make a more informed decision about whether or not a particular hotel is right for them.

In 2014 there were two occasions where hotels had fined guests because of bad reviews or negative comments that were posted on review sites.

First, in August it came to light that a guesthouse in Hudson, New York, had a policy that stated that for every negative review left on Yelp regarding a wedding booking, the bride and groom would be charged a fine of $500. The policy also stated that the fine would be refunded when a bad review is taken down.

It's not much of a surprise that when this hit mainstream media the guest house received a barrage of complaints, and more bad reviews, from social media users who were disgusted by the policy. One reviewer said 'This is the worst business practice I have ever heard of'.

Second, in November a hotel in Blackpool, UK, fined a couple £100 for leaving a negative review on TripAdvisor in which they referred to the hotel as a 'filthy stinking hovel'. The 'fine' was taken from their credit card a few days after their stay. Again, this story hit mainstream media and the hotel was widely slammed by the public.

This practice is unethical and, in the cases above, backfired as the hotels received significant negative press as a result of their policies, with many seeing the policies as a way of bullying guests. These incidents further illustrate the dangers of trying too hard to control what people say about your brand or company on social media. There will inevitably be negative comments about your brand, but trying to control what people say online is not the answer.

SOURCES: www.telegraph.co.uk/finance/newsbysector/retailandconsumer/leisure/11011278/US-hotel-fines-guests-500-for-bad-reviews.html
www.bbc.co.uk/news/technology-30100973

Copyright

Questions around copyright are often raised when considering social media or marketing in general. While many marketing professionals will be aware of the constraints to the use of copyrighted material, others in your organization may not be so well versed in the risks of copyright infringement, particularly when it comes to the use of imagery.

If you're looking for an image to add to a report or a presentation, it's a bad idea to simply use Google Images. It can be hard to determine who owns the copyright for any particular image and whether or not you are allowed to use or reproduce it.

If you take a photograph of a beautiful sunset while you are on holiday, for example, you own the copyright for that image. Nobody can use that image for any purpose unless they have obtained your permission to do so. This may seem pedantic, but when it comes to business, infringing copyright can be a very costly mistake to make. There are a number of 'stock imagery' websites where you can buy images for commercial use. There are often a number of different licences available depending on how you want to use the image, and the costs of the image may depend on the physical size (in pixels) of the image itself. Some licences will allow you to use the image only online, another licence may extend the terms to include print, some licences might be for specific countries, and others might be worldwide.

There are tools available that can search the web to find instances where your own images have been used – if the person does not have your permission to use the image, you can request that they remove it, or in some circumstances even request compensation. Social media is a great place to share your marketing material but, the point here is to ensure that you own the rights to use whatever imagery you choose in whatever fashion you choose to use it.

The topic of copyright extends further than just images and is just as relevant when considering the content your users share within an enterprise social network. Your users may come across reports or research related to your industry and may decide to upload the report to your enterprise social network to share more widely with their colleagues. However, the user should check for any copyright marks on the document, and if it is copyright protected they should seek permission from the copyright holder before uploading it. If they don't you may find that your enterprise social network turns into a repository of illegally hosted copyright material. In my experience, most users don't realize that by uploading a document to an enterprise social network they are actually creating a copy of the document which may infringe copyright. The simplest solution to this is to educate the users of the risks of copyright infringement and encourage them to submit a link to the report or document, rather than uploading the actual document itself.

If it comes to your attention that users have uploaded copyright information, I recommend that you contact them, firstly to make them aware of how copyright can be infringed by uploading documents to an enterprise social network, and secondly to ask them if they have obtained the permission of the copyright holder to store the material on your network. I would include a note to say that you will automatically remove the content if you do not receive adequate assurances that the material does not infringe copyright within 30 days. If the content is within a group, it is worth copying the message to the group owners as well. More often than not, the user will simply acknowledge the mistake and replace the document with a link.

Data quality

What is it and why is it important?

Believe it or not, data can be of a good quality or a poor quality. At first, this may seem an odd concept as surely data is just data…? But no, data is not just data. In today's society, data is being created constantly. That includes such things as when we pay for something using our credit card, when we send messages to each other, or when we 'like' a social media post. So, what is data, and is it the same as information? The following is an example of some data:

31, 30, 31, 30, 31, 31

On its own, data is meaningless and is, therefore, not information – it's just some data. The data above becomes information when I say that it is the number of days in March, April, May, June, July and August. Incidentally, you'll notice that I deliberately started from March as February would have just over complicated matters…! It's true that the word 'data' is often used interchangeably with the word 'information', but for the purposes of this explanation let's think about them as being separate. Information is data with a context – without a context or any way of knowing what the data is, it's just considered data.

The problem of data quality comes when we start thinking of larger amounts of data. If you asked 100 people to fill in a form with details of where they live, you might find that a large number of respondents reported to live in London. So, it's logical to think that if you wanted to analyse this data in some way, you could say 'Show me all of the people who live in London'. However, you might find that some people typed 'london', others

'LONDON' and some might have mistakenly entered 'Llondon'. In this example, we have quite a lot of dirty data and need to perform a data cleansing exercise. This is the process of cleaning the data and making it accurate and in the same format. While a human might be able to compare 'London' and 'Llondon' and deduce that it is the same place, a computer cannot. Thus, if you look at how many people live in 'London' in this example, a computer may give a lower number as it is not intelligent enough to work out that the two are, in fact, the same.

So, data quality is all about how uniform and accurate any given data set is. Other issues can exist too; for example, just because five people stated that they live in 'London' and that 'London' is in the same format within the data set, it does not mean that the data can be fully relied upon – someone may well have answered London because they misread the question in some way or because of the difficulty of defining geographical boundaries. For reference, in data analysis a margin of error would normally be applied to counter this and make the results more accurate, but this is not relevant to this particular topic.

The reason that data quality is important is because, in today's world, we are all far more reliant on data when making decisions than we were in the past and, indeed, companies make many business decisions based on data. If a certain data set (for example, sales data) was being relied upon for decision making (say, to compare with marketing spend), but the sales data was of poor quality (perhaps it included duplicates), then the decisions made based on this data are likely to be poor and have negative consequences for the business.

There is a vast amount of data within social networks and there are many tools and packages available to help you analyse that data and gain insight to help you make decisions. It's important, therefore, that you understand the data you are analysing as well as the quality of that data. Ensuring that you maintain good quality data offers many benefits. When it comes to negotiating budgets, having confidence in your numbers and being able to cut the data in different ways to show different insights can be extremely valuable.

Later in this chapter we will look at how you can measure the success of a social media programme and what metrics you can use. A good consideration and awareness of the quality of your data will help cut down on the number of unexpected surprises that you may face. It's likely that you'll have a number of key performance indicators (KPIs), which you will use to assess how effectively your social media programme is running. Understanding the data that drives these KPIs will give you greater confidence and more reliable insights into the data.

Types of data: structured and unstructured

There are two types of data: structured data and unstructured data. Structured data has defined attributes and is presented in a consistent manner. Data within a database or a spreadsheet is considered to be structured data as it is held within various fields within a table or column in a spreadsheet. Therefore, a postcode would be stored in a postcode field, a name would be stored in a name field, and so on. Sometimes structured data will include references to other fields or pieces of data; for example, an order reference number may refer to order data in another database table or spreadsheet. Structured data is, therefore, usually stored in some kind of logical and uniform fashion.

Unstructured data, on the other hand, usually refers to data where there is no structure or logic. For example, a field containing 'I'm reading a great book about social media risk and governance' would be classed as unstructured. It's not possible to easily analyse the contents of the field because it could contain absolutely anything – there is no structure to it. While the format of a postcode is standard, the contents of a text field, or a social media post, is not standard.

Figure 5.5 provides some examples to illustrate the differences between structured and unstructured data.

FIGURE 5.5 Structured and unstructured data

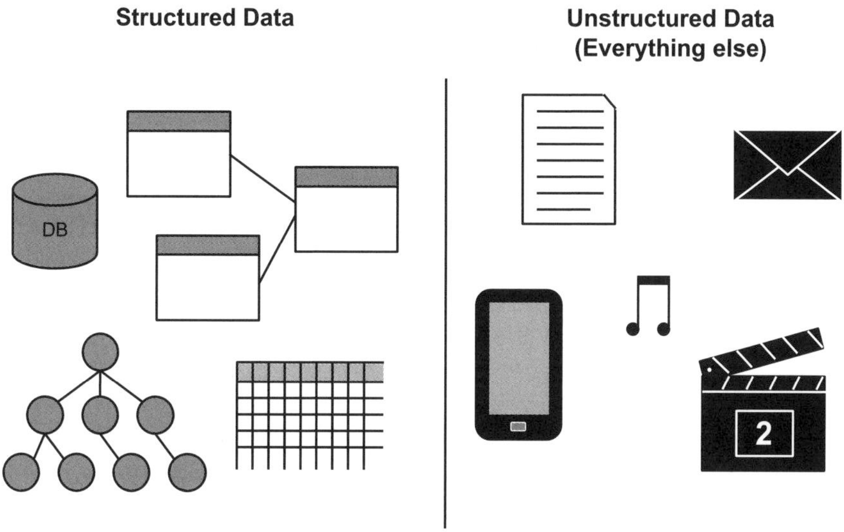

Sentiment analysis

Sentiment analysis is the term given to the analysis of a social media post in order to determine the 'sentiment' of the post. The sentiment is usually expressed as positive, negative or neutral, or is displayed on a scale, to describe mood. The purpose of sentiment analysis is to determine whether social media posts about any given term or criteria are generally positive, negative or neutral. Therefore, if you want to determine the overall sentiment towards your brand during a particular timeframe you could use sentiment analysis.

Many people try to use sentiment analysis in order to measure how people feel about a brand or company. Sentiment analysis is inherently difficult to do accurately due to the complexities of the languages we speak. This is mainly due to the fact that the data you can analyse from social media posts is usually in an unstructured format. For example, a post that says 'I love the products from company X' would show positive sentiment, 'I hate the products from company X' would show negative sentiment, and 'I just bought a product from company X' would show neutral sentiment. The complexities in the languages that we speak can make it very difficult for a computer to understand the real meaning of the words. Sarcasm is notoriously difficult for computers to understand. Most of us would probably understand a post saying 'massive queues at all of the tills – brilliant!' to be negative, but computers have a tough job identifying such linguistic nuances and may class this as positive due to the use of the word 'brilliant'.

There are many applications and platforms available that claim to be able to analyse sentiment towards a brand, however you should be careful how much trust you put into the algorithms that drive the sentiment scores due to the inherent difficulty of language analysis. If you use sentiment scores as part of your regular metrics you should be wary of how accurate (or inaccurate) the score can be.

CASE STUDY   Risk in action: UKIP – sentiment analysis difficulties

The United Kingdom Independence Party, commonly known as UKIP, is a eurosceptic, right-wing political party in the United Kingdom. In May 2014 the party decided to use a hashtag, #WhyImVotingUKIP, to give their supporters a way of voicing their support for the party and give them the ability to articulate the reasons for their vote.

It all started innocently, with UKIP members and supporters tweeting about why they were voting for the party. Unfortunately for UKIP, however, the idea backfired and the hashtag was quickly hijacked by other Twitter users who used it to poke fun at the party. Many tweets marked with the hashtag #WhyImVotingUKIP contained obviously sarcastic, and sometimes offensive comments.

I don't wish to comment on UK politics, however, the hashtag hijacking was fairly easy to predict by anyone who regularly uses social media.

This example of a hashtag hijacking effectively illustrates how difficult it is to accurately analyse sentiment. When I read down the tweets containing the hashtag it was generally clear when I was reading a sarcastic tweet. Other tweets, however, were more difficult to determine and required me to look at the user's profile to try to determine whether they were being sarcastic or not.

The point is that if a human is finding it difficult to determine whether something is sarcastic, and determine whether it includes positive or negative sentiment, then it must be considerably more difficult for a computer to accurately assess the sentiment.

Examples of Twitter hashtag hijackings are common and are often predictable, yet companies still fall foul of them. Social monitoring tools can give you a good awareness of current perceptions of your brand or company and should inform your decisions on which hashtag you create.

SOURCE: www.theguardian.com/politics/2014/may/21/whyimvotingukip-when-a-hashtag-goes-wrong-nigel-

Taxonomy

Taxonomy is the way in which social media content or posts are classified. In traditional social media, the most common tool for classifying content is through the use of hashtags, which are preceded with the hash (or number, or pound) symbol, '#'. The idea of the hashtag is to make it easier to find content or posts related to a specific topic because you can search for the hashtag and pull up all posts that contain it. There are no rules as to what a hashtag can be – social media users have total free reign to make up whatever hashtag they wish.

Many organizations create specific hashtags to accompany marketing or awareness campaigns about their products or services. You may have also noticed that it's becoming popular for a hashtag to be shown on screen at the start of some TV programmes to allow viewers to discuss the programme on social media. If you are considering what hashtag to use, it's worth doing some research and getting some opinions. You should search the major social networks to see if the hashtag has been used before and, if it has, in what context, so that you can avoid accidentally associating your organization with something unsavoury or irrelevant.

It's also worth looking to see if there are any other meanings of the hashtag in question. One entertaining example of a hashtag gone wrong was when it was used to promote the launch of the album of UK singer and Britain's Got Talent contestant, Susan Boyle. The hashtag that Susan's PR company chose to use to promote her album party was #susanalbumparty. Unfortunately, instead of reading #SusanAlbumParty, it could also read #SusAnalBumParty. Hashtags don't include apostrophes and so it quickly got noticed by many social media users and was reported in the media, causing it to be changed shortly afterwards. If you're planning to use an acronym as your hashtag it's worth doing some research to ensure that there aren't any rude connotations that might cause harm to your brand.

Content within an enterprise social network also needs to be classified in some way to help the users of the platform find what they are looking for. Most networks allow content to be shared within specific groups and categorized in some way. Often group administrators have the ability to create their own categories within their group so that new content can be marked as part of a specific category. Furthermore, most networks allow content to be tagged with keywords or hashtags. These tags are important because when a user types in a search term, the tags that have been assigned to content will drive the search results.

Some users will find it frustrating to have to type in tags or keywords when they post content to an enterprise social network. However, including instructions and guidance for content categorization and tagging within your training will encourage proper use of tags, and will help your users find the content they are looking for more easily.

Like traditional social media, tags within an enterprise social network are not usually controlled, so any user can choose any tag they wish for a piece of content. This can cause problems, however, because what might seem like an obvious tag to one person may not be so obvious to another. Some users may use abbreviations for their tags, others may use the full text. In this scenario, there may be two tags which mean the same thing, but which are spelt differently. This links back to the issue of data quality because having content which is not categorized in a standard way will mean that the data is difficult to search or analyse. Therefore, you should give consideration to how your taxonomy will be managed. Things that should be specified include:

- how many tags should be created;
- whether or not abbreviations should be used; and
- how many words a tag can consist of.

This guidance should be available to the users of the network so that they can refer to it and create correct tags from the outset. Some users, of course, will ignore the guidance and create their own tags that do not conform to the standards outlined in your taxonomy. When this happens, you may find it worthwhile to clean up the tags. Your chosen vendor should be able to provide you with extracts and mappings so that you can more easily view all of the tags that are being used within your network and the number of items they are tagged to. This will help you identify which tags need to be updated. By completing this exercise regularly, it will help your users to navigate the content within your network more easily and, in turn, find the content that they are looking for.

Figure 5.6 shows how a taxonomy can be designed and documented in a tree form so that it's easy to see how many levels of categorization there are, which sub-categories fit in which categories, and so on.

Monitoring

Why is it important to listen?

Social media is a place where conversations are happening every minute of every day, with people all over the world discussing any topic that they are interested in. There's a huge amount of data being generated all of the time which can make it difficult to understand how to monitor the conversations which are relevant to your organization. Monitoring, or 'listening' as it's often called in social media, is an important and ongoing task. As I have said before, social media is not a broadcast channel for your marketing material, it is a place where people connect and have fluid conversations.

You obviously can't monitor every post in social media so to start off you should complete an assessment to work out which people or organizations are engaging in content related to your own brand. You should determine who the influential users are. Influential users could be celebrities, other prominent figures, journalists or bloggers. These people may have a large following and they may also be followed by other influential people. By

FIGURE 5.6 Taxonomy tree diagram

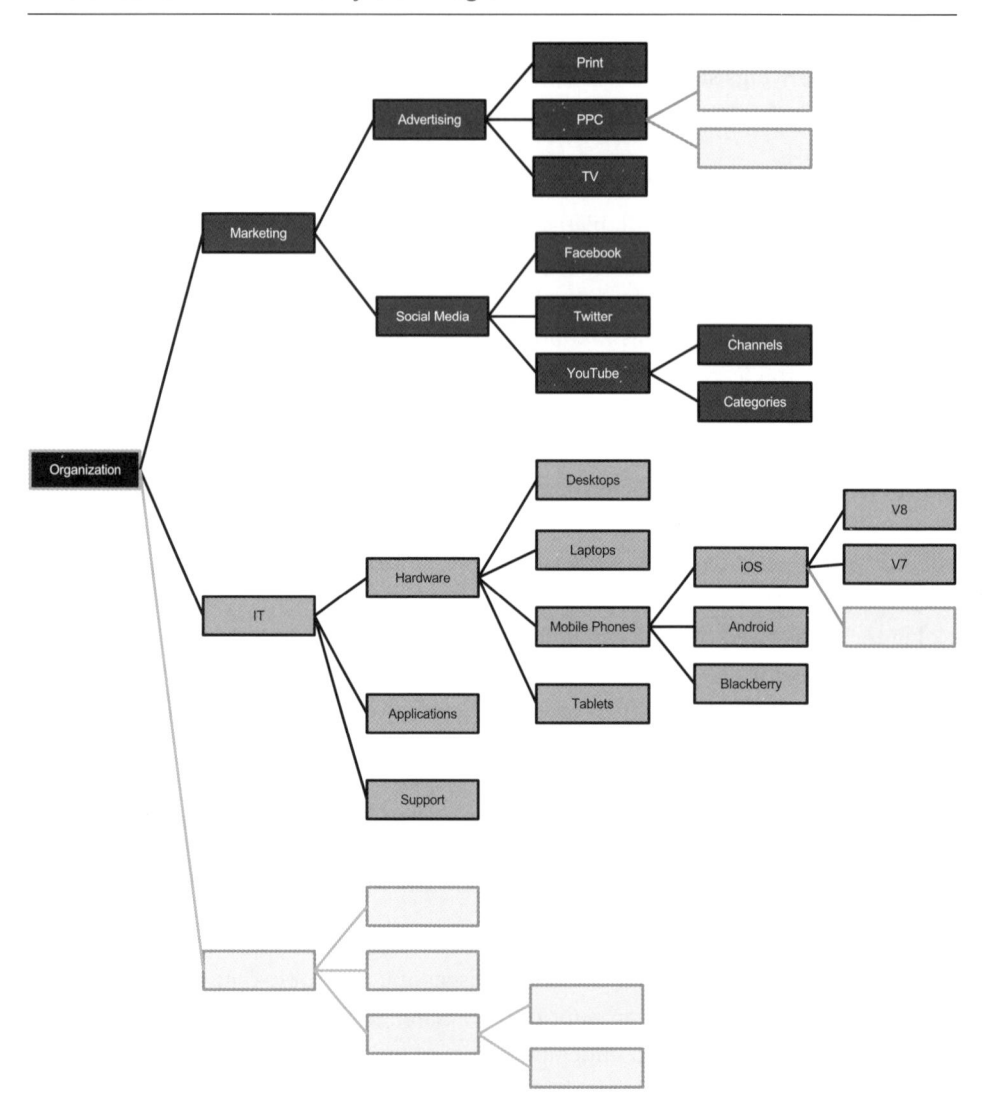

performing an assessment of the conversations taking place in social media you'll also be able to tell what topics resonate more with social media users within a specific network. This valuable information can then flow into your content strategy to ensure that when you do post content and engage with social media users that your posts are relevant and of interest to your targets.

By monitoring social media effectively you'll be alerted to any potential issues or opportunities much more quickly, and in turn be able to promptly address the issue or exploit the opportunity. A lot of social media is about timing, similar to news. News that's not current is no longer news, and people tend to engage on social media about things that are current and happening now.

Monitoring and listening tools

There is a very wide range of social media listening tools available on the market. Some of the popular platforms are Salesforce Radian6, ViralHeat and Talkwalker, however there are many, many more options available. Many social media management platforms include some analytics and listening functionality; some for free, some at a price.

The key things to consider when assessing which social media listening platform is right for you are your requirements, your current infrastructure, and your future ambitions. It may take time to implement and configure your chosen platform so you will need to document your requirements and perform an assessment of the tools available. Language is another important consideration. If you operate globally and have multiple accounts that post in foreign languages, you'll probably want to purchase a tool that can handle these complexities.

Some of the tools on the market only work with specific social networks, or work more effectively with certain social networks than they do with others. If you want to perform historic analysis on trends over time, you may want to purchase a tool that gives you access to the so-called Twitter Firehose. The Twitter Firehose guarantees 100 per cent of tweets for a given criteria, whereas the Twitter Application Program Interfaces (APIs) impose limits on the amount of data that can be processed. An API is a set of routines, protocols and tools for building software applications. Developers can easily access the Twitter APIs for free whereas access to the Firehose can be very costly. In summary, it's important to consider your monitoring requirements in advance to ensure that you make the right choice when purchasing a monitoring tool for your organization.

Performing social media analytics can be a time-intensive task as it often requires somebody to research the reasons for any significant changes or unexpected results. The social media landscape also changes quickly – the people that you engage with may change too, and new influencers may appear and others disappear. To keep on top of this I recommend giving someone the responsibility for social media analytics to ensure that the task gets the focus it deserves. A little later we will look at the metrics and performance indicators that you might choose to track.

Monitoring employee use of social media

The question of whether employers can or should be able to monitor their employees' social media usage is a complex one and often something that requires specific legal advice. I'm not going to address the specific legal points to employee monitoring here as I'm not qualified to do so, however, we will explore some of the issues more generally. Some other legal or regulatory issues will be addressed in Chapter 9, such as the ownership of social media accounts or the use of social media in recruitment.

In short, it is technically possible to monitor employee social media usage, in the same way that it is possible to monitor email or internet usage, and there are commercial tools on the market which will allow you to do this. I believe that the real issue, however, is one of ethics. I question why an employer would want to monitor an employee's social media usage, or why they feel that they have the right to in the first place. Up-to-date policies for social media or IT usage are less intrusive forms of controlling social media use. Within these policies you should clearly set out what is acceptable and what is not acceptable. While it is understandable that employers will want to protect their organization's reputation, as well as protect their other employees from things such as cyberbullying, most of this can be done using policy controls.

One of the common reasons cited by organizations that want to monitor employee use of social media is to counter loss of productivity. Some employers choose to block social media sites on company devices to try to stop their employees from accessing them. Nowadays, however, most people have access to their social media networks through their personal smartphones, so I question how effective blocking social media on work computers actually is. Outside of work, of course, it's highly likely that your employees will use social media and may indeed make posts related to their work.

Some employees have found themselves in trouble because, having phoned in to report that they are sick, they then post photos of themselves having a nice day out somewhere. If a post like this is reported to the employer and investigated, the employer may well be within its right to discipline the employee in question. However, if the organization had been secretly monitoring its employees without having received adequate legal advice, and without appropriate policies and controls in place, it gets trickier. Privacy is a topic many people feel strongly about, so any tactics that may be seen to infringe someone's privacy are likely to be met with hostility. Privacy policies are a way of setting out what an organization does with the data it collects about employees, and this topic is discussed in more detail in Chapter 6.

Another challenge that employers face in employee monitoring is complying with different laws around the world. If your company is global you will need to ensure that you comply with all necessary local laws. There are, for example, considerable differences between what is acceptable in the United Kingdom and what is acceptable in some of the individual states of the United States.

After receiving independent legal advice, if you do decide to engage in social media monitoring of your employees, you should do so in an ethical manner. This means that you should be open about the purpose of the monitoring, and what you'll be monitoring. Monitoring employees through deception is considered to be unethical and should be avoided. An example of deceptive techniques for employee monitoring might be creating fake social media accounts that you use to request a connection with an employee for the purposes of monitoring them. In November 2008 a 31-year-old Swiss woman who worked for Nationale Suisse called in sick one day due to a migraine. She reportedly accessed Facebook from bed and was then fired by the company due to a breakdown of trust. The company claims that a co-worker who she was friends with her had noticed and informed management. But, the woman believes the company had created a fake account, made friends with her through it and used the account to spy on her.

In general, I would discourage companies from monitoring their employees' social media usage unless there is a specific need to do so, where the employee is aware of the monitoring and where it is ethical. If you plan to implement a tool to monitor employee social media usage I strongly advise that you seek legal advice before doing so.

Metrics and performance indicators

What can you measure?

Accurately measuring return on investment in social media is difficult, but there are a number of metrics that can be monitored to measure the success of a social media programme.

KPIs fit into four main categories:

- *Reach*. Reach describes how many users see the content that you post, which drives awareness over time.
- *Engagement*. This category defines those actions performed by users where they are actively engaging around you or your content.

- *Influence.* Those with authority have more influence than others. If you are seen as a leader in your field then you will have greater influence.

- *Advocacy.* When users actively support you and recommend you, your brand or your content to their own connections, this is classed as advocacy.

It's important to monitor the success of your social media programme regularly, and to report the metrics to social media working groups as well as the programme sponsors. This can focus effort in the right place to improve poor metrics, and help to ensure that focus is directed in the right place in any given time period. It may well be that, over the course of a year, certain metrics are more important than others. For example, at the start of a marketing campaign, awareness may be more important than engagement; however, towards the end of the campaign, advocacy may be more important.

Often, the objective of social media posts is to drive users to your own website in order for them to either engage in some of your content or purchase products or services. Social media metrics should not be looked at in isolation; instead they should be reported along with broader website metrics. By linking the two metrics you'll be able to get more insight into where your users are coming from and which posts are more successful than others. By regularly reviewing the metrics, over time you'll begin to understand which pieces of content drive certain actions. This information can be extremely useful and will go a long way to helping you reach your goals.

Social media doesn't sit still, though. Your followers will change; posts that might have high engagement rates one month may not generate the same interest the next month. This may be due to outside factors, such as popular news stories at any given time. This emphasizes the importance of having a robust social media monitoring programme in place, as discussed earlier in this chapter, so that you can constantly tweak your posts and hit your targets. The fact that a post gets X number of retweets means little on its own. You need to analyse why that was, what it was that engaged the users, and which users were engaged by the content. Sometimes content is retweeted for the wrong reasons.

When mistakes happen and something gets posted by accident that causes embarrassment to a company, often it will be retweeted or shared by a huge number of people in a short space of time. In isolation, it may look like your performance indicators for engagement are very successful. Until, that is, you delve into the detail and uncover the real reason for the high number of engagements.

Table 5.1 shows the key performance indicators for four of the most common social networks. Note that some metrics can be part of multiple categories and that the ultimate category is subjective.

Metric visualization

With so much information available, it can be difficult to visualize performance. This makes it challenging to ascertain whether or not a social media programme is reaching its targets. For those who are aware of social media and its importance, but don't necessarily understand how each network works or how users are engaging with an organization, it can be quite intimidating to see a long list of metrics.

To bring the metrics to life I recommend using data visualization techniques and dashboards. This can be as simple as plotting a graph or chart using your metric data, or more complex, such as a tool which allows users to drill down into the data and manipulate it in different ways.

Once you have an agreed set of metrics and performance indicators you will report on regularly, then you can begin to design how they will be displayed. Many social media monitoring platforms come with ready-made visualizations; however, you are then constrained to the visual representations created by the vendor of the platform. To overcome this, you should build your own dashboards to extend the functionality and reports available within your chosen listening platform.

The first step to building a dashboard for your social media metrics is to define the data you will use. You want to get to an end result where you have a dataset or spreadsheet containing all of the data you will use to calculate your metrics. Once the format has been established it should not change, unless you decide to tweak your reports at a later date, at which time you may need to update your dashboard too.

There are a number of good data visualization tools on the market, the main ones being QlikView, Tableau and Spotfire. All allow you to build dashboards that you can use to display and manipulate data by applying filters, date ranges and so on. You should consider how your data will be refreshed, meaning how often you will take a new cut of the data and load it into your dashboard. The advantage of building your own dashboard is that, once created, all you need to do is load an updated dataset in order to refresh the dashboard.

It's possible to get deeper insights into your audience by looking at splits in gender, location, age, and so on. Many of the common social networks provide analytics and allow you to export data about your posts.

TABLE 5.1

Platform	Reach	Engagement	Influence	Advocacy
Twitter	# of followers	# of retweets # of favourites # of replies	Klout* score Influence of followers	# of mentions Sentiment
Facebook	# of friends/fans # of shares # of check-ins # of page views	# of likes # of user comments/posts # of repeat check-ins	# of page likes/fans	# of shares
YouTube	# of views # of channel views	# of connections # of likes/dislikes	# of embeds	# of channel subscribers
LinkedIn	# of comments # of views (on posts) # of members (in group) # of discussions (in group) Size of network	# of post comments # of post likes	# of followers	# of shares (on posts) # of mentions # of recommendations # of endorsements

* Klout is a third party tool which aims to measure influence using a scale of 0 to 100.

These extracts often include information about the demographics of your audience, such as gender or geographical location, which is extra insight that you can build into your dashboard. Figure 5.7 is an example of a metrics dashboard.

False metrics

In the pursuit of targets, it can be tempting to manipulate the metrics in some way to make it look as though performance is better than it really is. This is not only unethical, it's also a bad idea in the long term and may hamper your future success. One of the most common ways that social media users, as well as companies, manipulate metrics in order to appear more successful is through the purchase of followers or likes. There are a large number of people out there who will increase your total number of followers for cash. However, the new followers are likely to be 'bots' or fake accounts created solely for the purpose of increasing the total number of followers an organization has.

Firstly, this practice goes against the terms and conditions of most social networks, and engaging in it increases the risk that your account will be banned. Furthermore, it is relatively easy to spot accounts that have paid for followers, because they may have a suspiciously high number of followers in relation to the amount of content posted. It's also possible to analyse an account's followers to gain insight, such as the geographical location of the majority of followers. The location can imply that followers have been purchased because many of the people who offer to increase your followers control thousands of accounts in specific countries – India, for example. If your organization does not operate in India and you have a strangely large number of Indian followers, it's a sign that followers are likely to have been purchased. So, why does this matter? Well, it shows that you engage in practices that are based on deceiving other social media users into thinking that you are more influential than you actually are. This will likely cause a breakdown in trust between you and your target social media users, which may backfire and cause users to turn against you and your social media programme due to this unethical behaviour.

Purchased social media followers are not real, and therefore will not engage with your content. Therefore, your metrics will suffer because your total number of followers will increase but the ratio between followers and interactions will decrease. Building a strong social media presence takes time and shortcuts are likely to hamper your efforts and harm your reputation. By executing your strategy and engaging in ethical social media

FIGURE 5.7 Metrics dashboard

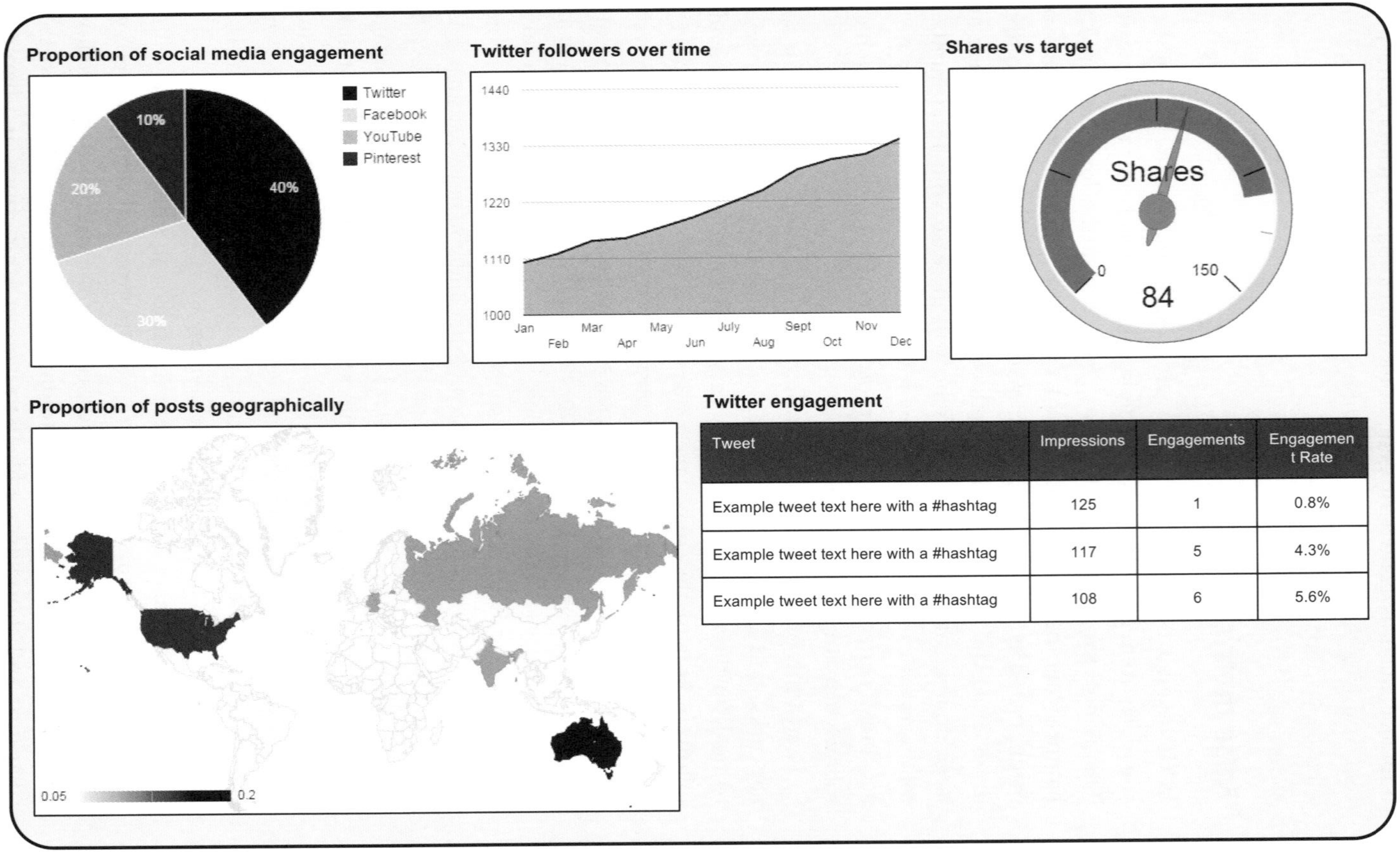

practices you are more likely to build a stronger social media following and, over time, reap rewards far into the future.

Operating procedures

Documented operating procedures are an important element of good governance as they set out the processes that should be followed for certain tasks. For example, what is the process for creating a new user on your enterprise social network or social media management system? Having processes like this clearly documented will make it easier for others to complete their tasks quickly and accurately. It also means that if a regulator or enforcement body requests information about how you manage social media risk you'll be able to provide the documentation that they need easily.

You should also think about the processes for data, other than just those processes that require human interaction. Earlier in this chapter we looked at data quality. By documenting processes that describe how data flows from one application or system to another, you'll be able to pinpoint issues far more easily. In Chapter 4 we covered data archiving and included an example figure to illustrate how data archiving works. Having up-to-date documentation about your archiving processes will help you when the time comes that you need to access archived data quickly.

Flow diagrams are a useful and common way of visualizing any given process. To design a process you should consider:

1 Your starting point.
2 What you will achieve in the end.
3 The steps that you need to take in order to get there.

A process will consist of a number of actions that need to be completed before you can move on to the next step in the process. There may be decisions to be made, and the decision will dictate subsequent actions. Figure 5.8 illustrates some of the most common symbols that are used in process flow diagrams.

The symbols are:

- *Beginning or end.* This is the symbol to illustrate the start or end of your process flow.
- *Process/Activity/Task.* An activity is something that must be completed before you can move to the next section of a flow chart;

FIGURE 5.8 Process flow diagram symbols

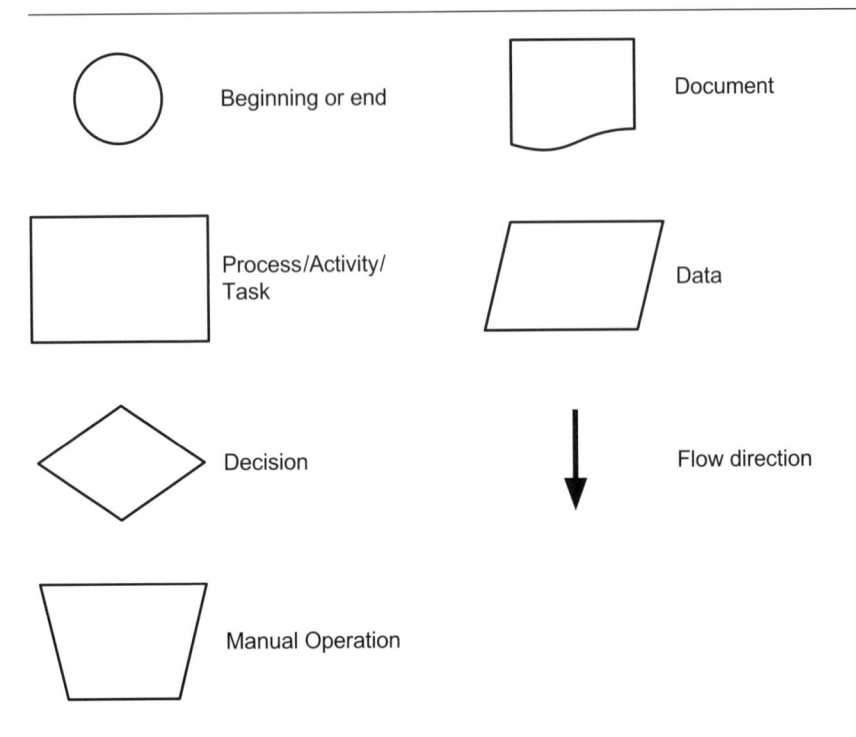

○ Beginning or end

▱ Document

▭ Process/Activity/Task

▱ Data

◇ Decision

↓ Flow direction

⏢ Manual Operation

it could be something like 'send email', 'delete post' or something similar.

- *Decision.* The decision symbol allows you to direct the flow chart in one or more directions, based on the decision. Decisions with a 'Yes' or 'No' outcome are most common; for example, a decision of 'is the contract signed?' would give two possible options.
- *Manual operation.* This symbol illustrates a step in a process which must be completed manually, not through automation. The manual review of a piece of content by a human.
- *Document.* This symbol can be used to illustrate a document, such as a policy document or contract, usually the input or output of a process.
- *Data.* Either an input or an output, the data symbol can be used to illustrate where data is received, such as receiving an email or generating a report.

I recommend that all of your most important or high-risk processes be documented in this manner. This way, you can quickly and visually see what tasks need to be completed in order to achieve a particular goal. It's also a much clearer way of documenting complex processes than attempting to type them out using words, particularly where there are multiple decisions or multiple possible outcomes.

New user process

One area of risk that can impact your organization is the operating procedures around user administration. In any organization you will have joiners and leavers and it's important to have documentation available that shows what tasks need to be completed in any scenario. The processes around new joiners or leavers are likely to have significant overlap with the HR and IT departments, both of which will almost certainly already have defined processes and policies. Many organizations generally have good documentation around new employee onboarding, such as 'request security pass', 'request computer user account', 'request access to various different systems' and so on. Often, social media can be overlooked so it's worth ensuring that you have robust processes that cover what tasks need to be completed when someone new joins your team. It may be that controlling access to social media accounts is your responsibility so it's important to document robust processes to manage risk.

To do this, you might use a 'role description form' which sets out who the person is, what role they will play, how long they are expected to be in the role, what privileges or access rights they will have and so on. This is important to ensure that they are given the right access because getting their access level wrong could expose you to additional risks. This is relevant to both enterprise social networks as well as traditional social media, for example where a social media management tool is used.

An advantage of having well-documented policies, procedures and governance in general is that it will greatly assist new joiners to your team. What seems obvious for you or your team may not be obvious to a new joiner. They won't know anyone in the team, nor will they know the systems that you use or how your team works.

Checklist for new users

- **Role description forms**
  Have relevant role description forms been completed, reviewed and approved?

- **Account access**
  Have you determined which accounts the user will have access to?

- **Account privileges**
  Do you know what privileges the user will have within each account?

- **Access provisioning**
  Do you know who will provision user access and when this will happen?
  Do you know how the user will be notified of their account details?

- **Training**
  Do you know what introductory training the user will receive, and when? Do you know if their role will require any additional training?

- **Policies**
  Has the user read and agreed to all applicable social media policies and guidelines? Has the user been provided with a copy of the policies and is their acceptance recorded?

- **Processes and procedures**
  Is the user familiar with the relevant processes and procedures they will need to follow?

- **Examples**
  Have you included examples of good and bad behaviours?

- **Key contacts**
  Does the user have a list of key contacts so they know who to reach out to for support?

- **Extra resources**
  Have you considered what other resources might be helpful for the user to refer to during the onboarding process?

Leaver process

As with the new joiner process, a well-defined and documented leaver process is essential. In fact, it's more important than the new joiner process as it carries more risk. If someone leaves your organization and their access to corporate systems or accounts is not revoked, they will be able to continue to access your confidential information after they have left. In the case of social media, they may be able to continue to make posts on your official social media channels, as has happened many times in the past.

I have heard stories where someone has left a company and everyone apart from one poor individual in IT has gone to the pub for leaving drinks. The person left behind has the arduous task of changing the passwords for all social media accounts because no management system was in place. Of course, if you do use a management system you won't need to reset all passwords, but you will need to ensure that you disable the leaver's account to prevent them accessing it. If there are any other group accounts that you use, however, you'll need to remember to change the passwords manually. We dive deeper into account management practices in Chapter 8 but it's important here to understand all tasks that should be documented as part of the leaver process.

You may also need to remove personal information about a leaver from your enterprise social network. They may have included personal details about themselves, including a photograph, on their profile. We've already covered data privacy and protection in Chapter 4 so you'll know that it is your responsibility to keep personal information up to date and to delete it when it is no longer required. This applies to your enterprise social network too, so you'll need to include any tasks that need to be completed in relation to your enterprise social network in your leaver process documentation. The data or content that the user produced, such as discussions on the enterprise social network, probably won't need to be removed because it's likely that your employment contracts and policies include clauses which note that any content produced during the period of employment is owned by the employer. But, this is an important clause to check!

A question that has come up in the past is one of ownership of social media accounts. The question as to who owns corporate accounts, such as '@YouCompany' or '@YourCompanyCustomerServices' is fairly straightforward, but there have been instances where an employer has asked that an employee hands over access to their own social media account to their employer, or that they provide details of all connections to the company.

The legalities of this are outside the scope of this book, and are points that should be assessed by qualified legal professionals. However, I strongly question an employer's perceived 'right' to access an employee's social media account, let alone to 'hand it over' to the employer. First, it is a breach of the terms and conditions of most social networks to give anyone access to your account (for example, through password sharing), so by giving your employer access you would be in breach of these terms. Second, if you are worried about the effects of an employee leaving and taking their contacts with them, there are other measures you can put in place to minimize the impact of the employee leaving. For example, you could mandate that any professional contacts, whether they originated from human interaction or social media interaction, be logged on the company's contact management system. That way, the company would still hold the details of the key contacts, which would minimize the effect of someone leaving.

My view is that an organization has no rights to any of its employees' personal social networking accounts or connections, and it seems unethical to think otherwise. You should seek independent legal advice if this is a particular concern.

Change process

Things change: people come and go, new products are launched; old products are discontinued; new software replaces old software. The process for making changes to IT systems, policies or processes needs to be tightly governed to ensure that any new or existing risks are assessed and managed appropriately. It's likely that over time your social media policies and procedures will need to be refreshed and updated. The best indication that it might be time to update your policies or procedures is if you start to receive requests for clarification or when new technologies are adopted at your company. When this happens, you will need to ensure that new changes are proposed, validated, reviewed, approved and then take effect at an agreed date. Your own process for change management may differ and may be more or less complex, however, it's important to have a change management process defined and documented so that you don't make changes that introduce new or heightened risks to your operating environment. All documentation should include a change history that details any changes that have been made to a document since its inception, who made those changes, who approved them and when they took effect. This is a useful audit trail as it will allow you to see the history of changes and, if required, to easily look back to a previous version.

You should have a change process defined for updates or amendments that you make to your social media platforms, such as your enterprise social network. If you have opted for an off-the-shelf package with absolutely no customization, you may choose never to implement custom changes. However, if you do want to make changes, it's likely they will require some form of development in order to add or enhance some functionality.

The standard process for developing, testing, and releasing changes to IT systems is detailed in Figure 5.9.

FIGURE 5.9 Application change process

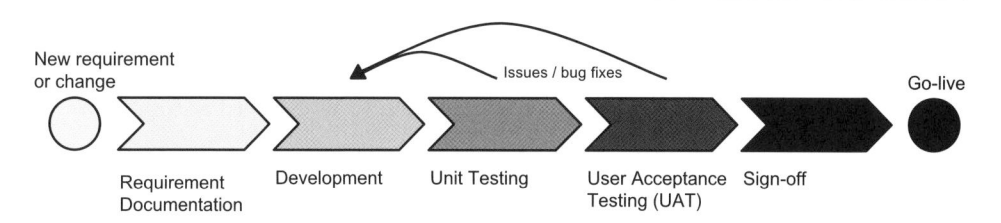

New requirement or change → Requirement Documentation → Development → Unit Testing → User Acceptance Testing (UAT) → Sign-off → Go-live

Issues / bug fixes (loop back from UAT to Development)

The first stage is to document your requirements. It's advisable to define a standard change request template that can be used for all changes as it should ensure that all of the information required by your developers is included. When dealing with developers or development teams, it's vital that your requirements are documented thoroughly and accurately. Developers will usually follow requirements precisely – if you include obvious typing mistakes, for example, they will be included in the finished product. It's therefore important to review requirements thoroughly, as making additional changes can be very costly.

Once the developers have received the requirements they will follow their own processes, such as the development of technical requirements. They will then develop the change you requested and, once complete, will perform what's known as 'unit testing'. Unit testing is testing which the development or technical team complete to try to identify and fix any bugs before they release it for testing by you.

You will then perform what's known as User Acceptance Testing, or UAT. Normally you will develop testing scripts based on your requirements which detail, step by step, how you will test the new functionality. Your testing should also include 'regression testing', which is the term used to describe testing the wider functionality of your application to ensure that the new change has not had an adverse impact on another part of your application or network. Any bugs that you uncover should be documented and sent back to the developer who will address the issue and release another change for you to test.

Once testing is complete, you will sign off the change. By doing this, you are confirming that you are happy with the changes and that you are ready for the change to 'go-live', which means for it to be released to your production (or 'live') environment.

The final step will be completed by the developers, who will agree a schedule for when the 'go-live' should take place. The application or network may incur some 'downtime', which is the time that your application or network might be unavailable while the updates are made.

The documentation around application changes is important as it shows how an application has changed over time and, should you run into issues later, it can be useful to review when trying to work out the root cause of any seemingly mysterious issues.

Summary

In this chapter we looked at the stakeholders who have an interest in social media governance and methods for engaging them through working groups or committees. We then looked at some of the mechanisms and controls you can implement to manage risk and support your projects, such as moderation.

We covered the different types of data which you might capture or analyse, and looked at some of the difficulties in analysing unstructured data or sentiment. Monitoring is one of the hotly debated topics, which we covered in detail, before moving on to the assessment and measurement of social media. The metrics you implement will depend on your requirements and your goals.

Finally we covered the importance of operating procedures and how they can be documented. In the next chapter we will cover the different types of policies that you could implement to manage social media risk and look at what content the policies should contain and what format you might use to document them.

Policy, training and awareness

06

Overview

Policy is often thought of as the silver bullet when it comes to social media risk management. While this is a simplistic view, policy is still a very important control that can help you manage social media risk, encourage appropriate behaviours and enable you to achieve your social media and business goals.

In this chapter we will cover both social media policy and privacy policy. We'll look at the key points that should be included in the policies as well as how the use of language can make your policies more accessible to your employees. Having a policy is essential, but even more important is how your employees engage with that policy and demonstrate the behaviours you encourage. Therefore, we'll also look at how to embed these behaviours throughout your organization through training and awareness campaigns.

The purpose of a social media policy

A social media policy is not a complex legal document that you hope your employees will read and abide by as part of their ongoing employment at your organization. A social media policy should be an easy-to-read document that sets out what you expect of your employees when they use social media. A good social media policy will be read and understood by your employees and will empower them to engage in social media in the manner that you expect.

Hopefully the fact that you need a social media policy doesn't come as a surprise; however, if your organization is not as forward thinking as you would like and perhaps doesn't see the benefits of engaging with social media you may hit resistance from others when you try to write and launch your social media policy. A defence to this is that most regulators will request copies of your documented policies and procedures if you ever suffer a significant incident related to social media. Therefore, it's vital that you have documented evidence that shows that you have assessed social media risk appropriately and that you have implemented a suitable policy to manage social media risk.

The first thing I want to cover is the name of your policy. Is calling the document a 'policy' going to have your desired effect? Many people think of policies as boring documents they are required to adhere to in order to do something. All over the web we are required to agree to policies, terms and conditions when signing up to websites or services. This has led many to ignore the policies altogether. So, you may wish to title the document 'Social media guidelines' or even a 'Social media playbook' to avoid having your employees think it's just another one of those boring documents which they need to accept and which they don't bother reading. There's nothing that requires you to name the document a policy; likewise, there aren't any requirements that dictate what your policy should contain. For consistency, I'm going to refer to the document as a policy throughout the rest of this chapter, and indeed this book!

I'm often asked if I can provide a generic, or template social media policy, which an organization can simply adopt without change. Unfortunately, it's not quite that simple and this misses the point of the document. The policy should be aligned to your own business goals and the goals of your social media programme, taking into account any applicable laws or regulations in force in your country or industry. The policy should describe your own operating model and the rules and procedures that you have implemented to support your goals. Taking a generic social media policy from the internet or copying an existing one from another organization will not address the points that matter to you. It won't encourage the right behaviours or align to your own culture and may just confuse your employees.

Language is powerful, so the language that you use in your policy should be appropriate for your objectives and the culture of your organization. Some organizations choose to use very legal-sounding language that would be more familiar in a contract, but is this really necessary in a social media policy? Having overly formal language around the rules of how employees engage on a predominantly informal platform such as social media is likely to confuse employees and encourage behaviours that don't match your goals.

Consider which of the following two pieces of text is easiest to understand and delivers the point best:

1. Breaches, or suspected breaches, of any confidential information, as defined in information security policy section four paragraph two should be reported immediately to your line manager and failure to do so may lead to disciplinary action against you, including dismissal or, in some cases, criminal proceedings.

2. Share with care: some things need to be protected and you should never post confidential information on social media. If you are unsure if something is confidential or not, read the information security policy for more guidance [*include link so employees can easily access the policy*].

It can be tempting to use overly formal language in policy documents but if you can say something in fewer words, while keeping the same meaning, you should do so. Avoiding legal-sounding language and long sentences will make it far easier for your employees to understand the rules. Remember, the *existence* of a long policy with intricate and precise details won't protect your company. Instead, how your employees *interpret* and abide by the rules in the policy will protect your company.

You obviously want people to read and understand your social media policy, so you should try to keep it short and succinct. As soon as a user sees that a document is pages and pages long, they might just skip reading it altogether. Keep your policy to only a few pages and instead of including detailed information within the policy itself, refer to, and include links to, other company policies. Your social media policy should link well with other policies such as your code of conduct, IT security policies and other HR policies. For example, in your policy you might ask your employees to act in a professional manner when they use social media. This point might benefit from a link to your code of conduct, where the reader can find out more about what it means to act in a professional manner.

Creating an effective social media policy

Structure of the policy

Your policy should not be a long document that gives detailed guidance on every possible social media scenario which you can think of. If you compare the social media policies from different organizations you'll notice that the language, structure and rules are different in each and there is no standard format accepted by all. That said, in my view the key sections to include are:

- *Introduction.* This section should define the audience and set the scene for the content within the rest of the policy. Bear in mind that you may have people within your organization who are totally new to social media, so including definitions of key terms will help their understanding. Include the objective of your social media programme early on so that your employees know the purpose of their engagement in social media.
- *Main content.* Paragraphs of text, each with their own heading, which set out what you expect of the employees when they use social media, are a good way of setting out and breaking up the main content of your policy. Pictures are also a good way to bring your content to life; for example, including screenshots of ideal social media profiles or good and bad social media posts.
- *Do's and don'ts.* Including a list of do's and don'ts, usually side by side, will help to emphasize any key points you feel deserve particular attention.
- *Frequently asked questions (FAQs).* A list of frequently asked questions will allow your employees to quickly skim through the policy to find the answers to any particularly common problems.

Top and tail of the policy

Policy documents change over time, particularly those that refer to social media. Because of this, it's best practice to include a change history at the start of all policy documents. The policy should be dated and include details about who is responsible for maintaining the policy as well as details of who approved it and when it came into force. The change history should show a table that includes high-level details and comments when changes were made, when those changes were made and who approved them.

Regardless of how long you spend writing your policy, there will always be some people who have specific questions about what they can or cannot do in social media. Because of this, you should include contact details at the bottom of the policy to allow your employees to seek further guidance should they need it.

Content of the social media policy

The actual content that makes up a social media policy is hotly debated. The stories range from those companies which have adopted policies consisting of only four words, 'Don't Do Stupid Stuff', to those who have issued 100-page documents. In my view, the key points a good social media policy should cover are as follows:

1 *What to post (and what not to post)*. This is your opportunity to encourage your employees to share positive information and news about your company. By providing clear guidelines on what is acceptable and what is not, you'll help your employees, and especially those who are new to social media, to engage effectively. A good way of articulating this would be to ask them to always protect your organization, backed up with references to your code of conduct.

2 *Confidential or sensitive information.* You should draw attention to the fact that employees should never post any confidential or sensitive information on social media. This will help protect you from any unfortunate data breaches or breaches to contractual terms.

3 *Profile information.* What should employees include in their profile? Will you allow them to identify themselves as employees of your organization? Will you require them to include a disclaimer, for example to state that views and opinions expressed are their own and not those of their organization? You should also remind your employees that they should review the privacy settings for all of their social media accounts. The default settings are often changed by the social networks themselves so it's worth reminding them to review and update them.

4 *Interpersonal etiquette.* Some people see social media as a 'wild west' where anything goes. You need to set out how you expect your employees to interact with other social media users. This can include not criticizing others, not engaging in 'trolling' (deliberately starting arguments or offending others on the internet), respecting others' opinions and so on.

5 *Sharing content.* Highlight that you want to encourage your employees to share content about your organization, for example by retweeting the company tweets. What other content do you want them to share? For example, do you want your people to share interesting news or reports from your competitors?

6 *Think before you post.* You need to remind your employees that once they have posted something on social media or the internet, it can be extremely difficult, or in some cases almost impossible, to remove it if

they change their mind later. Your policy should tell employees to think about the consequences of every post and consider whether it could be misunderstood or misinterpreted by other social media users. There have been many examples in the past where a social media user has intended to send a private message to someone, but accidentally posted it publicly. You need to make them aware of this to ensure that they think before they post. In 2014, this mistake was even made by one of the top executives of Twitter, which goes to show how easy it is to make this mistake!

7 *Personal responsibility.* Your policy should set out the fact that it's the employees' own responsibility to use social media well. You should encourage them to be themselves and use their own voice and style but remind them that what they post is their responsibility.

8 *Add value.* Encourage your employees to use social media effectively. Your policy should include examples of best practice so that your employees know how to use social media well and appropriately. For example, you should discourage them from simply posting hundreds of links to websites that they like, with little or no qualifying text. This adds no value and will, at best, be ignored by other social media users. At worst, it'll be seen as spam (posting irrelevant messages indiscriminately).

9 *Don't be deceptive.* Have you noticed that your friends always look great in the photos that they post on social media? The reason for this is that most people won't post unflattering photos of themselves online and will 'un-tag' themselves from unflattering photos uploaded by their friends. I'm not suggesting that this should change (I'd face a personal backlash from many of my friends if I did!). However, it's important to tell your employees that it's not acceptable to try to deceive other internet users. Your need to be transparent and trustworthy. Acknowledging and responding to negative feedback can actually work in your favour as it shows you're listening and want to improve. Therefore, you should not allow your employees to post fake information about your products or services online and nor should you allow them to delete comments or reviews they dislike.

10 *Personal vs work.* You need to set out boundaries in your policies so that your employees understand when they are posting in a personal capacity and when they are posting, or might be perceived to be posting, in a work capacity. For example, if your employees post a mix of official content about your organization as well as controversial posts about politics or their personal views, these associations might harm your brand. Furthermore, you should set out some basic guidelines about the use of your company brand. Your employees may be proud to work at your company and may want to include your logo on their page, or even to design their whole profile in your corporate colours and branding. Would you allow this? If so, you need to set out the conditions, and if not, explain what your brand restrictions are.

It can be helpful to include examples within your policy in order to bring to life the rules within it and ensure that your employees understand the reasoning behind the rules. Case studies and 'do's and don'ts' are also a good way of painting a picture to the reader to illustrate what you expect from them and what you won't tolerate.

Sometimes your employees will want to refer back to your policy during their day-to-day work. The employee might face a particular challenge and want guidance on what they're allowed to do in social media so you should include a Frequently Asked Questions section at the end to cover any common points your employees may struggle with. Examples of frequently asked questions might be 'Can I connect with competitors in social media?', 'A competitor recently released a report which is gaining a lot of attention. Can I refer to their report in social media?' or 'Can I set up a dedicated social media account for my team?' The answers that you choose for these questions will depend on your social media strategy as well as your overall business objectives.

Policy checklist

- Writing style and content
  Is your policy written in a way that is easy to follow and which does not include overly legal-sounding words and phrases?

- References to other policies
  Have you included references (and ideally links) within your social media policy to your other policies, such as your IT security policy or HR policies?

- Frequently asked questions
  Have you included a list of frequently asked questions?

- Practical examples
  Have you included practical examples of where social media has been used well and badly?
  Have you pointed out the reasons that something is considered a good use of social media vs a bad use of social media?

- Format and accessibility
  Is your social media policy easy to find, and is it in a format which is easily accessible?

- Change history and further queries
  Have you included a change history, details about who is responsible for the policy, and whom to contact if someone needs extra guidance?

Location and format of your policies

You should consider how your employees will read or find out about your social media policy, where they will be when they are reading it and what they will be using to read it. Having a hard copy of a policy somewhere in the office, pinned to a notice board is unlikely to be an effective place for it. Consider making your social media policy as accessible as possible by making it available in a number of different formats, such as a PDF, a web page, or even a video to really bring the content to life. You could also use posters to make sure that it's easy to engage with. If you have an enterprise social network, I strongly advise that you ensure that your policy can be accessed easily regardless of which page a user is looking at. You could do this by including a link to it in the footer at the bottom of every page.

Most enterprise social networks can be configured to force users to read and accept your social media policy the first time they log into the network. It's also possible to force existing users to reconfirm that they have read the policy. Therefore, if you make some significant changes to your policy, it's worth making them reconfirm their agreement with the policy when they next log in.

The purpose of a privacy policy

A privacy policy is a notice that tells users who you are, what data you are going to collect about them and how you are going to use it. The use of privacy policies is best practice, as well as a requirement in many countries. However, being clear about what you are doing with users' data will also make your organization more transparent and trustworthy.

The issue of data privacy has become a hotly debated topic. In 2013, Edward Snowden, an IT consultant, leaked classified information from the US National Security Agency (NSA). The documents he leaked suggested that both the NSA and the UK's General Communications Headquarters (GCHQ) had developed a global surveillance programme. This led to a great number of stories in the media and helped to further fuel the public debate about privacy.

Also, in 2013 the EU's Court of Justice made a landmark ruling against Google Spain, which was brought by Mario Costeja González. Mr González had demanded that Google remove links from its search results relating to his past social security debts, which had since been cleared. The ruling has come to be commonly known as the 'right to be forgotten' and demonstrates how important the issue of data privacy has become. Both public and private sector organizations are going to come under more and more pressure to be transparent about the data that they are collecting and what they are doing with it. Privacy policies are one of the things that organizations can use to explain how they use user data and in turn be more transparent about their activities.

Enterprise social networks, as well as other public-facing IT systems, such as customer forums, need to include privacy policies because of the personal data they capture and process. An explanation of what constitutes personal data and the challenges that it brings has already been covered in Chapter 4, Data privacy and control. By publishing a privacy policy, you will be openly telling your users what you plan to do with their data. This transparency will allow you to build trust with your user and this knowledge will give the user the choice to use your system or not. However, don't get worried that it will deter users, because a well-written policy will give confidence that you are handling their data appropriately and with their consent.

There is a big difference between a social media policy and a privacy policy. A good social media policy sets out the rules that your employees must follow when using social media, and it should encourage appropriate behaviours. A privacy policy is an informative notice to make users aware of what data you are capturing about them and empower them to take action if they want to. For example, it's very common for website operators to use tools to track how a user got to their website (ie which link the user clicked in order to arrive at your website). You might have noticed this type of thing yourself when the adverts you see on websites mysteriously show products that you have recently been researching. These tools don't pose a risk to the user as they aren't able to identify exactly who is viewing your website, just that 'someone' clicked on a link and arrived at your website. But, you should explain this in your privacy policy and provide instructions on how they can opt out if they wish to.

Creating an effective privacy policy

In the same way that a generic social media policy cannot be downloaded from the internet and used as-is, a privacy policy is not a generic document that you use simply to meet requirements around data protection. The privacy policy that you implement should be a description of your operating procedures and should highlight anything that has an impact on privacy and personal information.

While drafting a privacy policy, you should keep the following in mind:

- What information you are collecting?
- Why are you collecting it?
- What are the implications for the user?
- Would the user object to you using their information in this way?

Not every user will want to read your entire privacy policy and may be more concerned about how they simply use your tool. They may just want the high-level details about what data you collect. Because of this, it's best practice to offer users two version of your privacy police: a short one, and a longer and more detailed one. The short version of the policy should set out the key points that you think will be of most interest to your users and the longer version should explain the key points from the short version in more detail. For example, one of the points in your short version of the policy might be that you will take great care to protect any information that users provide and that you won't share any of this information without their permission. The longer version should go into detail, explaining what data you capture, how you protect it, and in which circumstances you might share their information with a third party.

Like a social media policy, a privacy policy should be easy to understand and avoid overly complex or legal-sounding language. What you include in your privacy policy will depend on the way that your enterprise social network or external community is configured and the features that you have included. However, the point is to be as open and transparent as possible about what information is being captured about the users of your network and the risks that this poses. Remember that this applies not only to the data that you are capturing about the users, but also the data that is being captured by any third parties. For example, if you have included functionality to allow users to 'Like' some content on your website on their social networks, it's likely that the social network itself will be able to tell that the user has been on your website. As this functionality is widespread on the internet, you can assume that it does not pose a threat; however, a privacy policy is the ideal place for you to bring it to the attention of your users, should they be interested.

In the first section of Chapter 4 I referred to privacy impact assessments, and I recommend completing one before drafting your privacy policy. However, the following list will help you consider what information you are going to include in your privacy policy and the sorts of questions that you should ask:

- Who has access to the information in your enterprise social network? Just your organization, or the group of companies that your organization belongs to? If you allow external people, clients or vendors to use your enterprise social network, what information can they see about your users?

- How long will you retain the data in your enterprise social network? Is the data backed up and, if so, how often is it backed up? Where are the backups stored and who has access to them?

- What happens if an employee leaves your organization? What will happen to their profile and the data within it? What about the comments or discussions they had posted? You'll probably want to keep the comments, discussions or other work-related data that they posted, so you should include these intentions within your policy.

- Do you track logins to your enterprise social network or the pages that your users have viewed? A common and valid reason to do this is to personalize the user experience in some way, such as by showing search results tailored to them, based on their previous searches. If you do capture this type of data, you should explain what you capture and why.

- What have you done to ensure the security of the network and to guard against any data breaches? Have you gained accreditation or performed security testing? If so, these are valid things to note to give your users confidence that you are securing their data.

- If you are a global organization and your enterprise social network is used by your people around the world this will mean that the users' personal data may be viewed in foreign countries. If this is the case, details should be included in your policy.

- Does your enterprise social network capture location data? If so, it might be possible for you to track a user's movements. Whether you do track their movements or not, you should let the user know if you are capturing this data and explain what you are doing with it (even if you do nothing) and why.

- The information that users include in their profiles will be visible to other users. Can the user change their privacy settings and, if so, how do they do this? It's likely that if a user includes details about their skills and expertise within their profile, another user might contact them to ask for their advice. So that this doesn't come as a surprise, you should include this as an example of how their personal information might be accessed and used.

In addition to the questions above, you should also point out to your users that they are responsible for the personal information they choose to share:

- You should not encourage your users to share sensitive personal information on your enterprise social network, as defined in Chapter 4, 'What is personal data?'

- You should push the responsibility for maintaining personal data onto the user and include instructions for the user to follow if they want to delete their account.

As you can see, a privacy policy includes a lot of technical information about how your organization operates its enterprise social network or other social systems. You'll need to connect with your IT and legal departments, as well as your data protection officer, to ensure that the information you include in your privacy policy is correct. In Chapter 5, Governance, we covered strategies for linking up the key stakeholders who have an interest in social media. Drafting your privacy policy is an activity that should have oversight from your social media working group so you may wish to refer back to Chapter 5 for more details on how to set up and run a social media working group.

Technology changes rapidly, so in the same way that you update your social media policy, you should keep your privacy policy up to date and let your users know that you will change the policy from time to time without warning. Finally, you should always include contact information so that users can request further information should they need it.

Training and awareness

Training

Many organizations require their employees to complete some form of training on an annual basis. This could be because of a requirement from a regulator for compliance purposes or because the organization has identified a particular risk area and needs to ensure their employees are trained accordingly.

Because of how quickly social media develops, I believe social media should be included in mandatory annual training. This is an excellent way of ensuring that your employees know about any major changes to your policies and procedures, and also gives you an opportunity to rearticulate the objectives of your social media programme. If the annual training process is well managed, you'll also be able to track who has, and who hasn't, received training so that you can catch any teams that might have slipped through the net.

An effective and popular way of rolling out training is through the use of eLearns. ELearns are electronic self-service courses that employees can access and complete at a time convenient to them. Good eLearns usually incorporate text, exercises, pictures, diagrams and videos. Some people find visual aids more engaging while others are happier reading text and answering questions. By getting a good mix of content into the eLearn you'll be more likely to engage all of your employees. There are, however, two downsides to eLearn. First, it requires your employees to complete the training on a computer, something that might not necessarily be an easy task for all of your staff. Second, the cost of developing an eLearn can be quite high.

There are other alternatives though. In Chapter 3 we discussed the advantage of engaging an advocate community to support your social media programme. While you will need to justify the time taken to deliver training, the cost of using advocates may be significantly less than developing an eLearn. Of course, this will depend on the size of your organization and the resource that you have at your disposal. Your advocate group should be trained up so that they can deliver your social media training updates and push the key messages out among their peers and teams.

Your social media training should familiarize your employees with your social media policy and provide practical examples of how they can use social media, while remaining compliant with your policy. You should highlight examples of good and bad practice, preferably from your industry sector. Quizzes and discussions are also effective; for example, you might include

FIGURE 6.1 Example social media posts

1. What is the best way of managing social media risk? http://bit.ly/18qDuZP
   Retweet   Favourite   Reply

2. Risky tweet? I think not! Backlash on Twitter? No way! Here's how you manage #SocialMedia risk http://bit.ly/18qEcGl
   Retweet   Favourite   Reply

3. Nice! #SocialMedia governance http://bit.ly/18qEcGl
   Retweet   Favourite   Reply

some examples of tweets and ask them to debate which tweet will have the best effect. An example of this is shown in Figure 6.1.

Figure 6.1 should provoke some good discussion. While there's nothing wrong with the first tweet, the second one might have more impact as it's interesting and entices you to click on the link. The third tweet doesn't really tell Twitter users what it's about so is unlikely to engage the users.

CASE STUDY   Risk in action: US Airways tweets pornographic image to customer

In April 2014, US Airways made quite a spectacular mistake on Twitter. In response to a tweet from a passenger who was complaining about a delayed flight, US Airways tweeted back 'We welcome feedback, Elle. If your travel is complete, you can detail it here for review and follow-up...' They then included a link which was supposed to go to a form where the user could submit a complaint. Fairly harmless, you would think. However, the link that they included was actually an explicit photo of naked woman with a toy plane somewhere... that you probably wouldn't expect it...

It shouldn't come as a surprise that the tweet was retweeted many times before it was deleted about an hour later and was reported in media channels across the world. US Airways then tweeted an apology for the inappropriate image and said that they were investigating.

The image had apparently been tweeted to the US Airways Twitter account earlier and the person responsible for the account had accidentally included it in the tweet. US Airways said that they would not fire the person who sent the tweet as it was an honest mistake; however, it was reviewing its processes to stop this sort of thing happening again.

SOURCE: www.huffingtonpost.co.uk/2014/04/15/social-media-fail-us-airways-tweets-model-plane-in-vagina-passenger-picture_n_5150948.html

Awareness campaigns

When commencing a social media programme, an important part of the project is an awareness campaign. The purpose of the campaign is to tell your employees about your social media programme, to raise awareness about what you expect of them and to familiarize them with the policy.

I recommend that you include some of the following ideas in your campaign in order to drive awareness:

- *Posters*. Put them everywhere you can! Eye-catching, colourful posters with bold headings can be a great way of getting your employees' attention. Include key messages and perhaps even a question for them to consider, as depicted in Figure 6.2.
- *Drop-in sessions*. A drop-in session is an opportunity for people to 'drop in' to get one-to-one help on any particular social media issue they might have. They're like training sessions, but are usually less formal and might take place over lunch. I've personally found that offering free doughnuts at these sessions is a very effective way of enticing people to attend! The sessions could easily be run by your advocates, which would be a good way for them to raise their profiles and won't require much time from your core team.
- *Internal communications*. Most organizations have company-wide internal communications which include key information or news. Write a selection of texts, each with catchy titles, about the launch of your social media programme or your updated policy and feed these into the company-wide internal communications each week. Be on the look-out for real success stories from around your organization which you can showcase.
- *Webcasts*. Webcasts are becoming commonplace. A webcast is a presentation that takes place virtually and means that people from across your organization, regardless of where they are physically situated, can join the webcast and participate in the presentation.

- *Advocates.* Contact your advocate community and make sure that they are all aware of the changes to your policy. Reinvigorate them and encourage them to push out the key messages to their own teams.

FIGURE 6.2 Awareness campaign poster

It's time to GET SOCIAL!

BUT, how you use social media is your responsibility!

Our social media policy has been updated

Check it out at: //socialmediapolicy

For more information, please contact internal communications on #1234

The awareness campaign is important because without it, you run the risk of your social media policy being just another one of those documents people cast their eyes over once or twice as part of their annual training. The ideas above can have a big impact, but I recommend you and your team explore other creative ways to push out your key messages in the most effective way for your organization.

Summary

In this chapter we looked at two important policies: the social media policy and the privacy policy. We covered the purpose of the policies and why you need them. A social media policy is a key document that can empower your employees to use social media effectively and help them understand how they can avoid making embarrassing mistakes. A privacy policy is an informative notice to users of a social network which explains what data will be collected about them and why it's being collected. A privacy policy is not an overly complex legal document. It's a document that is easy to read and that will demonstrate transparency and build trust with your users.

Finally, we looked at techniques for driving awareness about your policies throughout your organization, such as communications campaigns and training. In Chapter 3, Strategy, we also looked at how advocates can encourage positive behaviours. This is something that is particularly relevant when thinking about how to push out the key messages from your social media policy.

Unfortunately, no matter how much work goes into managing the risks of social media, at some point in time an incident is likely to occur. In the next chapter, we'll look at crisis management and cover what you can do to plan for and manage incidents.

Crisis management

07

Overview

A key element of effective social media governance and risk management is crisis management. Crises can hit any organization with little or no warning and can have devastating effects. In today's world, rumours and news spread at incredible speeds over social media, which can make an incident escalate faster than ever. In the past, perhaps only large international incidents would hit the mainstream news; however, with so many people using social media around the world, an incident doesn't need to hit mainstream news for it to get the attention of thousands of your customers.

In this chapter, we'll look at how crises develop, how you can assess a crisis when it happens and how to implement a strategy to manage the crisis effectively. We'll also look at how human behaviour changes when faced with stressful situations and consider how well-laid plans and a well-executed crisis response strategy can help an organization avoid disaster.

Planning and preparation

What is a crisis?

A crisis is an incident that has a high impact and has either already occurred or has a high likelihood of occurring. An organization may experience a high number of incidents in its normal course of business, such as making a social media post and including a link that doesn't work. A crisis, on the other hand, is an incident that has a much higher impact on the business. To continue the example above, an erroneous link embedded in a post would cause only minor annoyance to social media users; however, if an offensive image had accidentally been included in the post it would have a much higher impact on the company and is more likely to go viral, resulting in the company's reputation being damaged by a large backlash from social users. This happened for real to US Airways in April 2014 and is covered as a case study in Chapter 6.

In Chapter 2 we looked at how a risk matrix (Figure 2.1) can be used to assess risk. The risk matrix shows the relationship between the impact of a risk and the likelihood of it occurring. A crisis will be any event classed as 'extreme' in the risk matrix.

There can be a fine line separating an incident from a crises. All crises will begin as incidents but not all incidents will spiral into full-blown crises. To assess a crisis you need to consider what the impact could be of an incident occurring to understand what might happen. Some examples of incidents that could turn into crises are as follows:

- *Hacked social media account.* This will almost certainly be classed as a crisis because during the time that you lack control of your account, the hacker could post a huge amount of negative material that could quickly attract the attention of the global media.

- *Inappropriate social media post.* Many companies have experienced incidents where someone accidentally posts something inappropriate on social media. A good example of this was when a tweet was posted from the American Red Cross account which said 'Ryan found two more 4 bottle packs of Dogfish Head's Midas Touch beer…. When we drink we do it right #gettingslizzard'. While this is an embarrassing mistake for someone to make (likely mixing up their personal and work accounts) and attracted a lot of attention across the internet, it could have been a lot worse. On the other hand, if the post had included more offensive language or imagery, and if it had stayed up for a long period of time, it would be more likely to escalate into a crisis.

- *Website goes offline.* If your website goes offline unexpectedly in the middle of the night for a few minutes it might not have a big impact on your company; however, if you're a multinational online retailer, any downtime could cause a real crisis, harm your reputation and negatively impact both revenue and investor confidence.

- *Data breach.* Data breaches would normally constitute a crisis; however, if an attacker had only managed to access your internal data you might be able to avert a wide-scale crisis. If, on the other hand, a hacker had gained access to the personal data of your customers or employees it could be considerably more serious, have a harmful impact on your reputation and attract fines from regulators.

In the above examples it's clear that not all incidents will have the same impact. Likewise, what one organization sees as a crisis another might see as just another day in the office. Some organizations are targeted regularly by activist groups or hackers and have become used to dealing with a wide range of incidents.

Human response to a crisis

It can be tempting for someone who is experiencing a crisis to act differently to how they would ordinarily. In the course of their normal work they will follow policies and procedures diligently, for example by seeking approval for new content posts and documenting their actions as they go. However, in a stressful situation these tasks can appear menial when compared with the crisis that the person is experiencing. This can make them change their behaviour by not following required processes and procedures. The person may feel that they're doing the right thing and are prioritizing effectively. However, these actions can actually make a bad situation worse.

Picture this hypothetical scenario: a number of abusive images and offensive content are accidentally posted on the company's social media account. Not realizing what had just happened, the social media team goes out for a pre-planned team lunch to a pub down the street. The pub has very poor mobile phone reception and no wifi. An hour into their lunch, a colleague runs into the pub and explains what has happened. Tensions heighten almost instantly. Questions start popping into everyone's head: 'what do we do next?', 'how could this have happened?', 'what has the response been from other social media users?', 'who's to blame for this?' or 'Oh no, this might be my fault, who can I try to blame?'. The team hurry back to the office and start trying to rectify the situation. They're receiving lots of posts every second and they try to respond to as many as possible. Normally, all content and replies need to be reviewed by the team leader before they can be posted, but due to the heightened stress levels, members of the team started making more posts, defending themselves and claiming that it wasn't their fault. This annoyed other social media users and made the crisis worsen – it was then picked up by mainstream media and reported on the TV and main news websites.

We can relate to the team because there will be times when even the most laidback people have experienced stressful situations. However, if appropriate technical controls had existed and a crisis response plan initiated it would have helped to manage the crisis and avert an escalation. It can feel counter-intuitive to assess the options and plan the next steps when faced with a crisis because many people will want to act. Even after controls have been implemented, the teams that will have to deal with crises should be given appropriate training. Training is important to ensure that the team are familiar with crisis situations and know how they should act. Crisis simulations are an effective and fun way to test a team's response to any given crisis and can help improve your crisis response strategy. Crisis simulation is covered later in this chapter.

Avoiding a crisis

The best way to deal with a crisis is to avoid it in the first place. An effective risk management function and a risk-aware culture will go a long way to safeguarding your company from unfortunate incidents. As we discussed in Chapter 2, you should spend time thinking about where the risks are to your business and what you can do to manage them. For example, if you have engaged a third party to manage your enterprise social network, you are exposed to a risk that the third party may experience issues that have a knock-on effect to your company. If the third party's IT network goes down, it may take your enterprise social network down with it. A common way to guard against this is by completing a due diligence exercise where you assess any third parties that you work with to gain confidence that they have appropriate processes and procedures in place to avoid any impact to your own business.

Your procurement team should already have due diligence processes in place, but if you're purchasing an enterprise social network or a social media management tool, you should complete your own additional due diligence to ensure the tool meets your needs. Purchasing a social media tool without appropriate due diligence is risky because you are at the mercy of the supplier to provide the tools. Things you should consider are:

- *Security testing*. Have the provider's infrastructure and applications been independently security tested? Has the provider achieved appropriate accreditation that shows that they have assessed security risks and implemented mitigating controls? Can you comfortably rely on the security offered by your provider and does it meet your own requirements?
- *Availability*. You should ensure that the provider has agreed to an acceptable level of availability of the tools or applications you are purchasing. When is it acceptable for the application to be unavailable? How quickly will the provider respond to unexpected

down time (when the application is unavailable)? At what times and on which days will maintenance be carried out? The systems should have an appropriate level of redundancy, for example to avoid downtime from unexpected events such as power cuts. To do this, 'uninterruptible power supplies' can be used, which will provide power for a short period of time while the main building power is off.

- *Support.* What support arrangements will be in place? How quickly will the provider commit to responding to any support requests and how long will they take to resolve?
- *Data protection.* Is the provider aware of their responsibilities with regard to data protection law? Has the provider implemented controls to safeguard personal data? Where will the data be hosted/stored geographically? Will the data be transferred and, if so, have controls been implemented for this to happen legally?
- *Archiving.* What data is archived? What is the process and schedule for archiving data? When will data be deleted?
- *Backups.* How quickly can the provider access backups, should they need to? Will backups be stored on-premise or off-site? (If the building burns down and the backups are in the building, it's not likely you'll get access to them...) Who has access to the backups? How are the backups secured?

A problem with one of the challenges listed above is something that could lead you into a crisis, which is why oversight of these is vital. However, for all the planning and preparation that you do, nobody has a crystal ball and it's impossible to guarantee that you won't face a crisis at some point in the future. Therefore it's important to put plans in place to deal with a variety of incidents quickly and effectively to stop them from becoming a crisis.

CASE STUDY Risk in action: Twitter Q&As backfire, attracting barrage of public criticism

Twitter Question and Answer (Q&A) sessions, or 'ask me anything' events, can be a really effective way for organizations to connect with their customers. They give customers an opportunity to pose questions to a company's senior leadership and, when executed successfully, can increase customer engagement and improve a business's reputation. Unfortunately, however, there have been a number of examples of companies that have started a Q&A only to be faced with a barrage of public criticism.

One such example is UK gas company British Gas, which organized a Twitter Q&A in October 2013 and invited Twitter users to ask questions to British Gas Customer Service Director Bert Pijls, using the hashtag #AskBG. Unfortunately for British Gas, they decided to run their Q&A session on the same day that they announced a 10.4 per cent increase in electricity prices. The session immediately started trending on Twitter as users joined in to voice their grievances over the increase in prices and the impact that it would have to their families. One user asked:

> @britishgas is it true your top shareholders heat their homes by burning loads of £100 notes they have from excessive profits?

Another Twitter Q&A event which caused a stir on social media around the same time was planned by US bank JP Morgan. In this case, however, the bank received such a barrage of negative tweets before the event even began that they cancelled it. Even after the Q&A had been cancelled, messages continued to be posted with some highlighting how JP Morgan had failed to embrace social media as an effective PR tool. At the time, JP Morgan was facing a record fine of $13billion for mis-selling bad mortgage debts to investors prior to the 2008 financial crash. One user posted:

> #AskJPM is the greatest social media fiasco ever contrived. A lesson in being completely self unaware of public perception.

According to Topsy, a company that analyses tweets, at least two-thirds of the 80,000 tweets sent using the AskJP hashtag were negative. After a few hours the bank reversed its decision to hold a Q&A session online and posted:

> 'Tomorrow's Q&A is cancelled. Bad Idea. Back to the drawing board.'

The key takeaway from both of these examples is around the timing of the Q&A sessions. It's hardly surprising that, at a time when both companies were already receiving negative press, users took to social media to publicly complain about them. Social media analytics could have been used to show overall sentiment over the brands and could have fed into their decision to run the Q&A, or not.

SOURCES: http://metro.co.uk/2013/10/17/british-gas-twitter-qa-backfires-on-day-of-huge-price-increases-4150204/
www.telegraph.co.uk/technology/twitter/10448715/JPMorgan-cancels-Twitter-QandA-after-tirade-of-abuse.html

Assessing an incident

The crisis lifecycle

Crises are unexpected, can happen at any time, and are inevitable. Because of this, organizations not only need plans in place to deal with them, but to assess them after the dust has settled. Performing an analysis of how the organization responded to a crisis will help make existing crisis management procedures more effective and will help prevent future crises.

FIGURE 7.1 Crisis lifecycle

Preparation → Assessment and analysis → Response → Prevention

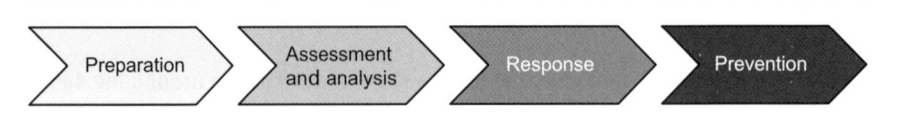

Figure 7.1 shows the four stages of a crisis lifecycle:

- *Preparation.* As the saying goes, 'if you fail to plan, you are planning to fail'. Smaller businesses may be able to cope with a crisis with minimal planning because it's quicker and easier to get all key stakeholders in a room to discuss next steps and response. A large organization, on the other hand, needs to plan in advance because when more people are involved, it is more difficult to respond to a crisis.
- *Assessment and analysis.* When an incident occurs, you need to perform some analysis in order to assess how the incident might impact the organization. Clearly defined plans as to how to manage different severities of crisis will enable an organization to take the right actions at the right time. A thorough analysis of a crisis will also allow an organization to estimate how a crisis might escalate, allowing it to ready its response, should the crisis indeed escalate.
- *Response.* Responding to a crisis should be well executed, with key tasks completed at the right times by the right people. An effective response will stop a crisis from escalating and will give the organization control over it.
- *Prevention.* Once a crisis has been dealt with, it's important to assess how the organization reacted, when plans worked well and when they failed. By doing this, the organization will have a better chance of managing future crises effectively.

Assessing crisis severity

There are five classifications of crisis severity, as depicted in Figure 7.2. A crisis can start at any severity level and move in either direction, becoming less or more severe based on how the crisis develops. Assessing a crisis is subjective, however Figure 7.2 allows you to consider an incident to understand where it sits on the scale. In turn, this will dictate how you respond to the crisis. As a crisis moves from level 1 through to level 5, the intensity of the crisis increases and the impact on the business as a whole gets more serious.

The five levels of crisis severity are as follows:

- *Level 1 – Limited.* At this stage, the impact to the business will be confined to specific teams or projects and will not have a wider impact on the continuity of the business. Only a small group of people within the company will be affected and, while it will cause some disruption to the business, it will not be a public event which impacts external stakeholders.
- *Level 2 – Moderate.* At level 2, the impact of the crisis starts to go beyond a specific team or project and begins to have an impact on the business's overall goals, albeit only in the short term. A larger group of people inside the company will be affected with an impact on some systems and processes. This will lead to a minor financial impact on the business.
- *Level 3 – Significant.* At this stage, significant control will be lost in key systems and processes, which will impact the business's medium-term goals and pose a higher threat to its financial performance. A significant crisis may involve minor injuries to people inside or outside the business and may attract attention from large groups of people and the media.
- *Level 4 – Severe.* A severe crisis will bring into question the business's long-term continuity. Major financial impacts are likely and damage experienced during the crisis may be irreparable. People may experience serious injuries or even fatalities. This will result in news outlets picking up the story, which will further increase the scrutiny over the business.
- *Level 5 – Extreme.* At this stage, the organization is stressed to the max. Failure or collapse of the business looks imminent and the knock-on effect could impact other companies. The story will be reported in mainstream media and attract widespread negativity. Loss of control in key systems will be sustained, which will further

FIGURE 7.2 Crisis severity levels

Level 1	Level 2	Level 3	Level 4	Level 5
Limited	**Moderate**	**Significant**	**Severe**	**Extreme**
Short-term impact affecting only one project or business area.	Potential short-term impact to the overall business.	Potential medium-term impact to the overall business.	Potential long-term impact to the overall business.	Failure of the business imminent.
Incident impacts only a small number of people inside the company.	Incident impacts a large groups of people inside the company.	Impact to a large group of people inside and outside the company.	Impact to groups inside and outside the company with attention from local news outlets.	Significant negative public sentiment and attention from national news.
	Minor financial impact likely.	Moderate financial impact likely.	Major financial impact likely.	Significant financial impact experienced.
	Partial loss of control over some systems and processes.	Significant loss of control over some systems and processes.	Loss of control over multiple key systems and processes.	Sustained loss of control over multiple key systems and processes.
		Small number of minor injuries.	High risk of serious injuries or fatalities.	Multiple injuries or fatalities.
			Irreparable damage to large parts of the business.	Significant knock-on to other business or industry likely.
				Regulatory and law enforcement investigation likely to result in significant fines or imprisonment.

hamper efforts to rectify the situation. Multiple injuries or fatalities may occur. The business, or its leadership, will face regulatory scrutiny and may even face criminal proceedings.

Reporting a crisis

A useful way of capturing key information during a crisis is to use a crisis report template. Crisis reports should be used to describe what has happened, when it happened and outline the key tasks that need to be completed. A crisis report should be sent out to all the key stakeholders during a crisis and will allow everyone to work together towards a common goal.

Some crises may last many hours or even days, so new crisis reports should be issued regularly to provide official updates about the progress and to highlight the tasks each team is working on. Including a status against the key tasks will make it easier to see where extra resource or attention might be needed and it will help to identify areas of higher risk. Using a crisis report template also cuts down on rumours that may start to work their way through the organization because it is a standard and official report distributed internally.

Figure 7.3 shows an example template that you could use to document a crisis.

Implementing a crisis response strategy

Your crisis response strategy should be documented and distributed to all key stakeholders who might be involved when a crisis hits, such as department or team leaders, communications, senior management, legal and so on. The first step in a crisis response strategy is to include details about how a crisis can be assessed to determine its severity. The severity level will dictate the tasks that you will need to do and when they should be completed.

To establish a crisis response strategy I recommend that key stakeholders hold workshops in order to debate what content should go into the strategy. Checklists are a helpful way of ensuring that key tasks are completed and are not forgotten. Figure 7.3 shows a checklist for a significant crisis (level 3), including an indication of when the tasks should be completed. Your strategy should also include an appendix of useful documents, such as the crisis report template and crisis severity definitions.

FIGURE 7.3 Crisis report template

Crisis Report Template				
Time / date of incident:				
Author of report:				
Time / date report completed:				
What happened?				
Teams impacted:				
Related tasks				
Activity		Person responsible	Due Date	Status
Additional comments:				
				Confidential. For internal use only.

Crisis management | 151

Crisis response checklist

Hour 1	Crisis communication and analysis	
	Complete crisis report and send to key stakeholders	
Hour 1	Roles and responsibilities	
	Assign an official spokesperson for the crisis who has the appropriate media training	
Hour 1	Response team	
	Hold meeting with key stakeholders to agree planned response	
Hour 1	Monitoring	
	Monitor social channels, accounts and news websites.	
Hours 2–5	Internal communications	
	Send internal communication statement to employees	
Hours 2–5	External messaging	
	Publish press statement on company website	
Hours 2–5	Social media response	
	Continue to respond to users and share updates about progress (including cross-links to company website)	
Hours 2–5	Response team	
	Update crisis report, send to all key stakeholders and hold update meetings or calls	
Hours 6–24	External messaging	
	Publish further update online	
Hours 6–24	External messaging	
	Proactively share updates regarding expected time of resolution of crisis	
Day 2	Post-crisis	
	Complete a post-crisis analysis	
Day 2	Post-crisis	
	Update crisis response strategy based on post-crisis analysis	
Day 2	Post-crisis	
	Hold stakeholder meeting to reflect on how the organization managed the crisis	

You should also take into account geography when considering how to respond to a crisis. If you're a global company, you might be hit with a severe crisis in only one of the countries you operate in. Your crisis response strategy should take into account the fact that people within that country will want regular updates on your response. People on the other side of the world, however, might want to know what you're doing, but won't require or want to know each and every detail as it unfolds. Social media is an excellent tool to do this effectively because you can target which users will see your posts. If you have a main corporate social media account as well as individual native-language accounts within the various countries, the local accounts should provide far more information than the main corporate account. This gives social media users the option to follow your local accounts if they want extra information, but if they don't, they can still get intermittent updates from your main account. Of course, when implementing a global crisis response strategy you'll also need to consider time zones and language. That way there's less chance that you'll wake up a colleague on the other side of the world just to give them an update that there is no change in the situation.

Media materials

Any crisis will require you to communicate with outside stakeholders such as media organizations, your customers or the public, and it's likely that shortly after the crisis begins your organization will be contacted for comment. You should pre-empt these requests by creating template holding statements or press releases that can be quickly and easily adapted to include all relevant information. The statement should be published wherever it will gain maximum exposure. To do this, a defined list of approved communications channels should be included in your strategy detailing how to go about publishing the information. For example, if a press release will be published on your website, the document should include details about who it should be sent to and any other relevant details, such as information about the typical amount of time that it would take to publish. For social media channels, a list of the key individuals who look after your official accounts and their contact details will make it easier for the person issuing the statement to get it pushed out.

It's also a good idea to keep an up-to-date list of journalists or news outlets that your company has a relationship with and to include details about how to obtain this information within the strategy. Contacting news outlets and journalists directly with updates about your response to a crisis will be a quick way of getting information out to the public.

Roles, responsibilities and logistics

It's important to have roles and responsibilities clearly defined within your crisis response strategy so that there can be no ambiguity as to who is responsible for what. Any uncertainty could delay your response and result in a crisis being escalated unnecessarily while your people scramble to work out who should do what.

You should maintain a list of approved company spokespeople who are authorized to make comment to the media about the crisis. These people should be identified within your strategy and should have received appropriate training to ensure that they are capable of dealing with the media. Your strategy should also make it clear that only those people who are approved company spokespeople are allowed to make any comments to the media about an ongoing crisis.

It's also worth considering the mechanics of how you will operate during a crisis. For example, which room will you use to coordinate your response and where will it be located? Getting as many of the key people as possible in the same room will make decision making much quicker and will allow everyone to keep up-to-date on any developments. You might want to include social media feeds and a news channel on a big screen. In some cases, you might need to set up a dedicated telephone line that customers or members of the public can phone if they need assistance or further information. All of this logistical information should be included within your strategy, as well as a list of key contacts who can assist with setting up telephone lines, access to the internet and so on.

Responding to a crisis

Having assessed the severity of a crisis, documented the cause and communicated it to your key stakeholders, you can move on to actually responding. Your crisis response strategy will be invaluable here and it's important to refer back to your well-laid plans before charging ahead. The cause of the crisis, the current political environment, your business strategy and other events will all have an impact on how you respond and what tasks you will build into your response.

One of the first things that you should do to respond to a crisis is to assess your options. What was the cause of the crisis? Is there something that you can do to easily rectify the situation? Not everything can be addressed quickly and easily, but if it can what will you do next to communicate your response internally and externally? For example, if the cause of the crisis was a bad choice of advertising that ended up offending huge groups of

FIGURE 7.4 Crisis response process

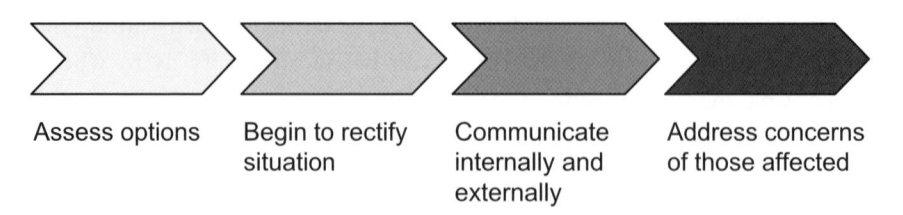

| Assess options | Begin to rectify situation | Communicate internally and externally | Address concerns of those affected |

people, you will have a few options. You could attempt to remove the offending advertising, or you could try to justify it. Justifying it might be dangerous because saying that 'it's not my fault' can cause more anger and escalate the crisis. If you want to remove the advertising, you'll need to plan how to do this. If it's online advertising, what channels is it on? Who are the people that you need to contact to get it removed. If it's printed advertising, you'll need to consider a communications strategy to apologise and explain. Once the advertising is removed, how will you engage with those groups who had been offended by it? The process for assessing your options and responding to the crisis is illustrated in Figure 7.4.

Social media may be a great way to quickly reach your customers or the wider public to communicate your response. But you need to consider where your target audience is and which platforms they are using. For example, if you experienced an incident in Russia, you won't want to rely solely on Twitter and Facebook because most Russians use local social networks such as vk.com or odnoklassniki.ru. Will your audience even use social media? If you sell stairlifts to the elderly you might find that a social media communications campaign doesn't reach your target audience and may just inadvertently publicize the issues which you are experiencing to a wider group of people.

Regardless of whether or not you will be using social media as your main communications channel, you'll need to carefully monitor it. Rumours on social media spread incredibly fast so you'll need to be prepared to respond if needed.

Having well-documented escalation processes is essential when you face a crisis. Teams who are dealing with a crisis need to understand at which point they need to escalate an issue to another team or to someone more senior and how they do so. Inappropriately escalating issues will bombard other teams and take their attention away from more serious issues they need to address. The process should outline criteria and situations that require the issue to be escalated to another team. Details of who in that team the issue should be passed to should be included.

Crisis management

CASE STUDY   Risk in action: Greggs bakery logo vandalized

If you search for a business in Google you may have seen the panel that appears on the right displaying key information about the business including its logo, address, phone number. On 19 August 2014 social media users noticed that if you typed 'Greggs', the UK's largest bakery chain, into Google, a fake logo with an offensive slogan was displayed instead of their official logo.

It didn't take long for Greggs to be flooded with posts and comments via Twitter. Greggs faced two issues: 1) they needed to work out how to fix the issue and get their proper logo to appear again; and 2) they needed to deal with the barrage of tweets from customers.

How Greggs reacted was impressive. They created the hashtag '#fixgreggs' and tweeted a photograph of a large plate of doughnuts to Google UK with the text:

Hey @GoogleUK, fix it and they're yours!!! #FixGreggs

Google UK then tweeted back:

Sorry @GreggstheBakers, we're on it. Throw in a sausage roll and we'll get it done ASAP. #FixGreggs.

For hours while they waited for Google to fix the issue, Greggs was responding to hundreds of tweets from their followers. They didn't respond with generic 'we're looking into it' messages the way other brands have done in the past. Instead, they responded with appropriate and sometimes witty posts. They didn't ignore their followers and didn't shy away from what had happened; they rose above it.

Greggs managed to get in touch with Google California and after a few hours the logo was fixed, at which point Google UK tweeted:

That's all done now @GreggstheBakers, #FixGreggs is now #FixedGreggs

Even after the logo issue had been fixed, Greggs didn't stop there. They then tweeted a photo of sausage rolls laid out on a table spelling 'Google', with the text 'Aaaand relax! Maybe those kind folks @GoogleUK could give us the doodle tomorrow?' (The 'doodle' is the changing Google logo that you often see on Google's homepage.)

Not long later Google tweeted back with a photo of an almost identical desk scattered with what appeared to be sausage roll crumbs and the text 'Whoops! Sorry @GreggstheBakers'.

Google didn't give Greggs the doodle, but it was an entertaining story with a good outcome for Greggs. They received a lot of support from its followers throughout and were able to respond in a very human way. The way Greggs handled this potential PR nightmare was reported positively in many of the mainstream newspapers and resulted in a lot of positive press.

This goes to show that social media can be used effectively to manage a potential PR nightmare and come out on top.

SOURCE: www.telegraph.co.uk/news/uknews/11043644/Greggs-bakery-shows-how-to-handle-a-social-media-nightmare-after-offensive-logo-appears-on-Google.html

Reactive versus proactive communications response

When you face a crisis you can choose to respond either proactively, or reactively. In a reactive response you will wait to be contacted by customers or the media before you respond to them and you will only disclose as much information as you have been asked for. In a proactive response you won't wait to be contacted, instead you'll proactively push out messages on social media, contact the media and give regular updates on your progress.

The best response tactic will depend on the circumstances of the crisis, as well as how much you know about the incident versus how much the public know. If your company is well known and champions transparency and you become aware of an issue with a product or service you might choose a proactive response. This would help you avoid being accused of hiding information, reacting slowly or not seeming to care. You might choose a reactive response tactic if there are already details of an issue emerging in the media, but not all of the detail has been leaked into the public domain. In this example, you wouldn't want to go out and put all your cards on the table as it might prompt an even bigger backlash against your company. Instead, you'll monitor the situation to see what stories get picked up by the media and put your energy into responding to them rather than focusing on other issues that are not causing such a press sensation.

Post-incident review

After an incident has been dealt with you should review your own performance to understand how you can improve should you face a similar incident in the future. Questions that you could ask are:

- Was the crisis report template used and was it effective?
- Was the response timely?
- Were the policies and procedures followed?

- Were any amendments to the agreed procedures made?
- Were the amendments effective and should they be incorporated into the processes?
- Did the teams collaborate effectively?
- How has the perception inside and outside the company changed as a result of the crisis?
- Were any improvements identified?

Once you have the answers to these questions you should have a fairly clear picture of how well your teams responded to the incident. You will also be able to see more clearly where your team had trouble or responded slowly. This valuable information should be used to update your crisis response strategy so that if there's a next time, your response will be more efficient.

Crisis testing and simulation

Once you've crafted your crisis response strategy it will hopefully be a quite some time until you have to put it in action, if ever! But such a strategy is an unfortunate necessity. The organizational change many companies face as well as the constant changes in technology and social media mean that the strategy could quickly become outdated. To avoid this, your strategy should be reviewed annually and updated appropriately.

You should also consider running crisis simulations to test your response strategy. Crisis scenario testing can uncover issues in your strategy and helps people in your organization to understand what they should do and how they should act in a crisis. Such testing will inevitably require quite a lot of senior resource, but the benefits of familiarizing your people with the strategy and getting a view on how it can be improved will prove invaluable when the time comes to put the strategy into action for real.

The objective of a crisis scenario test is to simulate events that might happen during a crisis over the period of a day. This could involve phone calls from the press, IT infrastructure going down, or even parts of the office becoming inaccessible. Throughout the test you will need observers to document how your people react to different situations, the decisions they take and the impact they have. You'll also need a team of people who will play the roles of key individuals in the outside world, for example a journalist calling for information. At the end of the test you should analyse the results and report back to leadership to summarize what went well, what didn't go well and what aspects of the strategy need to be amended.

The key benefits of crisis scenario testing are:

- It gives the organization an opportunity to rehearse its response capabilities and builds confidence in people's roles and responsibilities.
- It gives the organization confidence that they will be able to deal with a crisis but also highlights areas for improvement.
- The testing is realistic rather than theoretical. People will need to send emails and make phone calls as part of the test, all within a safe environment. This will bring the scenario to life and is more effective than just thinking about the tasks. For example, you might assume that to write a press release will take 10 minutes when in fact during the test it could take double that time.
- If the response to the crisis involves teams in multiple locations around the world, it gives them a chance to work together and get to know each other.

Crisis scenario testing is a fun exercise and a break from the norm. The tests are performed in a safe environment because they highlight fictional problems; however, they will go a long way to preparing an organization to deal with a crisis effectively when it occurs.

Summary

In this chapter we covered crisis management, an essential part of safeguarding your organization against social media risk. Being prepared for a crisis will help you deal with it more effectively. On the flip side, not being prepared for a crisis could have devastating consequences for your organization.

We covered the four stages of the crisis lifecycle: preparation; assessment and analysis; response; and prevention. In the preparation stage, you consider what threats the organization might face and what measures you will implement in order to respond to a crisis if it materializes. The severity of a crisis can increase or decrease, so by defining the different levels of crisis severity you are able to implement response plans to deal with the crisis effectively regardless of how it develops. Your crisis response strategy will have all of the tools and guidance that you need to deal with a crisis. Crisis response strategies need to be updated regularly as standard as well as after a crisis in order to tweak the strategy and help prevent future crises.

Finally, we covered crisis scenario testing – a key way to test your crisis strategy and an opportunity to identify and fix any issues within it. Running crisis scenarios helps bring the theory to life and will be a memorable experience for all of those involved, which in turn will help people to either prevent a crisis from happening, or to respond appropriately if it does.

In the next chapter we'll look at social media security and how to implement measures to manage the risk of security breaches when faced by a cyber attack.

Cyber security 08

Overview

Cyber security is one of the biggest threats facing businesses, governments and individuals. In 2014 there were 42.8 million security incidents reported. This is the equivalent of almost 120,000 attacks every day. Cyber security is nothing new, but the threat has grown considerably over the last few years as we have grown more connected and as organizations have begun to rely more on their digital systems. In a survey from professional services firm, PwC, the cost of the average cyber attack against large companies in the United Kingdom in 2014 was between £600,000 and £1.15 million.

In this chapter, I will introduce you to the topic of cyber security and cover some of the basics to give you a base level of understanding. We'll cover who the main actors are and what their motivations and targets might be. We'll then move on to consider where the security risks lie in social media and what you can do to safeguard yourself against them. Cyber attacks are not necessarily highly sophisticated. Likewise, there are some simple but effective steps that you can take to ensure the security of your social media accounts.

What is cybercrime?

Cybercrime is the term used to describe criminal activity on computer systems. A hacker is someone who aims to exploit weaknesses in computer systems for some kind of gain. The hacker's motivation is not always monetary and there are a number of reasons why people engage in hacking. From teenagers getting up to mischief in their bedrooms to nation states waging cyber warfare, there are a number of different players and motivations.

Cyber risks pose a threat to both individuals as well as companies. Everyone is aware that fraud and identify theft are common crimes perpetrated in order to steal money. But there are less obvious risks posed to individuals.

For example, many people go on holiday and post photos on social media of themselves relaxing, perhaps enjoying a beer on a beach. Unfortunately criminals have realized this and have started targeting people who geo-tag their posts with their location. There have already been cases of people having their homes burgled while they were away on holiday because geo-tagged social media posts have alerted burglars to the fact they are not at home.

Who poses a threat?

Cyber risks pose a number of threats to businesses too. Whether it be to steal money or designs for their latest products, the risk is already high and growing. So, who are these 'cybercriminals' and 'hackers'? Figure 8.1 shows the key players in cyber security.

FIGURE 8.1 Key players in cyber security

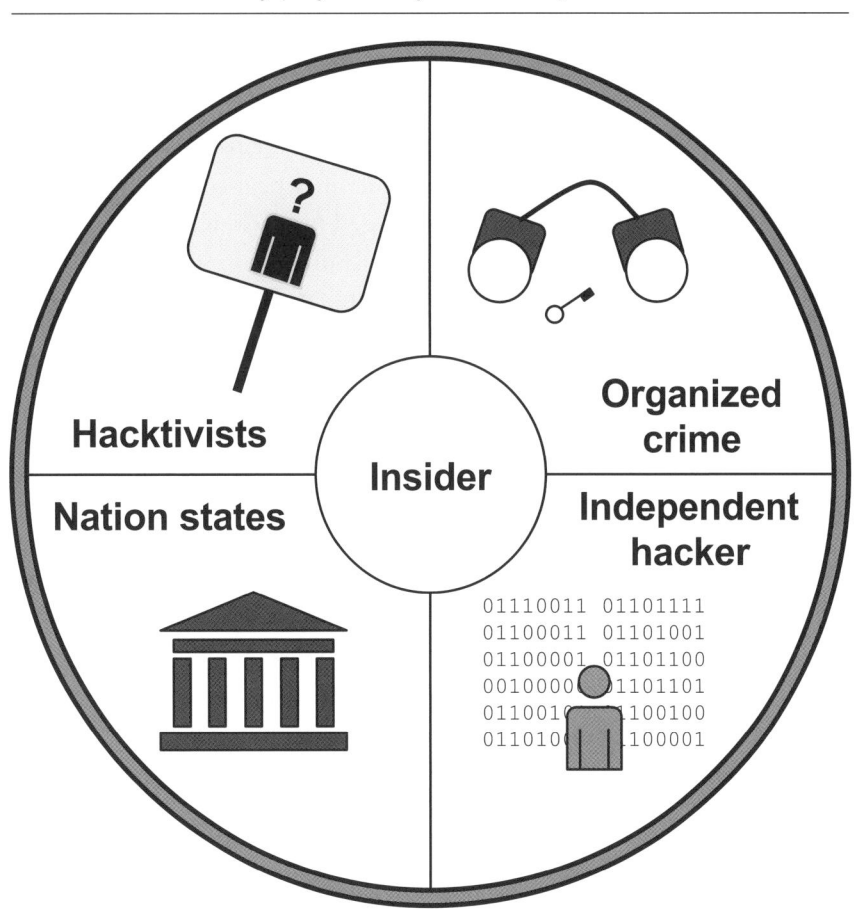

The key players are:

- *Organized crime*. Criminal gangs who engage in hacking for financial gain by stealing money from banks or personal information and intellectual property to sell on the black market.
- *Nation states*. The term 'cyber warfare' describes how nation states are using techniques to attack or defend against their adversaries. Nation states might use computers for intelligence gathering or develop and deploy cyber weapons that target a foreign country's utilities or infrastructure.
- *Hacktivists*. The word 'hacktivist' comes from the word 'activist' and usually defines groups of hackers who break security in order to publicize a social or ideological message. For example, some hacktivist groups are opposed to internet censorship, or indeed censorship of any kind, so launch attacks against governments or organizations who they see as supporting censorship. Some groups believe in the freedom of information and focus their energy on hacking to bring non-public, or confidential, information into the public realm.
- *Insider*. The insider is a special category and refers to someone inside a company or organization. The insider may be used as a mule, unaware that their account is being used for hacking. For example, an external hacker may send malicious software to someone within a company in the hope that they will install it. This software could give the attacker access to the insider's computer. Insiders therefore pose a big threat to organizations.
- *Independent hackers*. There are many types of independent hackers, however the main ones are:
  - 'Black hat' hackers: these are the hacker groups most commonly portrayed in popular culture or films. Black hat hackers break security for little reason beyond malicious intent or personal gain. Black hat hackers may break into computer systems to destroy or steal data, or to make the systems unusable.
  - Professional or elite hackers for hire: this group of hackers is highly skilled and often employed to uncover vulnerabilities in computer software and to write code that will exploit those vulnerabilities.
  - Ethical hacker: an ethical hacker, also known as a 'white hat' hacker, is someone who breaks security for non-malicious

purposes. This could be in order to a test a system's security and uncover weaknesses so that fixes can be applied. Ethical hackers perform 'penetration tests' or 'vulnerability tests', usually under contract.

- 'Script kiddies': these are relatively unskilled hackers who break into computer systems using tools created by black-hat hackers. Script kiddies can wreak havoc, but without their tools they have little understanding of the underlying computer concepts.

What's at risk?

As mentioned above, the threat presented by hackers goes beyond the financial. Figure 8.2 illustrates the key things that are usually targeted in a cyber attack.

FIGURE 8.2 Cyber security – what's at risk?

- Corporate secrets
- Personal data
- Business deal information
- Money
- Intellectual property
- Payment information
- Operational data
- Industrial control systems

The things that an attacker can target include:

- *Money.* Money is often a big motivator. Hackers may try to break through your security in order to access your bank accounts and steal money by transferring it out of your accounts.

- *Corporate secrets.* Corporate secrets are valuable: if they weren't, they wouldn't be secrets! What is valuable to your company would probably be valuable to others, whether that is a competitor, a government or an independent hacker who wants to sell your secrets on the black market.

- *Business deal information.* Information about business deals, such as planned mergers or acquisitions, is sensitive as any insider knowledge about the deal could impact the stock market or could be used by the opposing party. For example, if your organization is planning to sell part of its business and has set a minimum price, that information would be extremely valuable to the purchasing party. Again, information with a high value will always be targeted by hackers.

- *Personal data.* If someone were to get hold of all of your personal data, it would make it much easier to steal your identity, which is why personal data can have a large intrinsic value to criminals. Hacktivists may also target personal data because they want to expose it online in order to embarrass the company that controls it and cause uproar from all of its customers and employees. In this case, a hacktivist may not make money from the hack, but the company they targeted may be fined by a regulator. The hacktivist's goal is to cause as much pain to their target as possible.

- *Intellectual property.* Designs for your latest products or the inner workings of your existing products clearly have a high value, especially to your competitors. If hackers were able to get a feature list of your new product and pass it on, it would erode competitive advantage, which is why intellectual property is often a target.

- *Payment information.* Rather than stealing money directly from a company, it might be easier and more rewarding instead to steal the payment information of all of your customers. These payment details could either be used by the criminals to make purchases themselves, or they could be sold on the black market to other criminal gangs.

- *Operational data.* This may not seem obvious at first, but if a hacker was able to obtain data about how your business operates, they could use that information to their advantage for large cyber attacks

in the future. Alternatively, if an attacker can find out information about your delivery trucks, they might be able to work out the best time and place to rob them.
- *Industrial control systems.* The systems that control water filtration plants, the electricity network, power stations and so on are called industrial control systems. These systems are usually targeted by hackers for cyberterrorism. Their purpose is to disrupt a nation's utilities or to have a large impact on normal citizens, for example by manipulating water filtration systems.

Although not exhaustive, this list does help to show that there are a large number of incentives for cyber attacks. The key takeaway is to apply the same caution to your information assets as you would to your physical property. If something is valuable, it could be targeted, and should therefore be protected. If an attacker can gather intelligence about your company by stealing your operational data, then they will be able to use that data against you in the future.

Account management

Why is account management important?

I'm sure you'll agree that it would worry you if it was easy for a hacker, or anyone with malicious intent, to get access to your corporate social media accounts. Unfortunately, there have been lots of examples of this happening, and in many cases the reason has been poor account management. There are a number of tools and techniques available to hackers that they can use to gain access to your social media accounts. In this section we'll examine the ways that hackers achieve this, and look at what you can do to guard against it.

On the flip side, if inappropriate or offensive content is posted on your social media account, it might not be because of a cyber attack. It might be an innocent mistake made by someone in your team who mixed up your corporate account with their personal account. There are a lot of examples of this, so we'll look at what you can do to stop this from happening but you should also read Chapter 6 for guidance on how policy and awareness can reduce the risk of this happening.

The problem with many social networks is that they were initially conceived as tools to allow people to connect with each other. Only later did organizations start using social media to connect with their customers and promote their products. Because of this, many social networks only allow one username and password to be associated with a social media account. So, if you have a Twitter account with the handle @[your_company_name] and have a team of 10 who need to use it, you've really only got two options: 1) share the username and password among your team; or 2) use some kind of social media management tool to control access, as covered in Chapter 4. The easiest option might be to simply share the login credentials with your team; however, as discussed in Chapter 4, this poses a big risk to your organization.

There are other problems with sharing account credentials. Because everyone in your team is logging into the same account, it makes it almost impossible to control what is being posted. You have no control and if you want to block a disgruntled employee from the account, your only option is to change the password and communicate it to the rest of the team, provided that that employee hasn't already changed the account password to spite you.

The use of a social media management system, or a social risk and compliance tool, is an excellent way to manage your accounts. We looked at the advantages of these systems in Chapter 4 (see Figure 4.4). By implementing a social media management system you will not only be able to give each member of your team their own login but you'll also be able implement controls to ensure that your password policies are adhered to. For example, you can configure how often you want your users to be forced to update their passwords and set rules that dictate password complexity.

Another advantage of using a social media management tool is that it will provide a different interface for your team when logged in using their mobile devices. Figure 8.3 illustrates that more than one social media account can be connected to your smartphone. We often operate on 'autopilot', completing simple and common tasks while barely thinking about them. It's this behaviour that has caused some people to confuse the corporate account with their personal account. However, when a social media management tool is used, access to the corporate account will be controlled through the management system's own mobile application. This means that the personal account will be configured in the social network's native application on your phone. The interfaces are likely to be significantly different from one and other, which will reduce the risk of a mix-up.

Passwords

I don't know anyone who likes having to remember lots of different passwords or who enjoys having to regularly changing them. However,

FIGURE 8.3 Multiple accounts on one device

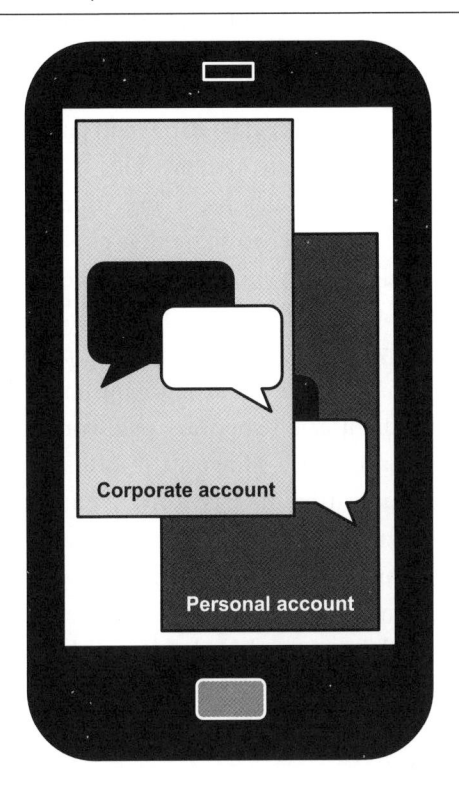

good password management is an unfortunate necessity. It's tempting to set them to things that are easy to remember, such as the birth date or name of your first child. But the problem is that it's now even easier than ever to find out information about peoples' lives: a quick look on someone's public social media profile can often give a very detailed picture of their life: when and who they married, when their children were born, their names, where they live, where they go on holiday and so on. It's complicated further by the fact that the average person now has a multitude of different online accounts, which makes it tempting to just use the same password for every account. However, the problem with this is that if any of those accounts get hacked, the attacker will have access to all of your other accounts. Even if you signed up to a website just once to see what it was all about and never returned, if you used the same password as you use for your other accounts then you are at risk of your main accounts being hacked, even though you only used the website in question once.

In our personal lives, there are a few occasions when we might disclose our passwords to someone else. In theory, this should never happen, but I'm sure there are times when we have shared our passwords, perhaps with a loved ones to allow them access to our emails or social network. In a corporate setting, one of the few occasions when passwords will be shared is when a new account is being created. Many companies operate a security model whereby the user has a global user ID (GUID) and password, which they use for all, or at least most, corporate systems. This is good because it means that the user doesn't need to remember a large number of passwords and there's also no need for them ever to share that password. However, not all applications will use this security model and an exception might be a social media management system. This means that every time you create a new user you will need a way of communicating the password to them. The management system may have built-in mechanisms to deal with this, for example, by emailing the user a temporary password and providing a link for them to change it on first use. However, if this isn't the case you'll need another way of communicating the password. As a rule, you should never use the same method to communicate the username and the password. For example, you might email a person their username and tell them their password over the phone. Alternatively you might text them their username and verbally tell them the password face to face. Whatever you choose, you should ensure that the username and the password are not communicated in the same way because it decreases the likelihood that the details could be intercepted.

Two-factor authentication

No matter how careful you are, there's still a chance that your password could be stolen or 'cracked'. Two-factor authentication differs from single-factor authentication because it authenticates someone based on something they know (such as a password) as well as something else that is inseparable to the user. Taking money out of a cash machine is an example of two-factor authentication because of the use of the bank card, which the user possesses, and a personal identification number (PIN), which the user knows.

Many online systems, including email providers and social networks, have adopted two-factor authentication as a way of overcoming the inadequacies of simple passwords. You may already use some form of extra device from your bank in order to log in to your internet banking, which is another example of two-factor authentication. Nowadays, most people own a smartphone, which has led it to become the go-to device used for two-factor authentication for online services such as social media.

How both single-factor and two-factor authentication work is illustrated in Figure 8.4. The single-factor authentication route to your social network is simply to log in using your username and password. Many social networks allow you to configure two-factor authentication using your phone. When enabled, you log into your social network account using your username and password, then the network sends an automated authentication code to your phone, often via a text message or via an app installed on your device. You then type the code into the input box on screen to gain access. The code will only be valid for a short period of time, perhaps between 1 and 10 minutes.

FIGURE 8.4 Single-factor vs two-factor authentication

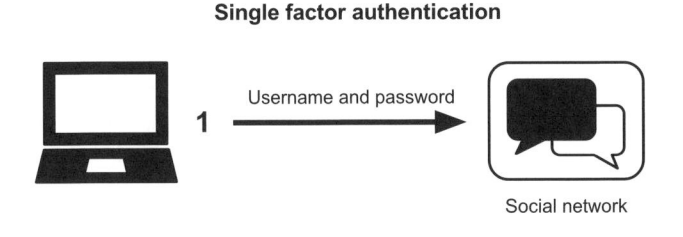

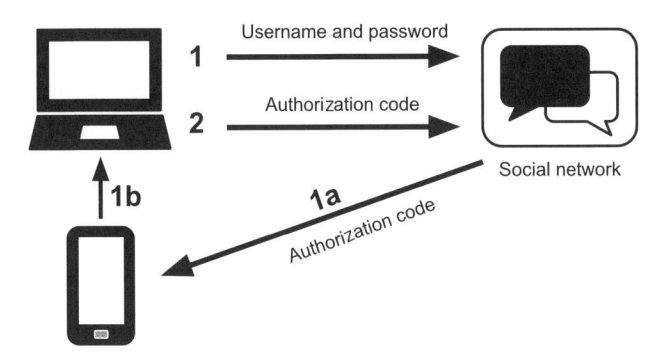

The beauty of this is that even if your password is broken, stolen or an attacker manages to get hold of it using some other means, they still won't be able to access your account unless they also have your phone.

It's obviously an extra hurdle and could be quite frustrating if you were in a location without any mobile phone signal, or without your phone, however, it's one of the best ways to significantly reduce the risk of your account being hacked. You should check the account and security settings on your social networks and other online accounts to see if two-factor authentication is an option. If it is, there will be details about how to register your phone and turn it on. Some online services try to make it even easier for you by letting you identify certain trusted computers that do not require you to continually log in.

Viruses, spyware and malware

Some of the tools hackers use against their victims are actually tools that unsuspecting users have running on their own computers. Often, malware (malicious software) is sent to users in phishing emails or can be automatically downloaded when a user visits a malicious website. Malware is the term used for any software installed on computers that performs unwanted tasks. There are different types of malware; the key ones are as follows:

- *Virus*. Viruses have been around for almost as long as personal computers started to appear in peoples' homes. A computer virus replicates itself on the infected computer and spreads itself to other computers, normally through a computer network or via email. A virus can damage an infected computer by corrupting the hard drive or by taking up all available memory to render the computer unusable.
- *Spyware*. There are many types of spyware but their main purpose is to covertly spy on a user's computer usage. Information about what the user is doing is then transmitted to servers controlled by the hackers. A 'Trojan horse' (or Trojan) is a type of malware that often acts as a 'backdoor' into the victim's computer. Some Trojan horses can give the attacker full control over the user's computer.
- *Adware*. Software that serves up irritating adverts on a user's computer, often bombarding the user and severely impeding productivity.
- *Ransomware*. Ransomware is a particularly vicious type of virus that encrypts a user's hard drive, effectively locking the user out of their own computer, and holding them to ransom. The user must pay a ransom (often in the region of around £250 but sometimes considerably more) to get the key to unlock the hard drive. Often a time limit is imposed whereby if the user does not pay up in the given time the contents of the hard drive will be permanently deleted. There's no guarantee that the decryption key will be provided if the user pays. Ransomware is not new, but became more popular among

cybercriminals around 2013 with the release of a widespread ransomware package called 'Cryptolocker'.
- *Keyloggers*. These are types of spyware, often included in Trojan horses, which record all keys pressed by a user. Usually the keylogger will run in the background of the computer and is difficult to detect by the average computer user. Because keyloggers record all keys pressed it means that they can capture all passwords entered.
The fact that passwords are usually hidden on screen does not matter if a keylogger is installed because they record every key.

The best way to avoid unexpectedly installing malware on your computer or network is to ensure that your anti-virus and anti-spyware software is up to date. You should also have a good firewall to protect you from attacks over the internet and to detect whether malware is attempting to secretly transmit to criminals. A firewall is a security system that controls inbound and outbound network traffic based on a set of rules. If malware is trying to submit information to an attacker elsewhere on the internet, a well-configured firewall will block the connection attempts. In the corporate environment, most of this should be the responsibility of your IT team, so unless you are in that team you shouldn't need to install these programs yourself. Malware is also attached to malicious phishing emails so you should avoid clicking any links in any suspicious emails. Phishing is covered in more detail in the next section.

A less obvious way that malware can get onto your computer is through devices connecting with it, for example a USB stick, a mobile phone or even a USB charger. Malicious devices can be programmed so that whenever they are connected to a computer (or mobile device), they automatically install malware. For this reason, many large organizations lock down the ability for users to plug anything into their computers by disabling USB or other inputs altogether. So, you might want to think twice the next time someone asks you to do them a favour and let them charge their mobile phone using your laptop or computer. That mobile phone may be loaded with malware that will silently infect your computer. Likewise, USB memory sticks are now very cheap and often given away for free at conferences. Be warned – by accepting the 'free' memory stick and plugging it into your computer you might be handing over control of your computer to a cyber criminal!

CASE STUDY Risk in action: 2 million passwords stolen and posted online

In December 2013 reports emerged that more than 2 million passwords for a wide range of online services had been stolen. The stolen login credentials were then posted online. The site, written in Russian, claimed to offer valid logins to 318,000 Facebook accounts, 70,000 Gmail, Google+ and YouTube accounts, 22,000 Twitter accounts and 9,000 Odnoklassniki accounts (a Russian social network).

The passwords appeared to have been stolen from computers infected with keylogging malware. Keylogging malware logs all keys pressed on a keyboard, then sends them to servers controlled by the hackers. Analysis of the stolen passwords by security firm Trustwave showed that the most popular password in the database was '123456', which was listed 15,000 times. Facebook said that all users found in the database had been put through a password reset process.

The moral of this story is that online users should be more careful with their passwords. Don't use the same password for all of your online accounts, make sure that the passwords you do use are not simple or easy to guess and ensure that you change them regularly. An extra level of protection would be to use two-factor authentication, which would significantly reduce the likelihood of your account becoming compromised if your passwords are stolen.

SOURCE: http://money.cnn.com/2013/12/04/technology/security/passwords-stolen/index.html?hpt=hp_t2

Social engineering

What is it?

Social engineering describes techniques used by hackers to deceive people in order to extract information or to encourage them to do things for them. Social engineering usually exploits an insider at a company, either by phoning or emailing them and making them think that the attacker is someone else, such as a senior member of the company. Social engineering is a very powerful way of manipulating people in order to bypass controls or break a company's security. An attack may consist of multiple attempts to manipulate users to build a picture of how an organization operates, get hold of names, phone numbers and other information that they can then incorporate into their deceptive techniques in order to make them more believable to their next victim. In the context of social media, there are two types of social engineering that pose the biggest threat to an organization: impersonation; and phishing.

Impersonation

Impersonation is when an attacker disguises their identity by impersonating someone else. The attacker may try a number of different techniques, such as impersonating senior members of staff or by claiming that they are calling from the company's IT department. The attacker can be creative and will normally spend a lot of time building a picture of what it's like to work at the company, who its suppliers are, who the key people are and so on. The more information an attacker can get, the more convincing he or she can be when they contact their victim.

The victim will often receive a phone call or an email from an attacker who is claiming to be someone else. The attacker's objective is to either extract information or to get the victim to perform certain tasks. For example, the attacker might claim to be a headhunter interested in hiring the victim. Once the victim gets talking they might expose information about the size of the team, the working hours, the types of social media accounts they have and so on. This information may seem harmless on its own, but it is extremely valuable to the attacker, as it allows them to build a more accurate picture of how the team operates. They could then use that information to call a new member of staff claiming to be the boss's boss and ask that the user hands over their login credentials, even issuing threats to the victim should they not comply. An attacker may also ask information such as the browser version which the employees use. This helps the attacker focus their attention on hacking the specific browser version in use at the company and discounting any others.

Other information that an attacker might want to gather from a victim could be the team's holiday schedule, or information about when nobody is in the office. This could then be used to launch attacks in a quiet time when there is less chance of it being noticed. Information about whether employees can access the corporate social media accounts on their phones could also be useful to the attacker. In some cases, the attacker might be able to persuade their victim to explain the process for setting up access on a mobile device. Internal documentation, such as policies and procedures, can also be useful to an attacker as they often include details about key contacts or instructions about how to complete tasks within the organization, such as how to submit new content for approval on a social network.

Social media can also present the risk of impersonation. If you or someone within your company is widely known, for example a well-recognized CEO, a reporter from a news agency, or a celebrity or film star, then members of the public can create false accounts in their name.

False social media accounts can be damaging in many ways, and there are numerous reasons impersonators may decide to set one up. A key motivator can be to satirize or mock the company or person, or to damage reputation in some other way (see the British Petroleum case study in Chapter 2). Fake accounts can also be created as part of a wider attack, for instance by mimicking a bank and contacting people through social media to tell them that fraudulent activity has been identified on their account in the hope that the user will provide their details.

Many of the social networks have tried to combat fake accounts by designating certain accounts in some way to show that they are official. On Twitter, for example, a blue tick appears beside official accounts which Twitter has verified. Other social networks have similar ways to help users identify official accounts.

Using deception to impersonate another person or organization is a violation of most social networks' terms and conditions so you should ensure that you follow the network's procedures to report the impersonated account as soon as possible. However, because many social networks support freedom of expression, many allow parody accounts to be created provided that certain conditions are met. For example, the social network may require that the parody is clearly identified as such by explicitly stating that the account is not official.

If you find that your company has been impersonated and you are not happy about it, the best action to take is to report it to the network. Unfortunately, the network may take a long time to review the reported account and, as stated above, may allow the account to exist if it complies with the network's terms and conditions. If this is the case, the best thing that you can do is to work harder to ensure that you attract supporters and that the content you create resonates with users. If you are facing criticism over a recent crisis it may be best to simply weather the storm and commit to producing high-quality content and engaging with your customers and followers effectively.

Phishing

One of the most common techniques that attackers use to hack into users' social media or other online accounts is phishing. A phishing attack involves an attacker sending an email to their victims that includes harmful content, such as an attachment that includes malware or links to fake or dangerous websites. If the user opens the attachment or clicks on the link, malicious code could be installed on the user's computer, which could either cause damage to the computer or spy on the user in order to gather sensitive information such as bank account details or login credentials.

It's important that your users are able to spot a phishing email to avoid falling victim to an attack. If you receive a phishing email you should report it to your IT department so they can attempt to block any future attacks, and delete the email without opening any attachments or clicking on any links. Figure 8.5 illustrates what a phishing email might look like.

FIGURE 8.5 Phishing email example

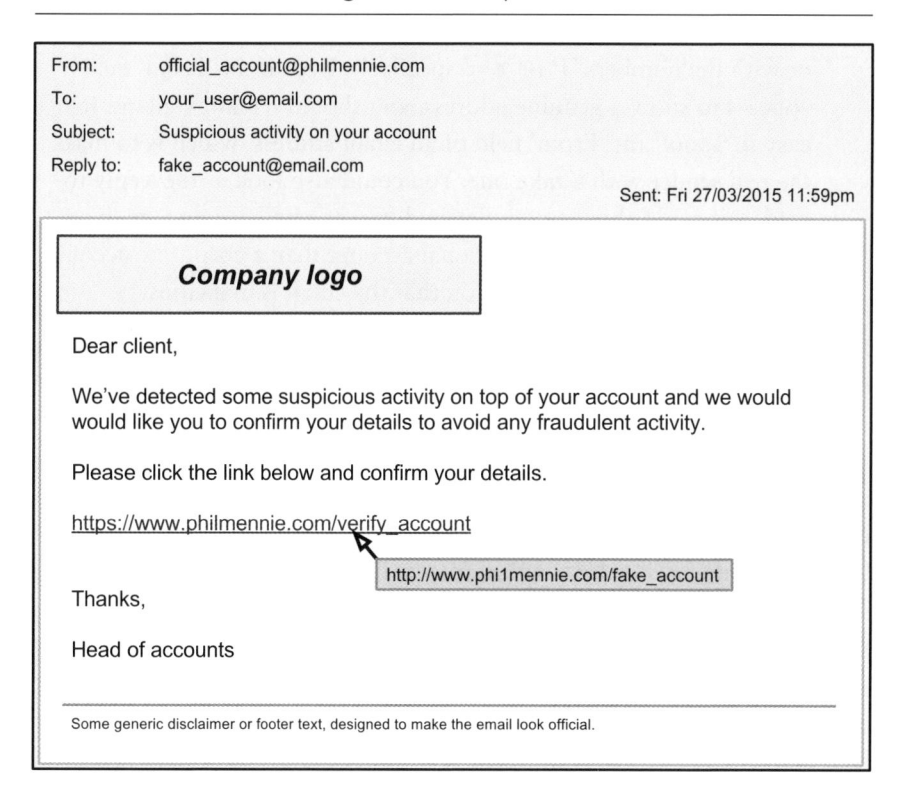

From:	official_account@philmennie.com
To:	your_user@email.com
Subject:	Suspicious activity on your account
Reply to:	fake_account@email.com

Sent: Fri 27/03/2015 11:59pm

Company logo

Dear client,

We've detected some suspicious activity on top of your account and we would would like you to confirm your details to avoid any fraudulent activity.

Please click the link below and confirm your details.

https://www.philmennie.com/verify_account

http://www.phi1mennie.com/fake_account

Thanks,

Head of accounts

Some generic disclaimer or footer text, designed to make the email look official.

If you suspect that you have received a phishing email you should consider the following:

- How does the email refer to you? If the email says 'Dear client' or 'Dear customer', it might be a phishing email. It's unlikely that official emails from your bank or your social network would refer to you using such a generic term.
- Be wary of links within the email. In Figure 8.5, you can see that the link looks genuine; however, if you hover the mouse over the link you might see that the actual target of the link is different.
- Poor spelling or grammar. It's unlikely that official communications from reputable companies will include basic spelling mistakes or grammar mistakes so this could be a good indication that the email is a fake.
- From field. Check the address in the 'From' field. The address might be subtly different, for example by replacing the characters 'l' or 'o' or with the numbers '1' or '0' respectively. Even if the 'From' field appears to show a genuine address, you should remain vigilant. It's easy to 'spoof' the 'From' field of an email address, which is to mask the real sender with a fake one. You could also look at the 'reply to' field as it could show a completely different email account, such as one that looks more like a personal account than a corporate account. This could be another indication that the email is malicious.

Finally, you may have a feeling that the email that you have received just doesn't seem right. You might have received it unexpectedly and it may include content or references that make you suspicious.

Sometimes, a phishing email may encourage users to click a link and log into a phishing website. A phishing website looks like a legitimate website but is in fact a malicious copy, designed to make the user think that they are logging into the real website when in fact they are logging into a fake. The login credentials used on the phishing website will be captured and used to hijack the user's account. This also illustrates how two-factor authentication, as discussed earlier in this chapter, can help protect a user from this type of attack. Figure 8.6 illustrates how a phishing website might differ from the legitimate site it is impersonating. At first glance the websites seem identical; however, if you look carefully you can see that the web address is slightly different. The letter 'l' has been replaced with the number '1'. The idea of this is that if the user glances briefly at the web address they might not notice the subtle difference.

Cyber security 177

FIGURE 8.6 Phishing website example

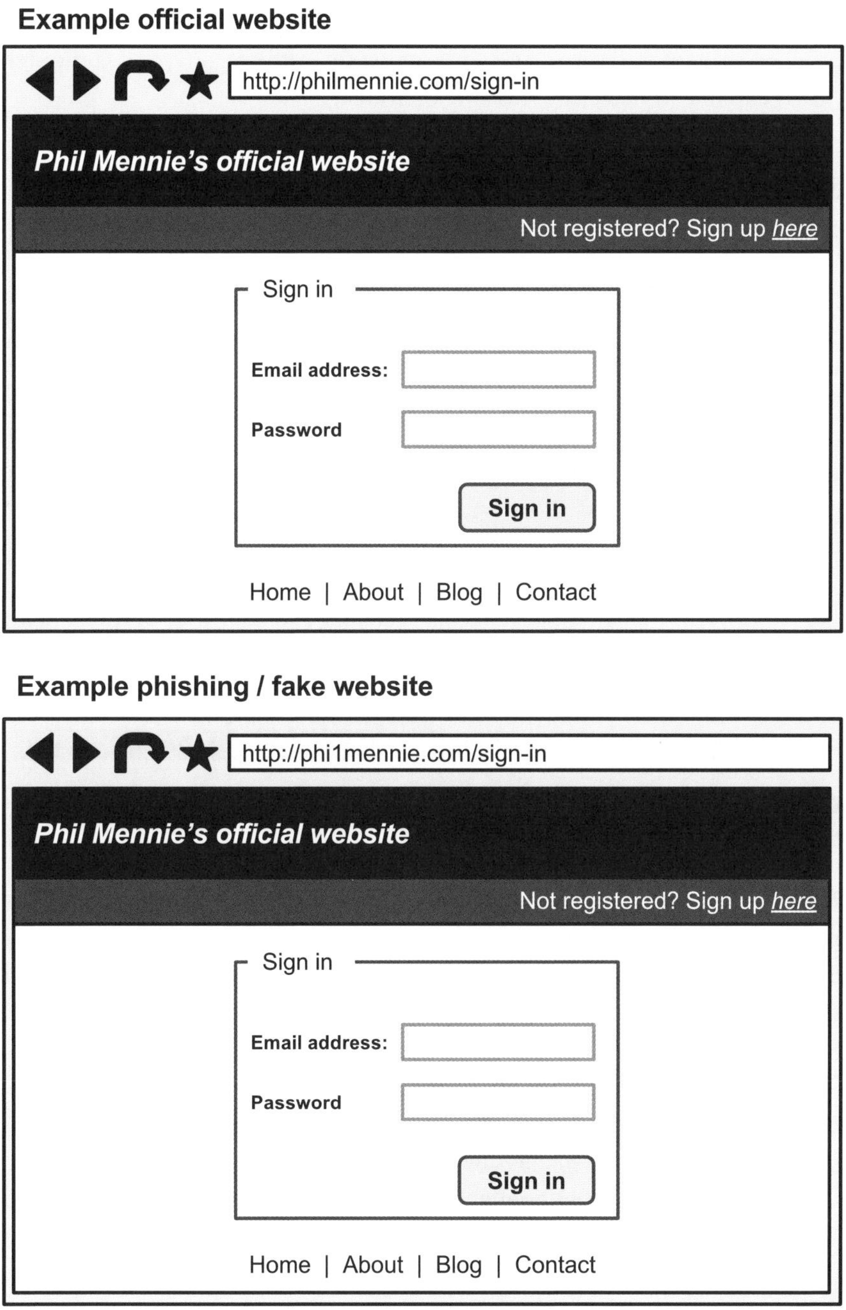

Example official website

◀ ▶ ↪ ★ http://philmennie.com/sign-in

Phil Mennie's official website

Not registered? Sign up *here*

Sign in

Email address: ☐

Password: ☐

[Sign in]

Home | About | Blog | Contact

Example phishing / fake website

◀ ▶ ↪ ★ http://phi1mennie.com/sign-in

Phil Mennie's official website

Not registered? Sign up *here*

Sign in

Email address: ☐

Password: ☐

[Sign in]

Home | About | Blog | Contact

It's worth pointing out that users should not rely on the web address alone because an attacker may have used other techniques to mask the web address. To guard against this, your IT department should ensure that you have up-to-date anti-virus and anti-malware software on your computer that is capable of detecting this sort of attack.

Spear phishing

Spear phishing is a targeted phishing attack against a specific user, or group of specific users, rather than a mass mail approach where a generic phishing email is sent out en masse with little direction. A spear phishing attack could be launched on specific employees within an organization and will normally include specific details that an attacker may have gathered using other social engineering techniques. For example, a spear phishing attack might target specific members in your marketing team by name and reference recent meetings or projects in order to fool the recipient into thinking that the email is legitimate.

Phishing emails have become popular with hackers who are looking to gain access to a company's social media accounts, and there are many examples of successful social media attacks as a result of phishing.

CASE STUDY   Risk in action: the SEA targets media outlets

The Syrian Electronic Army (SEA) is a group of computer hackers who support the government of Syrian President Bashar-al-Assad. The group rose to notoriety during 2013 when it hacked a number of prominent Western media websites and social media accounts, including Forbes, The New York Times, The Associated Press and The Guardian.

A lot of the SEA's hacks are not very sophisticated and instead look to trick people into clicking links within malicious emails. The SEA is known for using phishing attacks like this successfully.

One particularly noteworthy attack was against the Associated Press (AP). The SEA managed to hack the AP's Twitter account and post a tweet with the text:

Breaking: Two Explosions in the White House and Barack Obama is injured

This tweet had a particularly big impact because the Associated Press had nearly 2 million Twitter followers at the time so it was picked up and retweeted by other social media users almost instantly. It even had an impact on the stock market and one minute after the tweet was posted the Dow Jones Industrial Average started a short nose-dive. A Bloomberg reporter wrote that in the three minutes after the post the 'fake tweet erased more than $136 billion in equity market value' before recovering shortly afterwards.

About an hour after the hack, the SEA claimed responsibility. Reports in the media claim that the SEA gained access to the Associated Press Twitter account through a phishing attack. An innocent-looking email asked AP staff to click on a link, which then downloaded malware to their computer to spy on them. This goes to show that cyber attacks don't need to be highly sophisticated to be effective and, more often than not, humans are the weakest link.

SOURCE: www.washingtonpost.com/blogs/worldviews/wp/2013/04/23/syrian-hackers-claim-ap-hack-that-tipped-stock-market-by-136-billion-is-it-terrorism/

Securing your network and data

The more security you put in place, the more difficult it becomes for users to access your systems. The most secure computer is one that is without power in a protected vault in an unknown location where nobody can access it. However, the computer is clearly not going to be very useful this way. Therefore, you need to strike a balance between security and usability. When implementing an enterprise social network you'll need to consider how to configure your network. You'll need to assess the risks and make an informed decision about how users will be able to access it and what data they will be allowed to store within it.

Enterprise social networks are excellent collaboration and knowledge-sharing tools. Your colleagues are able to connect with each other and share documents, or even collaborate to create documents within the enterprise social network itself. Because of this, as time progresses the amount of valuable, and potentially sensitive, information within your network will increase. This will make the network an extremely attractive target for a hacker. If an attacker can gain access to your network they will have free reign to search and download a huge amount of information. Because of this, it's vital that you ensure your network is well protected.

In Chapter 4, we looked at data classification, which is a helpful way of defining different types of data. A data classification framework will help you set policy decisions about the types of data you will allow in your network.

For example, you may allow internal information to be shared freely on the network, but more sensitive data to be shared only within closed groups with extra controls in place.

You will need to consider how your users will access your enterprise social network. The network provider will offer different options, such as simple web-based authentication or more complex requirements around the use of a virtual private network (VPN). A VPN allows users to connect to the private corporate network across a public connection. For example, you may use a VPN to connect to your corporate network from home. The advantage of using a VPN is that it's an added layer of protection which authenticates your corporate users and allows them to access company systems, such as your enterprise social network, when outside the office. The disadvantage is that it requires extra configuration and support from IT in order to set up and run the network. It also requires the users to configure their devices to access the network.

From a user perspective, the simplest way to authenticate a user into your enterprise social network is to allow them to connect to it by using a web login. The problem with this is that without any additional controls, a user could go on holiday and decide to go to an internet cafe and access your enterprise social network. The computers in the internet cafe could be riddled with malware spying on the user's login credentials. Once the login credentials have been exposed in this way it will give the attacker an easy route into your enterprise social network.

Configuring your enterprise social network to only allow connection from within the corporate network, or via VPN, is an extra hurdle your users would need to jump through. However, I believe that the added protection that this offers is worth it.

Most enterprise social networks allow users to upload and share documents, as it is a very practical way of enabling effective knowledge sharing. However, some organizations make the decision to prohibit documents from being uploaded due to security concerns. The organization may be worried about losing control over sensitive documents uploaded to the network. If you decide to allow documents to be uploaded, you should consider what types of file you want to permit. For example, you may wish to prohibit executable (.exe) files from being uploaded because you want to reduce the risk that users might accidentally, or deliberately, upload malicious software to the network. Many good enterprise social networks have built-in features that scan any uploaded files for viruses. If you allow files to be uploaded, it's essential that this feature is enabled. You should also consider how the virus definitions (the rules the software uses to detect viruses) are kept up to date.

This may be a question for the vendor but is one that you should definitely raise during your preliminary discussion. If virus definitions are not updated regularly it could mean that newer viruses get missed by the software.

Summary

Security is an important part of social media risk management and governance. There are large numbers of hackers around the world who work tirelessly, so IT security professionals need to be ever vigilant in order to stay one step ahead. IT security is evolving, but in many organizations the 'traditional' IT systems get more attention than the newer 'social' systems. This can result in weaknesses that not only impact the social systems themselves, but also threaten a company's IT network more broadly.

In this chapter we introduced the topic of cyber security and looked at the key actors and their motivations. Good account and password management is one of the simplest things to get right; however, many people neglect best practice because they don't perceive the extra effort as worthwhile. However, even some of the most notorious hacker groups launch attacks using fairly unsophisticated techniques that have proven very effective.

We looked at some of the practical things you can do to protect yourself and your team online, such as enabling two-factor authentication on your social network accounts. Finally we considered how an attacker might target your enterprise social network and looked at some of the steps that you can take to secure your network, such as by prohibiting connections that do not use the corporate VPN.

In the next chapter we will look at the changing regulatory environment and how it impacts social media.

Regulation

09

Overview

In this chapter we're going to look at how regulation impacts social media. Regulation differs around the world, and the laws and regulations that are applicable to your organization will depend on the country, or countries, in which you operate, as well as your industry. As such, rather than include a long list of regulations that impact social media worldwide I'm going to highlight the key themes that these laws and regulations aim to control. In doing so, you'll get a broader view of what to look out for in the countries in which you operate and understand what practical steps you can take to manage social media risk and achieve compliance with these laws and regulations.

Ultimately, you will be responsible for researching, understanding and applying any particular regulations that might impact your social media programme. However, this chapter will equip you with the knowledge of the types of regulation that might impact your programme and provide ideas as to how you might fulfil any regulatory obligations.

The social media regulatory mix

Regulations that impact social media are more developed in some countries than others. In the majority of cases, however, laws and regulations have not had a chance to catch up with social media. This makes it difficult to understand how a particular regulation might apply in social media or how you might remain compliant with a regulation through your use of social media.

Most regulators have chosen not to change their rules, but to publish guidance about how social media can be used within the existing constraints of the rules. I often hear regulation cited as a reason for why an organization is not fully embracing social media, however, I believe that it's possible to use social media and experience its benefits while remaining compliant.

Regulations that impact social media can be split into three main categories. These categories overlap with each other because of the way that social media has grown organically and because it impacts so many people. The Social Media Regulation Mix, illustrated in Figure 9.1, shows the three categories and how they overlap with each other.

FIGURE 9.1 The social media regulatory mix

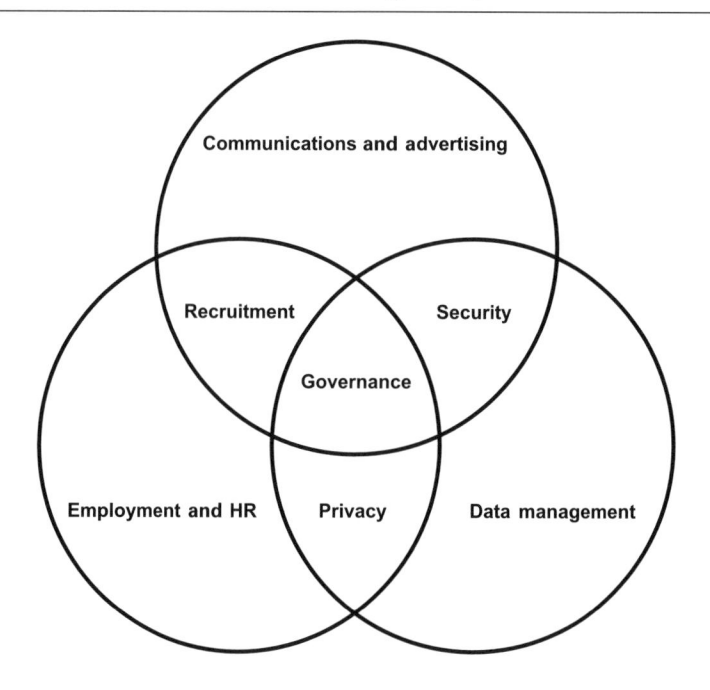

[Venn diagram with three overlapping circles: Communications and advertising, Employment and HR, Data management. Overlapping regions labelled: Recruitment, Security, Privacy, and Governance in the centre.]

Communication and advertising

Organizations need to comply with laws and regulations when communicating with their customers. The key points covered in this section are:

- advertising
- financial promotions; and
- disclosure.

Advertising

Many countries have laws that govern how a company can advertise its products and services. The purpose of these laws is to protect the buyer by ensuring that companies don't mislead consumers by making false claims about their products. Clearly, social media is a great place to advertise products and services; however, there are new constraints and challenges that organizations face. A simplistic example is that a company can post an advertisement on a bus stop, which complies with advertising, standards and hope that passers-by notice it. However, on social media, a company can do more because it can interact with its customers directly and can encourage other social media users to make recommendations about its products. For example, a company might give a celebrity free products in return for a positive social media post. This sort of behaviour gets a bit murky and is where some companies have got into trouble. The celebrity's followers might see their tweet and think that they genuinely do like the product they are recommending, when in fact they are recommending it only because they have been paid to do so. This can mislead the customer and is why regulations exist to help make consumers aware of this activity and not be unfairly influenced into buying a product or service. The same is true for other types of endorsements, such as retweets. In response to this, it is becoming common practice to include the hashtag #ad or #spon (sponsored) within advertising endorsements to highlight to social media users that the post is sponsored.

Financial promotions

Financial products are contracts that stipulate movement of money between two parties. Banks, credit card companies and insurers all offer financial products, such as bank accounts, mortgages, loans or insurance. There are strict rules around how financial products can be advertised and these rules apply to both online and offline advertising. However, space constraints make it more difficult for companies to include any necessary disclaimers that they would include as a matter of course in offline or print advertising. The most important point is that financial promotions should be fair and not misleading. Financial promotions should be balanced so that consumers have an appreciation not only of the potential benefits, but also of any relevant risks.

The reason that regulations that cover financial promotions are stricter than standard promotions is because of the impact that a bad investment decision can have on someone's livelihood. In some cases, a bad investment can make unlimited losses. Banks and financial institutions are not known for their innovative use of social media, mainly due to their caution when it comes to social media regulation. Financial regulation is complex and governs how financial institutions operate. Promoting financial products through social media has been seen widely as difficult or risky. For example, financial institutions are often required to include terms and conditions in any financial promotions, something that can be difficult in the space-constrained world of social media. In March 2015 the UK's financial regulator, the Financial Conduct Authority (FCA), published guidance on how to use social media for financial promotions. The rules themselves weren't a change to existing regulation but instead provided guidance to financial institutions on ways that they could use social media to promote their products and services while remaining compliant with existing regulation. Financial regulators understand the benefits of social media and want to encourage companies to use it, provided it's used fairly and rules are not broken.

Disclosure

Publicly listed companies, whose shares trade on the stock market, have extra levels of regulation that they need to abide by. One such example is related to the disclosure of investor information. Information about a company's performance will be of particular interest to investors because it might have an impact on the company's share price. Because of this, regulation exists to ensure that the disclosure of such information is done fairly. Social media is a communications medium and it's not surprising that companies want to use it to engage with their customers, the public and their investor community. If they've performed well during a particular quarter, they will want to share the story through social media, as well as through their traditional channels, such as press releases. However, most regulators are still catching up with social media; therefore, if they believe that information has been inappropriately released on social media before investors or shareholders had been informed, they might take action against the company. Regulators are, however, catching up and the US Securities and Exchange Commission (SEC) now allows companies to disclose information through social media, provided the company's investors have been notified to expect to see such information there.

CASE STUDY Risk in action: Netflix SEC disclosure

Netflix is a subscription service for watching TV programmes and movies. In July 2012, Netflix CEO and co-founder Reed Hastings posted on his personal Facebook account that for the first time in his company's history viewers had consumed over 1 billion hours in one month.

The US Securities and Exchange Commission (SEC) issued what is known as a Wells Notice to both Reed Hastings and Netflix, which meant that they intended to pursue enforcement action over inappropriate disclosure of investor information.

However, in April 2013 the SEC announced that it would not be bringing enforcement action against Netflix or Reed Hastings and issued a report which said that companies were free to use social media networks to announce key information, provided that investors had been told where to expect this information to be published.

This example shows the difficulty that many organizations face when engaging in social media but it also shows that regulators are changing the way that they view social media.

SOURCE: www.bloomberg.com/news/articles/2013-04-02/netflix-ceo-won-t-face-sec-claims-over-disclosures-on-facebook

Recruitment

The issues that arise from the use of social media for recruitment are mainly in relation to discrimination. Many countries have strict laws to combat discrimination. It's now common for employers to look at a candidate's social media footprint as part of the recruitment process. There are valid reasons to do this. A person's social media account can give insight into a job candidate's experience and character. In LinkedIn, recommendations from previous employers or connections are listed on the user's profile as well as a list of skills endorsed by colleagues and associates. I've heard many recruiters talk about how a person's LinkedIn profile is often a more accurate representation of a candidate than a CV. Job candidates tweak their CV for the job that they are applying for, but it's harder to tweak a LinkedIn profile for specific jobs because the recommendations and endorsements are provided by other users. But, reviewing a candidate's social media profiles without their knowledge is an area for concern. This concern is heightened when a company uses deceptive techniques to gain access to a candidate's social media profile, for example by sending connection requests to candidates from a fake account.

Companies face a risk when reviewing candidates' profiles due to the potentially large amount of sensitive personal information that might be available in the candidate's profile, such as their gender, age, religion, sexual orientation, political views etc. Organizations need to ensure that they do not discriminate against candidates as a result of information gleaned from social media, because an unsuccessful candidate could claim they have been discriminated against due to the personal information in their social media profile.

If you intend to review a candidate's social media footprint as part of the recruitment process, the best course of action is to inform candidates that you will be conducting a review. This is fair as it gives the candidate a chance to review their profile and remove anything they might want to keep private. You should also give the candidate an opportunity to defend any findings from your review as this will remove the risk of you making assumptions or decisions based on inaccurate information.

An example of this is the appointment of 17-year-old Paris Brown as Britain's first youth police officer and crime commissioner. After her appointment she was found to have posted offensive and potentially racist messages on Twitter. As a result, she resigned and Kent Police and Crime Commissioner faced criticism in the media for not having conducted appropriate background checks.

Employment and HR

Organizations need to comply with an array of laws and regulations relating to employment. In social media, the key issues that arise are:

- discrimination;
- employee monitoring;
- ownership of social media accounts;
- acceptable behaviour and conduct;
- bullying and harassment; and
- employee evaluation.

Discrimination

Discrimination, whether active or passive, will cause problems for companies. Because of the large amount of personal information in social networks, it's possible that employers might discriminate against recruitment candidates or their own employees based on their personal characteristics. Laws around the world prohibit discrimination and companies must ensure that they don't discriminate when engaging in social media. Companies need to provide equal opportunities for their employees, regardless of race, religion, gender, age etc.

Employee monitoring

Employee monitoring is a sensitive subject. Most organizations will already monitor their employees, perhaps through the use of CCTV cameras in and around their offices or through the monitoring of company emails. Some organizations may even have a regulatory requirement to monitor their employees in order to detect fraud or other illegal activity, such as insider trading. However, issues and risks arise when a company starts to monitor its employees' social media accounts without good reason and without their knowledge. While regulations allow organizations to conduct employee monitoring on social media, certain safeguards and rules may need to be in place. For example, policies need to include details of the monitoring to ensure that the employees are aware of what will be monitored.

Ownership of social media accounts

It can be difficult to determine the ownership of social media accounts. While corporate social media accounts are fairly easy to distinguish, uncertainty arises when an employee uses their personal account as part of their work. If that person has a prominent position in the company or if they have gained a large number of followers or connections, the company that they work for may feel that they can claim ownership of the person's account and that they should either have access to the account or that the account should be handed over if the person leaves the company. Regulations exist to make the rules around this sort of thing clear.

It's unlikely that an organization will be able to legally state a claim over an employee's social media account. If an organization requests access to an employee's social media account they are likely breaking both the law and the terms and conditions of the social network in question. Most social networks state in their terms and conditions that accounts cannot be transferred and that passwords should never be disclosed to anyone.

If you are concerned that an employee might leave your company and take with them a long list of contacts, the best way to combat this is by encouraging your employees to log new relationships on the company's customer relationship management (CRM) system. Many organizations require all work relationships to be logged and tracked through their CRM system, which means that even if the employee leaves, the company will retain details about the relationship including contact details. This may seem like quite an onerous task; however, you could incentivise your people to update the system by reporting on how many new connections, opportunities or sales each person or team made to encourage competition between teams.

Acceptable behaviours and conduct

Many employers have regulatory responsibilities to ensure that their employees maintain certain levels of professionalism. Most organizations already have codes of conduct in place that set out what behaviours they expect from their employees. These behaviours should also be reflected in the company's social media policy.

Bullying and harassment

Unfortunately, bullying and harassment exists in both society and business. Because of the perceived anonymous nature of social media, there have been many cases of abuse online, such as cyberbullying. Some people think that normal rules of politeness and human interaction don't apply in social media. In January 2014, two people pleaded guilty to sending 'menacing' tweets to feminist campaigner Caroline Criado-Perez, who had been campaigning for a woman to appear on a UK banknote. The court heard that one tweet started with an expletive and continued 'Die you worthless piece of crap'. Caroline was also told to 'go kill yourself'. Many countries have laws to stop this type of behaviour and organizations need to be aware of these laws and ensure that abuse does not take place within their organizations, either offline or online.

Employee evaluation

In some countries there are restrictions on how social media can be used as a tool for assessing employee performance. Germany is one country where such activities can be meet with opposition from works councils. A works council is an organization that represents workers and that complements national labour laws. Organizations that operate in Germany, or other countries that have the concept of works councils, should involve works councils in discussions from beginning to end to agree on how employees will use an enterprise social network or other social system. The works councils are entitled, by law, to be involved in any discussions around the use of security cameras or IT tools that are able to monitor and assess employee performance.

Privacy

In addition to the points that have already been raised in Chapter 4, Data protection and control, organizations must ensure that they comply with regulatory requirements related to consumers' rights to privacy. There can be a fine line between when a company is monitoring its customers or employees and when the organization is seen to be invading their privacy. A simple rule of thumb is that monitoring should be clear and fair and that deception is always wrong. An organization has the right to monitor its employees' social media use, provided that the employees are aware of what is being monitored. Similar to my earlier example, if an employer uses deceptive techniques to monitor the employee, such as through fake social media friend requests, this is likely to attract the regulator's attention.

Healthcare is one regulated industry that specifically requires any patient data to be kept private, for obvious reasons. For example, you should not share any information or make social media posts that might identify that a person has visited a particular clinic or hospital.

Data regulations around the world set out the specific requirements around privacy and data protection. A common requirement is that organizations implement robust privacy policies that explain what data is being captured about individuals and how it is being used, which we covered in Chapter 6.

Some regulations, such as the forthcoming EU General Data Protection Regulation, detailed in Chapter 4, affect many parts of an organization and the impact on social media is just one of these areas. Because of this, some organizations already have project teams in place that are tasked with addressing the requirements. This is clearly a good opportunity for you to link in with the project team to ensure that your own social media projects remain compliant, and it may mean that you work closely with the team to ensure that this happens.

Data management

Organizations must comply with regulations around record keeping. Certain types of data must be held for certain amounts of time, while other types of data cannot be stored for longer than they are needed. Organizations need comprehensive archiving and backup strategies in order to comply with these regulations. Because social media data often includes a mix of personal data and other business data, it can be difficult for organizations to categorize the data that they hold and deliver archiving programmes that meet their regulatory needs. Data archiving was covered in Chapter 4.

Regulators also have the right to request information to support their investigations or other legal cases. It can be difficult for organizations to respond to these requests, particularly if they are global companies, because a regulator in one country might require the organization to protect data about its citizens by not transferring it outside the country's jurisdiction. On the other hand, a regulator in another country may require the company to provide all data related to a specific individual because of an ongoing legal dispute. In this example it is difficult for the company to comply with both regulators, and this sort of scenario is one where the company's lawyers should provide guidance.

Many people copy and paste information from the internet and save online documents to their computers or email them to friends and colleagues. Copyright laws and regulations around the world protect works created by others, and organizations need to implement controls to ensure that copyrighted materials are not being hosted on company servers without permission. The issues around copyright are covered in more detail in Chapter 3.

Security

All businesses want to ensure that they protect against and avoid falling victim to cyber attacks. However, there are numerous regulations that require companies to maintain their IT security and some that specifically state requirements around how businesses should go about protecting themselves. Organizations need to be aware of laws and regulations around malicious communications, what constitutes malicious communication and what they are required to do if they receive such communications, or become aware that their employees are sending malicious communications.

Some regulators require companies to have robust security awareness programmes and to undergo regular security penetration tests. Security penetration tests are simulated attacks against a company's infrastructure or IT systems in order to uncover any weaknesses or security vulnerabilities. Once any weaknesses have been discovered, the company should run a remediation project to address these weaknesses. Other common security requirements imposed by regulators are for organizations to have processes to address deficiencies in information security policies as well as to detect, report and respond to security incidents. Security is covered in more detail in Chapter 8.

Governance

Some regulators have started setting out what they expect companies to do to manage social media risk through the provision of appropriate governance. The US Federal Financial Institutions Examination Council, for example, requires companies to have a risk management programme that enables companies to 'identify, measure, monitor, and control the risks related to social media'.

In addition, regulators will want to see documented policies and procedures as well as evidence that robust controls operate to manage social media risk. Training is a common requirement from regulators to ensure that the company's employees have an awareness of risk and so that they understand their own responsibilities in managing it. In addition to training requirements, some regulators also insist that employees who communicate through social media on behalf of the company are appropriately supervised. This supervision might take the form of systems and controls, such as social risk and compliance tools, which are configured to force content through approval processes.

This whole book should equip you with the knowledge to implement effective governance programmes to support social media and manage risk.

Dealing with character limitations

One of the main challenges to regulatory compliance on social media is that many social networks impose character limits on posts. For example, Twitter posts can include a maximum of 140 characters, videos on Vine are six-second loops, adverts on Facebook allow 25 characters for the title and 90 characters in the body. This makes it challenging to include both your key messages and any relevant terms and conditions or additional information within a single social media post.

There are a couple of things that you can do to overcome these limitations. Firstly, you can split your content across two or more posts, as depicted in Figure 9.2. Splitting content across two or more tweets is a common way of including more content than the 140 character limit allows on Twitter; however, to be effective the tweets must come in quick succession. Otherwise, a user might see the first tweet, but miss the second tweet, or vice-versa.

Another way to include extra content is by embedding an image within a tweet. So, you could include the headline in the text of the tweet and include a picture that includes more details as well as any necessary disclaimers, terms or conditions. An example of this is illustrated in Figure 9.3. However, it's possible for users to turn off images so it's important not to use an image for the disclaimers only; instead, the whole advert should be included within the image itself and the text should remain compliant on its own.

FIGURE 9.2

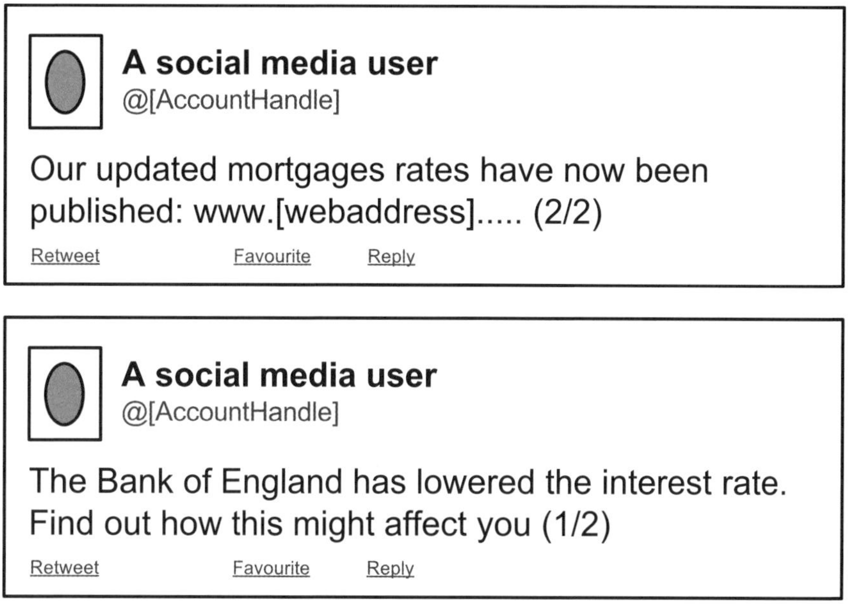

> **A social media user**
> @[AccountHandle]
>
> Our updated mortgages rates have now been published: www.[webaddress]..... (2/2)
>
> Retweet   Favourite   Reply

> **A social media user**
> @[AccountHandle]
>
> The Bank of England has lowered the interest rate. Find out how this might affect you (1/2)
>
> Retweet   Favourite   Reply

Finally, don't try to hide any disclaimers by making the font size so small that it's difficult to read. If you do this, a regulator will probably rule that the advert is neither fair nor clear.

Future of regulation

Regulators are catching up with social media, which is why we're already seeing them issuing guidance to companies about how they should use social media and manage risk. Social media and digital technology continue to evolve, with new social media networks gaining popularity and existing social networks adding new functionality. In January 2015 Facebook announced that it had begun testing a service, called 'Place Tips', which will deliver information about nearby shops and landmarks to Facebook users. If successful, this new functionality could offer businesses new advertising and marketing opportunities. Even if it fails, I have no doubt that other new developments and functionality will come along and change the dynamics of business–customer interaction.

FIGURE 9.3

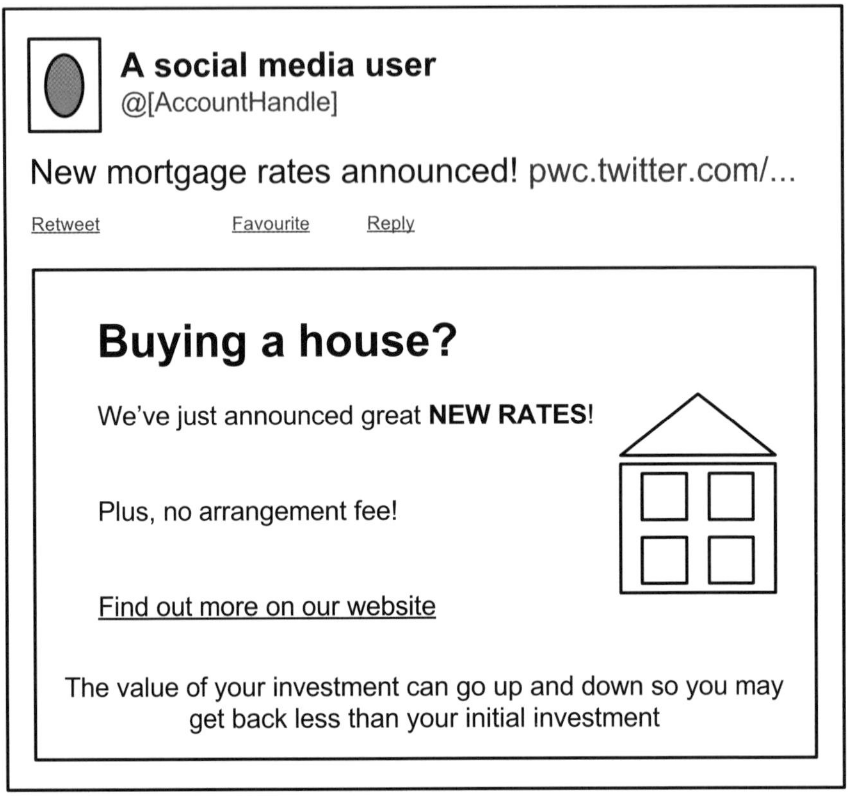

> **A social media user**
> @[AccountHandle]
>
> New mortgage rates announced! pwc.twitter.com/...
>
> Retweet   Favourite   Reply
>
> ## Buying a house?
>
> We've just announced great **NEW RATES**!
>
> Plus, no arrangement fee!
>
> Find out more on our website
>
> The value of your investment can go up and down so you may get back less than your initial investment

Changes in the social media and the digital landscape will continue to make regulators reassess the rules and guidance that they set out for businesses. Regulators don't like to make knee-jerk reactions to incidents and prefer instead to observe how companies and the public react. Because of this, regulators will remain behind the curve when it comes to regulations that impact social media and digital technologies.

That said, organizations will need to keep a watchful eye on any upcoming rules or regulations to ensure that they maintain compliance and safeguard the future of their business.

Summary

In this chapter I introduced the social media regulation mix, which is a useful way of categorizing the types of regulation that impact social media.

The laws and regulations related to social media around the world differ and the specific regulatory requirements in the countries where you operate will differ from other companies. You are now aware of what to watch out for and you should seek advice from your risk, compliance and legal colleagues for specific details about how to ensure that your social media programme remains compliant. There are practical steps you can take to help you deal with character limitations on social media, and elsewhere in this book I have highlighted other strategies to help you manage risk and maintain regulatory compliance.

In the next chapter, we'll look to the future by assessing emerging trends and technologies that might impact social media.

The future and its opportunities

Overview

In this chapter we'll look to the future to consider how social media might evolve and what it might mean for businesses. I believe that the future of social media holds a wealth of opportunities to increase engagement with your customers and your employees, drive efficiencies and encourage innovation. But where there is opportunity, there is risk.

Social media analytics will evolve and allow organizations to predict more accurately who will purchase their products and services and when they are most likely to purchase them. We will see the decline of email as the de facto communication tool, with more social-type systems taking their place. The kids will continue to be years ahead of us adults in their use of digital technologies and social networks, which will mean that more emphasis will need to be placed on educating them of the risks of the virtual world. Social media will evolve and more secure, encrypted services will emerge to protect users from unwanted monitoring. Our reliance on technology will increase, which will increase the impact of IT failures on our lives.

Social media analytics

Social media analytics is a topic that already attracts much interest and hype. The ability to understand which products your customers buy, which promotions and advertisements resonate with them best, and which social networks they spend time on is really useful to organizations looking to drive sales. A lot of work is going into improving sentiment analysis, which is the ability to automatically measure positive, negative or neutral sentiment of social media posts.

Predictive analytics takes analytics to the next level and instead of offering insight into events or behaviours in the past, uses large amounts of historical data trends to predict what might happen in the future. There are already many examples of predictive analytics correctly predicting future events. One of the best known is when US retailer, Target, 'predicted' that a girl was pregnant before her father had found out based on the products that she had purchased. The girl received coupons for baby products such as clothing and cribs which the father thought inappropriate until he realized that she was in fact pregnant. In this example, the retailer used information about the products she had purchased to predict that she had recently become pregnant, and similar predications can also be made by analysing social media posts or internet activity.

Predictive analytics is particularly interesting and powerful because of the vast amounts of data we share on our social networks every day. Not only do we share posts about our personal lives, we often geo-tag them with the location and 'tag' our friends in posts when we're 'checking in' to a nice restaurant for dinner. Furthermore, it's also possible for the social networks to track which posts a user has seen and how long they spent looking at them. All of this information is extremely valuable to companies who are looking to target their advertising more effectively.

Consider the key events of a couple's love story. They meet, get engaged, get married, get pregnant, have a baby, celebrate the baby's birthdays, their wedding anniversaries, and so on. Now, while not all of these things will happen in the same order (or indeed, happen at all), there is a typical trend a company can analyse. If our social networks know the date of our wedding anniversary, a company could make a prediction that adverts for flowers, chocolates or jewellery might be more effective during the weeks leading up to the date. So, a company may pay more for placement of their advertisements during these times, then cut the advertisement on or after the date.

Many analytics platforms have been built for a specific purpose to give insight into social media data and offer predictions using pre-built algorithms. The more technically advanced and accurate way to perform predictive analytics is to build your own algorithms. The advantage of this is that it allows you to pick what data you want to input and choose exactly what you want to predict instead of having to rely on off-the-shelf analytics packages that are available to everyone. The disadvantage is that there is a fairly high barrier to entry into the world of predictive analytics. You'll need to employ specialists such as statisticians or data scientists who will use advanced tools such as 'R' or 'python'. Building your own algorithms is likely to give you an advantage over your competitors because they will allow you to predict future trends more accurately. There is already high demand for job candidates who have skills and expertise in analytics and this trend will continue for years to come. Incidentally, Harvard Business Review named Data Scientist the sexiest job of the 21st century!

There are a number of 'use cases' for social media predictive analytics, such as:

- *Recruitment.* By using data from multiple social networks, including LinkedIn, it will be easier to predict if an employee is more likely to leave for another job. This can be useful for headhunters when targeting candidates or for companies looking to retain their staff.
- *Industry trends.* Extrapolating trends in social media data that discuss certain industries, such as utilities, could be used to predict spikes in energy usage.
- *Crime prediction.* Data that tracks where crime takes place might help authorities to increase their presence if incidents are predicted in certain areas. Likewise, the monitoring of social networks, however controversial, could alert authorities to individuals or groups who are planning to commit crimes such as terrorism. Law enforcement agencies around the world already use social media data to track fraud or predict where it is likely to occur.
- *Public opinion.* No longer will we need to rely on the polls reported during elections, instead relying on data from social networks to get a more accurate predictions on the outcome of elections.

Users are already becoming more aware of how companies mine their data in order to advertise products and services they might like. While this is good for customers, as it means the adverts that they see will be more tailored and relevant to them, users may view it as an invasion of privacy. The EU General Data Protection Regulation, as covered in Chapter 4, is going to have a huge impact on all businesses in the EU as well as companies around the world who process data on EU citizens. Because predictive analytics relies on vast amounts of personal data, we will see legal cases brought against companies who exploit predictive analytics to sell their products. Businesses will need to ensure that they are processing data ethically and in a manner users would not object to.

Farewell, email!

Although not everyone will agree, I believe email is wildly inefficient. We use it every day and many of us have to sift through hundreds of emails to work out which ones are for our information, which ones need us to do something, and which ones are just junk offering us a promotions for something that we just don't want or need. The big problem with email is that we've grown so reliant on it that it's difficult for us to imagine a world without it. Have you ever considered how difficult and long-winded it can be to make a decision among your team through email alone? Let's say that you need to agree a decision with your team members, so you email all of them. One member replies to you only with their comments, the others reply to all and one of the team also forwards the email to someone else for their input. The person who received the forwarded email replies to you and all, but has missed some of the emails from the other members. You then compile all of the responses and reply to all with a synopsis. This is complicated and could go on and on with multiple email trails breaking off and bringing other people into the conversation without your knowledge.

Figure 10.1 shows how enterprise social networks can enable this type of collaboration far more effectively than email. Using an enterprise social network, the team leader would make a post on an enterprise social network and ask their team to provide comments. If one of the team decided to include an extra person, that person would simply read the past responses and respond to the discussion. The response would then be seen by all and all comments would be captured in one place. If someone else was invited to join the conversation, they would be able to read all previous posts before responding. This sort of collaboration hugely increases the efficiency of decision making.

Many of the so-called digital natives, the people who grew up with social media, smartphones and tablets, don't use email. They communicate using social networks or instant messaging apps. Often, email is just one of those things that they need in order sign up for certain services in the same way that we all need a postal address so that packages can be delivered. However, many online services have started allowing users to sign up to their services by connecting their social network, rather than requiring an email registration. Doing this is a quick and easy way to set up a new profile on an online service as it only requires a few clicks and all of your information is pulled to the new service automatically. These systems will continue to contribute to the decline in email.

When I first mentioned my prediction to my wife that email will eventually die she said that I was mad. However, just a few days later, she asked her niece (a 19-year-old from Russia) to email her a document. The niece's response was 'email? Nobody uses email anymore! I'll send to you it via Facebook'. At this point my wife realized that maybe email isn't the great

FIGURE 10.1 Email vs enterprise collaboration

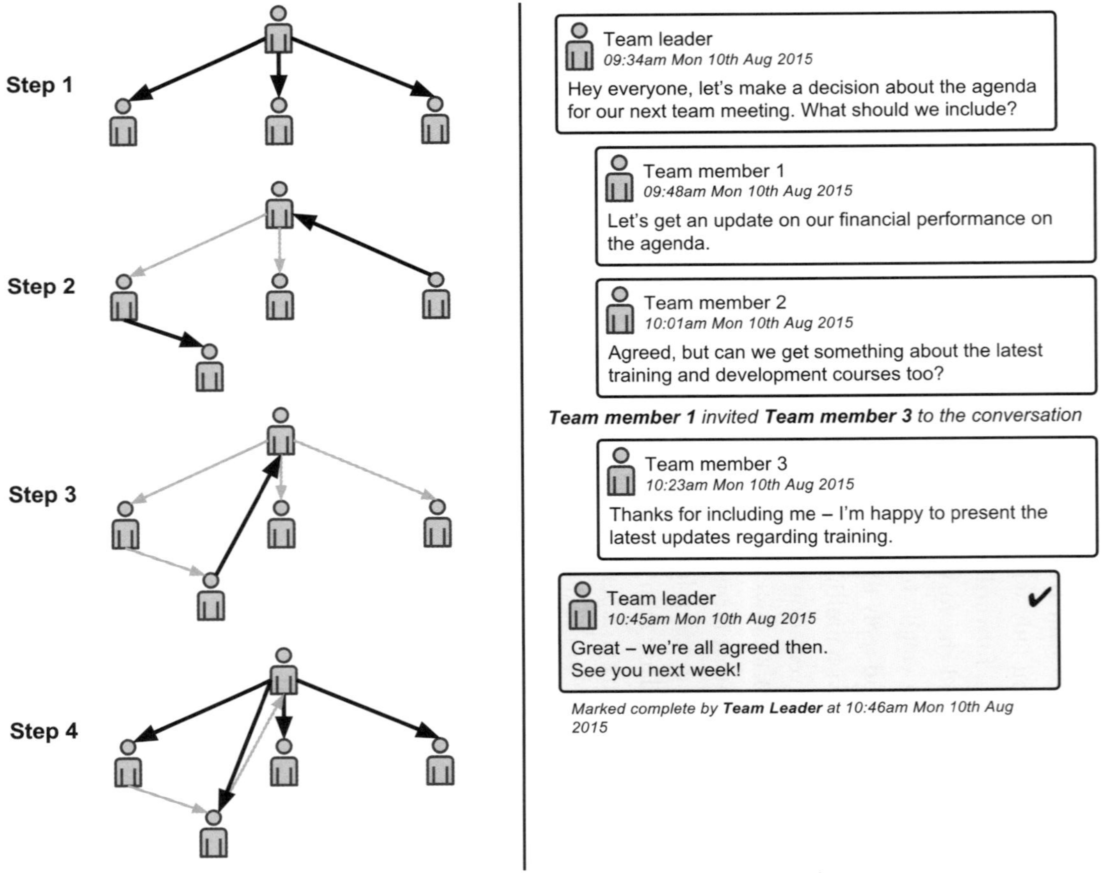

Step 1

Step 2

Step 3

Step 4

> **Team leader**
> 09:34am Mon 10th Aug 2015
> Hey everyone, let's make a decision about the agenda for our next team meeting. What should we include?

> **Team member 1**
> 09:48am Mon 10th Aug 2015
> Let's get an update on our financial performance on the agenda.

> **Team member 2**
> 10:01am Mon 10th Aug 2015
> Agreed, but can we get something about the latest training and development courses too?

Team member 1 invited Team member 3 to the conversation

> **Team member 3**
> 10:23am Mon 10th Aug 2015
> Thanks for including me – I'm happy to present the latest updates regarding training.

> **Team leader**
> 10:45am Mon 10th Aug 2015
> Great – we're all agreed then. See you next week!

Marked complete by Team Leader at 10:46am Mon 10th Aug 2015 tool that we've become so over-reliant on over the years and that perhaps something else will eventually replace it.

Of course, I don't think that email will completely die altogether. Good old snail mail has not completed died. After all, having a washing machine delivered to your house is far better than receiving a photo of one via social media, or indeed better than receiving instructions on how to 3D-print your own! Some people do take pleasure out of using a real-life pen to write a real-life letter, put it in an envelope, affix a stamp and send it to a loved one. But, you must agree that this sort of communication has declined significantly over the last few years. Many of my family members are abroad so at Christmas time I now expect electronic greeting cards that have a corny animation and cheap music instead of an actual physical card. Although receiving a physical card would be a nice surprise, it would probably mean that I would be obliged to send a physical card in return, and I'm far too digital for all of that paper nonsense!

Other advantages of social collaboration over email include:

- Centralization: everything is not stored across multiple mailboxes and is instead in one location, making it easier to refer back to at a future date.
- Audit trail: changes to documents or discussion on an enterprise social network are all logged with the time that they were changed as well as the person who made the change.
- Time saving: rather than sending emails and collating the responses, social collaboration does all the work for you.
- Space savings: If an email includes a large attachment, that attachment may be recreated every time a reply is sent, clogging up the inboxes of all recipients. If an enterprise social network were used, the attachment would be uploaded to the discussion thread and would be downloaded only by those who wanted to view it.

Hopefully I've convinced you of the inefficiencies of email and that *something* more 'social' will surpass it. The problem, however, is that I don't believe social networks, as they stand at the time of writing, are ready to replace email. Traditional social networks are public, meaning anyone can use them. But, each person needs to be a member of the same social network or platform to be able to send messages to each other. Email, on the other hand, allows a person to send a message to anyone else and it doesn't matter which email provider or email software they are using. Internally, people within organizations are already communicating using their company's enterprise social network, but this only allows communications within that network. So, if they want to contact one of their suppliers, they will have to resort to email and all of its inefficiencies. There is no standard system that everyone uses to get the benefits of social collaboration.

I believe that the solution to this is a new protocol that will emerge and allow social-type communications to be sent from person to person without the need for everyone to use the same social network. A new authority or network will emerge that will handle all social-type messages and become a hybrid between a traditional public social network and an enterprise social network. This is illustrated in Figure 10.2.

When this happens, I believe it will herald a whole new form of communication. Email is definitely wildly inefficient and there are already tools that go some way towards addressing these issues but they do not have the required security or ability to share content outside of the corporate network.

FIGURE 10.2 Communications 2.0

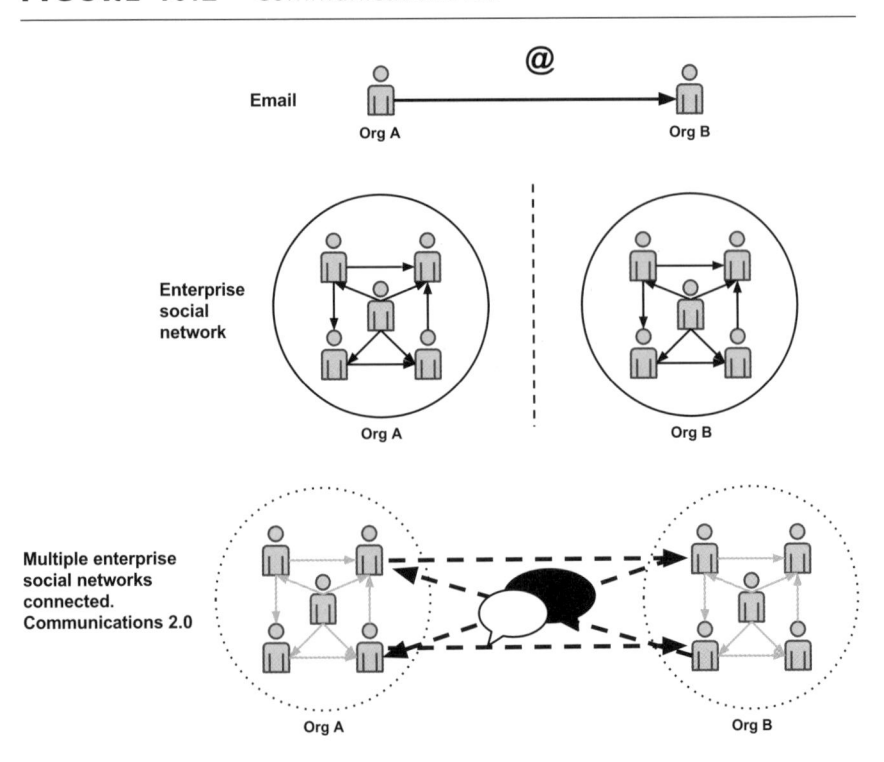

Education

Social media offers people, young and old, opportunities to stay in touch with friends and family, to collaborate and to share their thoughts and ideas. Many social networks and online services offer users the ability to hide their identity. The unfortunate side effect of this is that the anonymity can lead to some unsavoury behaviour. Some users hide behind the anonymity and act in a totally different way online than they would in the real world.

Social media and other digital technologies are usually adopted by the younger generations first. Only later do adults follow suit. At which point, the platforms become too 'uncool' because the parents have joined. This makes it difficult for parents to keep up with the technology that their children are using and makes it hard for them to determine where the risks lie.

Cyberbullying

Education is key and we will need to see far more of it to ensure our young people know how to use the internet responsibly and what to do if they ever encounter inappropriate material or behaviour. There have been a number of examples where both children and vulnerable adults have been exploited online or faced cyberbullying.

The scary difference of cyberbullying to playground bullying is that cyberbullying can give the bullies anonymity, enabling them to be even harsher than in the playground. Another issue is that while playground bullying may take place while the child is at school, cyberbullying can take place relentlessly at all hours of the day and night. There have been a number of sad cases where young people have taken their own lives as a result of cyberbullying.

Unfortunately, the internet has long been used by people to share indecent images, sometimes involving children. We're now seeing a worrying trend whereby children themselves are being exploited directly. Some of the new social networks allow users to send messages and photos that will allegedly be deleted a few seconds after they have been read or viewed. The system isn't 100 per cent effective though, as it's easy to take a screenshot when a temporary message or photo is received, thereby making a permanent record. Sometimes, children have sent indecent images of themselves to other users thinking that the other user is an attractive boy or girl of a similar age. Unfortunately, in these examples, the person sending and receiving the image has been a criminal who then uses the indecent image to exploit the child by threatening to post the photo online unless they pay money.

In February 2015, Google announced that it would be launching a version of its popular video sharing site, YouTube, for children below the age of 13. At the time of writing, only children who are 13 or over can create accounts on YouTube. This represents an interesting shift, in that it may signal a change where other technology companies begin to offer more services for children under the age of 13. Of course, it's easy for children younger than 13 to circumvent the age restriction by simply checking a box or lying about their age. But these age-specific versions of popular sites will rely on parental and network permission, which is clearly preferable. If successful it should make the internet safer for children as the content will be monitored to ensure it is age-appropriate. It also presents opportunities to advertisers who will be able to market their products and services to a younger age group, in the same way that they already do on television.

Oversharing

It's not just children who face the risk of cyberbullying. There have been a number of cases of adults being 'trolled', which is a term used to describe when someone is bombarded with offensive messages on online platforms. We covered an example of this in Chapter 9, which resulted in the Twitter troll being jailed due to a campaign of abuse on Twitter.

Many people are guilty of so-called 'oversharing', when they publish so much information about their personal lives that they put themselves at risk of stalking or burglary. Where stalking used to involve physically following someone, in today's world those people can track their victims using social networks far more effectively.

On a more positive note, social media is an effective tool to support distance learning. University fees are high in many countries, which often means that young people have to take out huge loans to pay their way through studies. Because of this, distance learning has grown in popularity. People who use distance learning engage with content, tutorials, video and other rich learning materials through the internet. They don't need to sit physically in a classroom and instead can form virtual groups with fellow students and work together over the internet using social media and other learning and messaging platforms.

Education will not only help raise awareness of the risks of the internet among young people, but it will also give them the skills needed to work in a more connected and fast-paced world of technology. Research from London First, a non-profit organization with a mission to make London the best city to do business in, shows that 80 per cent of companies in London's 'tech city' cite a lack of skills as the biggest single barrier to growth. The UK school's curriculum was changed in 2014 to ensure that children are equipped with the new skills that they will need when they enter work, such as programming and graphical design skills.

CASE STUDY Risk in action: Teenagers commit suicide because of cyberbullying

In 2013 tragic reports emerged in the media about teenagers aged between 12 and 17 years who had taken their own lives due to cyberbullying. Many of the teenagers were users of Latvian-based social network ASK.fm, which allows users to ask questions and post responses anonymously. While this may seem innocent at first, it turned out that many teenagers were being bullied on the site.

One such teenager who took her own life was 14-year-old Hannah Smith from Leicestershire in the UK. Hannah's father, Dave Smith, said that he found posts on ASK.fm from people asking her to die. The messages on the site urged Hannah to 'cut herself, drink bleach, and kill herself'. Mr Smith has called for tighter controls to be placed on social networks.

In another case in September 2013, a 12-year-old girl from Lakeland, Florida, committed suicide after receiving text messages saying 'You're ugly', 'Why are you still alive?' and 'Go kill yourself'. On the day that she killed herself she changed her name on a social network to 'That Dead Girl'.

In total, ASK.fm has been linked to six suicides.

UK Prime Minister David Cameron commented that the social networks must 'clean up their act' or face boycotts from users.

Peter Wanless, chief executive of the UK's National Society for Prevention of Cruelty to Children (NSPCC), said:

> *The cruel nature of cyberbullying allows perpetrators to remain anonymous and hide behind their screens.*
>
> *This is something that must be tackled before it gets out of hand. We must ensure young people have the confidence to speak out against this abuse, so they don't feel isolated and without anywhere to turn.*

These examples of cyber bullying are clearly worrying and shocking. Children need to be taught about the internet and how to stay safe while on it. Companies also need to be aware of these risk. Advertising is often purchased through agencies in 'bundles', which place their adverts on a wide range of websites.

Because of this, some companies were unaware that their adverts were appearing on ASK.fm beside such worrying content. Many advertisers later pulled out from advertising on ASK.fm as a result of the revelations in the media about child suicides.

SOURCE: www.dailymail.co.uk/news/article-2308395/Ask-fm-This-week-15-year-old-boy-killed-hounded-No-wonder-mothers-want-banned.html

Democracy 2.0

The revelations of Edward Snowden in 2013 caused a public backlash against the way that technology companies were passing information about their users to governments. The technology giants claimed to have been under pressure from governments to release information about their users so they publicly fought back by introducing the publication of so-called 'transparency reports'. The transparency reports detail the number of requests from governments for user data to be handed over or for data on the networks to be removed. The reports also show how many requests were fulfilled by the tech giants and how many were rejected. In February 2015, Twitter reported that it had seen a 40 per cent increase in the number of requests from governments since its last report in July 2014. Twitter received a total of 2,871 requests from governments across the world asking it to reveal data about 7,144 of its users during the second half of 2014. Twitter reported that it had fulfilled 52 per cent of the requests.

Governments in non-democratic states have to work harder to control their citizens' online activity. Social media is an inherently open place where people can post whatever they wish. A government censoring the internet will keep a constant watch on social media to understand public sentiment and to work out which pieces of content pose a threat and which it might therefore remove or censor.

Bitcoin and the dark web

It's difficult to tell what the future will hold for social media in the context of internet censorship. We've already seen social networks and other online services get banned in certain countries; for example, in 2013, Twitter was blocked in Turkey. Savvy users in countries where censorship is more pertinent know ways to get around these blocks. Two of the most common are:

- *Virtual Private Networks (VPNs)*. These are often paid services which route internet access through another country and encrypt the connection to the user's computer. This makes it far more difficult for a government to monitor a user's internet usage and it is also an effective way of bypassing local internet censorship.
- *The Onion Router (TOR)*. TOR is a tool that heavily encrypts a user's connection by routing it through hundreds of other computers (like the layers of an onion). Using TOR gives users access to the so-called 'dark web', websites that are accessible only through the TOR network, like a parallel internet. Using TOR allows users to avoid internet monitoring and bypass internet censorship. There are legitimate reasons to use TOR; for example, journalists might use it to report news from somewhere the internet is heavily restricted or censored. However, some of the dark websites that operate on the TOR network have become infamous black markets for illegal goods and services.

Transactions on the dark web marketplaces usually make use of crypto-currencies, such as Bitcoin. Crypto-currencies are decentralized digital currencies that use cryptography to secure transactions and control the creation of new units. The security that crypto-currencies offer means that criminals can make transactions on black markets anonymously. Since TOR is all about anonymity, the 'social networks' that exist on the dark web tend to be messaging boards where users are identified by their username or alias, rather than their full name. Many hackers use the message boards to discuss vulnerabilities in security systems and to organize cyber attacks.

If you want to find out more about the dark web, once connected to the TOR network you can visit the 'Hidden Wiki', which is a guide to the dark web: **http://zqktlwi4fecvo6ri.onion**

(However, there are potential risks involved, and I cannot be held responsible for materials located there.)

It's easy to understand why some governments want to control internet usage because we've already seen the effect that it can have. In July 2014, Russia announced a reward of 3.9 million roubles ($110,000; £65,000) for anyone who can who can crack the identity of users of the TOR network. The Arab Spring was a revolutionary wave of demonstrations and protests that began on 18 December 2010 and swept through countries of the Arab League and its surroundings. During it people used social media to organize demonstrations and circumvent state-operated media channels.

In August 2011 the London Riots were said to have been coordinated through social networks.

Incidents like these have led some governments to censor the internet and monitor its use. But, this move towards internet censorship and monitoring has prompted public scandal and opposition. It has also had a knock-on effect on how companies use data to track users and serve advertisements. New social networks have started to appear, such as Ello, which is a social network that claims to never sell user data to advertisers and to never show adverts. There's also Telegram, an alternative to Whatsapp developed by Pavel Durov, who is sometimes described as 'Russia's Mark Zuckerberg' after having launched vkontakte (vk.com, Russia's equivalent to Facebook). Durov stepped down from his company in 2013 amid wide speculation and rumours that he was forced out by the Russian government. His new venture, Telegram, claims to be highly secure and rely on complex encryption algorithms which make it far more difficult for governments to track usage.

Encryption

I believe that we're only at the start of the movement towards greater encryption and protection for user data in social networks. We will see more high-profile incidents and examples of excessive monitoring and censorship of the internet by governments and companies. This will increase the public's interest in internet and social media monitoring and will result in more social networks and platforms being created in order to safeguard free expression and protect user data.

Encryption will be key to this protection. Once data has been highly encrypted, without the password (or key) it takes an enormous amount of computing power to crack. It's possible to encrypt data so strongly that it would take even the most powerful supercomputers in the world years to crack the encryption.

Once social networks have developed their security to a high level it will make it extremely difficult for governments to monitor or censor the internet. This will mean that governments will find it more difficult to control or influence public opinion, which will in turn lead to more transparency, more freedom and thus a more pure form of democracy – what I like to call democracy 2.0. This isn't without risk though, because without effective monitoring it will be easier for terrorists to use encrypted communications to plan attacks. Because of this, encryption and anonymity remain hotly debated.

Identity verification and biometrics

As we discussed in the previous section, one of the issues with social media is that it's easy to hide behind anonymity. Many social networks try to stop users from being anonymous by imposing terms and conditions as well as by asking users to verify their identity by connecting their email address or phone to their account. However, it's easy to circumvent these types of controls. Many governments have ambitions to introduce digital methods for identity verification which, if successful, could even allow voting to take place electronically rather than in a polling station. Estonia is one such government that has already introduced electronic voting which builds on the Estonian ID card.

A secure database will authenticate someone, similar to the way that we authenticate ourselves to gain access to our internet banking. The big difference in the future, however, will be that when it's possible to authenticate someone with 100 per cent certainty, it won't just allow people to withdraw money from their banks, it could also be used to pay for things in shops or to vote in an election and it would mean the end of the dreaded password. There are dangers, however, because if the authentication was hacked, it would make it easy to steal someone's entire identity. If you are a victim of bank fraud, it's a serious matter, but if this form of identity verification could be circumvented it would prove a considerably greater risk. It's dangerous because it represents a single point of failure, a bit like putting all your eggs in one basket.

One new technological development that may go some way to solving the identity verification problem is the use of biochips and biometric data. In theory, biochips or other forms of biometric authentication, such as retina or fingerprint scanning, will make our lives easier. We will no longer need to struggle to remember all of the passwords for our various accounts, instead relying on something unique to us, such as our fingerprint or a microchip embedded under our skin. There have already been trials in Sweden where employees of a company experimenting with biometric authentication offered their employees the chance to get a biochip implanted under their skin. This meant that when performing simple authentication tasks, such as getting into the office or logging into a computer, they didn't need a password or a physical ID card, instead they just needed to swipe their wrist (the place where the biochip had been implanted). Hannes Sjoblad, Chief Disruptive Officer of the Swedish bio-hacking group BioNyfiken, which implanted the chips into the workers told *The Times*: 'We already interact with technology all the time. Today it's a bit messy – we need pin codes and passwords –

wouldn't it be easy to just touch with your hand? We want to be able to understand this technology before big corporates and big government come to us and say everyone should get chipped – the tax authority chip, the Google or Facebook chip.'

There will always be people who try to crack security systems and unfortunately there will always be criminals who won't think twice about killing someone to get at their biochip in order to steal all of their money. If a criminal is capable of killing someone in order to steal their bank cards today, are we to expect that if bank machines start to allow fingerprint scanning that criminals would start cutting off peoples' fingers?

There's no doubt that technology will continue to evolve at a rapid pace but whether or not it will change our lives will depend on the public's readiness to adopt new technologies, such as whether we will allow biochips to be implanted in our bodies. It will also depend on the technology companies' abilities to build security into their systems, products and services from the ground up.

CASE STUDY Risk in action: Silk Road, illegal marketplace on the dark web, shut down by FBI

In October 2013 one of the most infamous black market websites on the TOR network, Silk Road, was shut down by the FBI following a long search to track down its alleged founder, Ross Ulbricht, who went by the alias 'Dread Pirate Roberts'. Ulbricht was convicted on seven counts including narcotics and money laundering in February 2015.

Silk Road was an online black market that offered drugs, weapons, murder-for-hire, stolen credit card numbers and hacking tools, among other things. If you wanted to purchase something illegal, the chances were that it was for sale on Silk Road. Most transactions on the website used crypto-currencies such as Bitcoin in an attempt to keep transactions hidden from the authorities. The site reportedly generated $1.2 billion (£0.8 billion) in sales during the time that it was operational. When Silk Road was shut down, the FBI seized what at the time was around $25 million (£17 million) worth of Bitcoin, which it later put up for auction.

After Silk Road was shut down, it didn't take long for a new illegal market to take its place. Silk Road 2.0 was an almost identical copy of the original Silk Road site, which was also shut down by the FBI. It was reported that it had 150,000 active users and was selling $8 million-worth of banned drugs and other illicit goods a month. The FBI alleged that 26-year-old Blake Benthall from San Francisco was the administrator of Silk Road 2.0, going by the alias 'defcon'.

The scandals around these illegal marketplaces have helped shine a light on the secret world of TOR and have shown that even in a largely secret and anonymous network, the authorities still have ways to track down criminals. But, the authorities have a lot of work to do if they are to stay ahead of the criminals because, as we've seen, if they shut down one site, it doesn't take long for another to take its place.

SOURCES: www.wired.com/2013/11/silk-road/
www.forbes.com/sites/ryanmac/2014/11/06/silk-road-2-blake-benthall-fbi-shutdown/

Resilience and the need for trust

As our lives become more and more connected and our reliance on technology devices and digital systems increases, the need to ensure that these systems are resilient becomes more important. Digital systems need to be available the moment that they are needed. If you go online to book a hotel or a holiday and the website that you choose is unavailable, there is so much choice that you will likely just go to another website to book. The online retailers know this well and invest large amounts of money into keeping their systems available online. A website being offline for even a few seconds can result in a loss of sales. Likewise, if we go to our favourite social network and find that it's not available for some reason, it's likely to cause some annoyance. If it happens more than once, users might turn away to another social network. We become so reliant on many of the online systems we use, and we begin to build trust in those networks. Trust is one of those peculiar values which takes a long time to acquire but can be lost instantly. For example, as I write this, I'm sitting in a coffee shop on my table using web-based software. I love it because all the pages of my book sync between all of my devices automatically. However, it does mean that my entire book is hosted in the cloud on the provider's servers. As this is the final chapter of my book I can tell you that if for some reason their servers experienced a catastrophic issue that resulted in me losing all of my work it's fairly obvious that this would cause me significant pain and result in me losing all trust in them. Yes, I have taken backups (this is a risk and governance book, after all!), but even if I lost access to my work for just a few days I would lose confidence and look for another option.

Businesses rely on their internal systems to be available when they are needed. Many companies rely so heavily on their email system that if it went down, even for an hour, the disruption would be huge. The cost of loss of business and productivity would be massive. Because of this, many companies invest heavily in the resilience of their systems, ensuring that their infrastructure is equipped with redundant drives and servers that will come into action should a hard drive or server fail.

As email usage declines and we begin to rely more on our internal social systems, they too will need increased attention to ensure that they are resilient. In many companies, enterprise social networks are used as one of the primary forms of communication in order to avoid some of the inherent inefficiencies of email when it comes to collaboration. These systems allow teams to work on documents in real-time in a collaborative environment. Therefore, if they became unavailable it would not only stop teams from being able to communicate effectively but would also cut their access to key documents they need. As more and more internal systems start moving to the cloud, companies will experience issues because they are more familiar supporting their legacy systems. Many legacy systems have been around for 20 or 30 years, so there is far more experience within companies and industry about best practice for keeping these systems online, whereas in a cloud environment, there are more opportunities to simply blame the cloud provider.

The internet of things is, at the time of writing, the next 'big thing' that will rock our world. We think that we're pretty connected now, but when our fridges, thermostats, televisions and security systems are connected to the internet, we'll be in an entirely new world with new risks. In 2015 news reports started to emerge that one of Samsung's Smart TVs might be listening to everything that's said in a home and transmitting that information to a third party provider. It's not surprising that both consumers and the media met this news with shock. However, we will see many more cases like this in the future. Until security starts to be 'built in' and designed around technology components from the ground up, we will continue to hear stories about the security risks of internet-enabled devices. Our reliance on these internet-connected systems will undoubtedly continue to grow rapidly and new risks will emerge. There is a lot of talk and hype about 'driverless cars' which, as the name suggests, will drive us around the place like something from a science-fiction movie. But, in actual fact, many driverless car trials have been completed successfully and some states in the United States have permitted driverless cars on the road. It is not going to take long for hackers to target the systems on these vehicles and for news stories to flood the media about tragic accidents or cars having a 'mind of their own'.

Summary

In this chapter we looked at what the future will hold for social media and technology. There's a great deal of opportunity but there's a risk that if businesses don't keep up with the fast-changing technology environment, they will lose competitive advantage and be relegated to the past. The innovators of today may end up being the relics of the past unless they can continue to drive forward, assessing the opportunities and risks and adapting accordingly.

Throughout this book we've looked at the different types of social media risk and taken a deep dive into all the elements that make up good governance. A risk and governance mindset will ensure that your social media and digital projects succeed and safeguard the future of your business.

Social media does have its risks, admittedly. But, it can increase productivity, profitability and build a better workplace. Change isn't always popular, but it's a necessity for business in the modern day. By embracing social media today you'll be building the workplace of tomorrow, and you'll attract and retain the best talent. You'll stand head and shoulders above your competition and be recognized as the leader in our always-connected, digital world. The journey will be challenging at times but the ideas in this book will help you keep your cool, navigate risk and operate social media effectively. The potential benefits of social media are awesome. Embrace it, learn to love it!

FURTHER READING

Financial Conduct Authority (2015) FG15/4 – Social media and customer communications: The FCA's supervisory approach to financial promotions in social media, March 2015. Available from: www.fca.org.uk/news/fg15-04-social-media-and-customer-communications

Gilmore, G (2014) *Social Media Law for Business: A practical guide for using Facebook, Twitter, Google +, and blogs without stepping on legal land mines*, McGraw Hill, United States

Information Commissioner's Office (nd) Guide to data protection. Available from: https://ico.org.uk/for-organisations/guide-to-data-protection/

Levy, P (2014) *Digital Inferno: Using technology consciously in your life and work, 101 ways to survive and thrive in a hyperconnected world*, Clairview Books, West Sussex

Mennie, P (2015) Social Media Risk and Governance. Available from: www.socialmediariskandgovernance.com

PwC (nd) World in beta. Available from: www.worldinbeta.com/

PwC (2015) Data protection and privacy global insights blog. Available from http://pwc.blogs.com/data_protection/

PwC (2015) The data blog: Changing the way you think. Available from http://pwc.blogs.com/analytics_means_business

Scott, P and Jacka, M (2011) *Auditing Social Media: A governance and risk guide*, Wiley, New Jersey

Social Media Leadership Forum (nd) Available from: http://socialmedialeadershipforum.org/

Sollis, B (2015) The Conversation Prism. Available from: http://conversationprism.com/

Stepper, J (2015) Working Out Loud blog. Available from: http://johnstepper.com/

Zetter, K (2011) How digital detectives deciphered stuxnet, the most menacing malware in history, *Wired*, 11 July. Available from www.wired.com/2011/07/how-digital-detectives-deciphered-stuxnet/

INDEX

Page numbers in *italic* indicate figures or tables

advocates and mentors/reverse-mentors 50–55 *see also* case studies: risk in action
   attributes of 53
   engaging the rest of the organization 52–53
   tone from the top 50–52, *51*
   ways of motivating 53–54
Arab Spring 207–08
archiving 11, 80, 190 *see also* data archiving
   laws 29

Binding Corporate Rules (BCRs) 72
biochips/biometric data 11, 209–10
biometric authentication: retina and fingerprint scanning 11
Bitcoin 11, 206–07 *see also* democracy 2.0
budgets/budgeting 37, 50, 54, 89, 100

case studies (for) 4–5
   crisis management
      Greggs bakery logo vandalized 155
      Twitter Q&As backfire 144–45
   cyber security
      2 million passwords stolen and posted online 172
      the SEA targets media outlets 178–79
   data privacy and control
      Raytheon develops predictive analytics platform 67
      UBS 80
   the future: democracy 2.0
      Silk Road: illegal marketplace on the dark web, shut by FBI 210–11
   the future: education
      cyberbullying as cause of teenage suicide 205–06
   governance
      hotel fines for negative reviews 97
      UKIP – sentiment analysis difficulties 102–03
   policy, training and awareness
      US Airways tweets pornographic image 136–37
   regulation
      Netflix SEC disclosure 185–86
   risk
      BP fake Twitter account 24–25
      ChapStick – comment moderation 27–28
   social media
      the power of social media campaigns 4–5
   strategy
      MasterCard #Priceless Surprises 48
      PwC – advocate programme 55
Certified Information Protection Professional (CIPP) certificates 71
change 3, 9, 38, 53, 213 *see also* passwords
   history for policy documents 126, 130
   inevitability of 4
   organizational 157
   process of 120–22, *121*
   response to 13
chapter summaries (for)
   crisis management 158–59
   cyber security 181
   data privacy and control 81–82
   the future and its opportunities 213
   governance 122
   introduction to social media 12
   policy, training and awareness 139
   regulation 194–95
   risk 33–34
   strategy 64
the Cloud 4, 8, 71–72, *73*, 211, 212
   -based servers/systems 33, 68, 72
   and Dropbox 26
compliance when using social media, FCA guidance on (2015) 29
copyright 27, 62, 74, 97–99
   infringement 73
   laws and regulations 191
crisis lifecycle stages: preparation, assessment and analysis, response, prevention *146*, 146
crisis management (and) 38, 140–59 *see also* case studies
   assessing an incident (and) 146–47, 149, *146 see also* crisis lifecycle stages
   crisis severity levels 147, 149, *148*
   reporting a crisis 149

Index

crisis management (and) *cont'd*
  avoidance (through) 143–44
    archiving 144
    availability of tools/applications 143–44
    backups 144
    data protection 144
    security testing 143
    support 144
  crisis testing and simulation 157–58
  implementing a crisis response strategy 149, 151–53, *150*
    checklist for 151
    media materials for 152
    roles, responsibilities and logistics for 153
  planning and preparation (and) 140–45 *see also* case studies
    examples of potential crises 141–42
    human response 142–43
  responding to a crisis (and) 153–57 *see also* case studies
    post-incident review 156–57
    reactive vs proactive communications response 156
crowdsourcing (and) 56–62
  engaging external communities: customer advocacy schemes 60–61
  gamification 58–60 *see also subject entry*
  of ideas: ideation 56–58 *see also* ideation projects
  terms and conditions 61–62
crypto-currencies 11
cyberbullying 11, 203–04, 205–06 *see also* case studies
cyber security (and) 160–81 *see also* cybercrime
  account management (and) 165–72, *167*, *169* c/s 172
    passwords 166–68
    reasons for importance of 165–66, *167*
    two-factor authentication 168–70, *169*
    viruses, spyware and malware 170–71 *see also* malware
  securing your network and data 179–81
    and data classification frameworks 179–80
  social engineering 172–76, 178–79 *see also* case studies
    definition of 172–73
    impersonation 173–74
    phishing/phishing emails 174–76, 178, *175*, *177*
    spear phishing 178

cybercrime 160–65
  key players in 161–63, *161* see also hackers
  and targets at risk 163–65, *163*

the dark web 11, 206–08 *see also* democracy 2.0
data 76–77, *77*, 115, 144
data classification 73–76, *74*
  confidential 75
  exceptional 75
  highly confidential 75
  internal 74
  public 74
data privacy and control 65–82, 131–32 *see also* legislation (EU) *and* legislation (UK)
data management 71–77, *77*
  archiving 76–77, *77*
  classification 73–76, *74 see also* data classification
  storage and transfer 71–73, *73*
  implementing policy and technical controls 77–81 *see also* case studies
    access control within an enterprise social network 80–81
    social risk and compliance tools 78–80, *79*
  privacy and protection 65–71 *see also* case studies *and* privacy policy
    data protection principles 68–69
    law on 65–66
    legal definitions of personal data 69–70
    role of data protection officer (DPO) 70–71
data protection officer, qualifications for 71
data quality (and) 99–105
  data types: structured and unstructured 101, *101*
  definition and importance of 99–100
  sentiment analysis 102 *see also* case studies
  taxonomy and hashtags 103–05, *106*
data visualization tools: QlikView, Tableau, Spotfire 112
definitions (of)
  crisis 140
  data controller 68
  data processor 68
  data subject 68
  Generation Y/millennials 26
  social media 1
democracy 2.0 (and) 206–11 *see also* case studies
  Bitcoin and crypto-currencies 206–07
  the dark web 206–08

Index

encryption 208
evasion of censorship 206–07
identity verification and biometrics 209–11
riots and revolutions 207–08
The Onion Router (TOR) 207
virtual private networks (VPNs) 207
disasters
  Hurricane Sandy 42
  Malaysian Airlines flight 17 (2014) 25
  posting references to 42
driverless cars 212
Dropbox 26
Durov, P 208
  and Telegram social network 208

education (and) 203–06
  age-specific versions of sites 204
  cyberbullying 203–04, 205–06
    see also case studies
  oversharing 204–05
e-mail
  advantages of social collaboration over 199, 201
  decline/demise of 11, 196, 198–99, *200, 202*
  inefficiencies of 201–02
employee effectiveness, social media impact on 26
enterprise social networks 5–9, *7*
  see also social media
Estonia: electronic voting via ID cards 209
ethics 19, 20, 108
  and unethical tactics 20

Facebook 1, 5, 35, 43–44, 192
  and Place Tips service 193
figures
  application change process *121*
  awareness campaign poster *138*
  cloud storage: cross-border data transfer *73*
  Communications 2.0 *202*
  content calendar *41*
  content is king *41*
  crisis lifecycle *146*
  crisis report template *150*
  crisis response process *150*
  crisis severity levels *148*
  cyber security, key players in *161*
  cyber security – what's at risk? *163*
  data archiving *77*
  data classification pyramid *74*
  design for desktop vs mobile *44*
  email vs enterprise collaboration *200*
  images in Tweets *193, 194*
  metrics dashboard *114*
  moderation process flow *95*
  phishing email example *175*
  phishing website example *177*
  process flow diagram symbols *116*
  project management Gantt chart *47*
  risk assessment form *18*
  risk culture pyramid *20*
  risk matrix *15*
  single-factor vs two-factor authentication *169*
  smart phone: multiple accounts on one device *167*
  social media governance framework *90*
  social media posts (example) *136*
  social media regulatory mix *183*
  social media risk, five categories of *23*
  social media risk maturity model *22*
  social media stakeholders *88*
  social media working group dashboard *92*
  social networks explained through doughnuts *46*
  social risk and compliance tool *79*
  structured and unstructured data *101*
  tone from the top *51*
  what is social media? *2*
Financial Conduct Authority (FCA) 29
freedom of speech, safeguarding 11
the future (and) 196–213
  demise of email 198–99, 201–02, *200, 202 see also* email
  democracy 2.0 206–11 *see also* subject entry
  education 203–06 *see* subject entry
  resilience and need for trust 211–12
  social media analytics 196–98 *see also* predictive analytics

gamification 58–60
  legal challenges to 60
  virtual badges 59
  virtual points 58, 59
Gantt chart 46, 48, *47*
Germany
  employee evaluation in 189
  workers' councils in 60
Google Spain, EU Court of Justice ruling against 131
Google+ 5
governance 83–122
  data quality 99–105, *101, 106 see also* subject entry *and* case studies
  metrics and performance indicators 109–15 *see also* subject entry

Index

governance *cont'd*
  moderation   93–99, *95 see also subject entry and* case studies
  monitoring   105–09 *see also subject entry*
  operating procedures   *see* governance: operating procedures
  roles and responsibilities *see* governance: defining roles and responsibilities
governance: defining roles and responsibilities (and/of)   83–93
  approvals and processes   91, 93
  external stakeholders   86–87, *87*
    competitors   87
    customers   87
    investors   87
    media/press   87
    public relations/social media agency   86
    regulator   87
    suppliers   87
  internal stakeholders   84–86
    communications   85
    customer services   85
    human resources   85
    internal audit   86
    IT   85
    knowledge workers   86
    marketing   84
    recruitment   85
    risk, compliance and legal   86
    sales   85–86
  ownership and sponsorship   88–89, *90*
  working groups and oversight   89, 91, *92*
governance: operating procedures   115–22
  change process   120–22, *121*
  checklist for new users   118
  flow diagrams for   115–17, *116*
  leaver process   119–20
  new user process   117
  and User Acceptance Testing (UAT)   121

hackers   162–63
  'black hat'   162
  ethical   162–63
  and hacktivists   162
  professionals for hire   162
  'script kiddies'   163
hacking of Associated Press Twitter account by Syrian Electronic Army   30
hashtag-hijacking   20
hashtags   103–05
human resources (HR)   9, 35, 48, 49, 85, 96, 117
  data   33, 75
  and employment   187–89
  policies   125, 129

ideation projects (and)   56–58
  management override   58
  moderation   57
  review team   57
  stages of   57
information security risks   31–33
  access controls   31–32
  careless employees   32
  third parties   32–33
information technology (IT)   9, 129, 143, 157, 180, 189
  departments   35, 48, 85, 134, 173, 175, 178
  failures   196
  network   143
  outage   30
  purchasing systems   66
  as responsible for enterprise social networks   85
  security/security policies   125, 181, 191
  and social media   49
  system changes   120–21, *121*
  systems   71–72, 80, 131
  team   171
  usage policies   108
International Association of Privacy Professionals   71
internet browsers   43–44
internet of things   212

key performance indicators (KPIs)   100
  categories of: reach, engagement, influence, advocacy   109, 111, *110*

legacy systems   212
legislation (on)
  advertising standards   29–30
  local employment laws   60
legislation (EU)
  on data protection   29, 33
  Data Protection Directive 95/46/EC   65
  General Data Protection Regulation   65, 190
  ruling against Google Spain (EU Court of Justice)   131
  on transfer of data   66
legislation (UK)   109
  Data Protection Act (1998), eight principles of   68–69
legislation (US)   33, 109
  on discoverable information (eDiscovery)   29
LinkedIn   1, 5, 7, 37, 85, 186, 198

malware   170–71
  adware   170
  keyloggers   171

Index

ransomware and Cyrptolocker 170–71
spyware 170
virus 170
metrics and performance indicators (and) 109, 111–13, 115
  categories of KPIs: reach, engagement, influence, advocacy 109, 111, *110*
  false metrics 113, 115
  metric visualization 112–13, *114*
Microsoft 'Most Valuable Professional' programme 60
moderation (and) 93–99
  automatic (using dictionaries of terms) 94–96
  copyright 97–99
  censorship 96 *see also* case studies
  definition of 93–94
  peer 94, *95*
  of social media 27
monitoring (and) 105–09 *see also* social media
  employee use of social media 108–09
  listening 106–07
  listening tools 107

passwords 31, 77–79, 119, 120, 166–69, *169*, 171, 172, 181, 188, 206, 209
Pinterest 1, 5, 39
policy, training and awareness (and) 123–39
  see also privacy policy; social media policy *and* training and awareness
predictive analytics (and) 196–98
  building algorithms for 197–98
  future events 197
  legislation 198
  privacy 198
  use cases for 198
privacy policy 130–34
  purpose of 130–32 *see also* data privacy
  creating an effective 132–34

regulation (and) 182–95
  dealing with character limitations 192–93, *193*
  future of regulation 193–94, *194*
  social media regulation mix *see subject entry*
research on lack of skills as barrier to growth (London First) 205
risk 13–34 *see also* risk categorization *and* risk strategy
  and compliance 17, 35, 62, 86 *see also* social risk and compliance tools
  continuum 17, *18*
  and corporate culture 19–20, *20*
  social media risk categories 14
  social media risk maturity model 21, 23, *22*

risk categorization 23–33, *23*
  information security risks 31–33 *see also subject entry*
  innovation 28
  operational risks 25–27
    and moderation 27
  regulatory compliance risks 29–30
  reputational risks: fake accounts and world events 24–25 *see also* case studies
risk strategy 13–17
  approach to risk 14
  risk assessment 14–17, *15*
Russia 154, 172, 208
  personal data on citizens in 73
  and the TOR network 207

Snowden, E 131, 206
social media 1–12
  analytics 107
  controlling 8–9
  defining 1–2, *2*
  importance of governance and risk management 9–10
  listening and monitoring tools 107
  monitoring employee use of 108–09
  power of 3–5 *see also* case studies
  traditional 5–8
    vs enterprise social networks 5–8, *7*
    key characteristics of 5–6
    profiles 6–7
social media policy 123–30
  checklist for 129–30
  content of 126–29
  language used for 124–25
  location and format of 130
  name of 124
  purpose of 123–24
  structure of 125–26
  top and tail of 126
social media regulation mix 182–92, *183*
  communication 183–85 *see also* case studies
    advertising 183–84
    financial promotions 184–85
    disclosure 185
  data management 190–91
  employment and HR 187–89
    acceptable behaviours and conduct 189
    bullying and harassment 189
    discrimination 187
    employee evaluation 189
    employee monitoring 188
    ownership of social media accounts 188

social media regulation mix *cont'd*
  governance 191–92
  privacy 189–90
  recruitment 186–87
  security 191
social media risk maturity model 33
  five levels of 21, 23, 22
social media: use-cases 36–37
  connecting employees 36–37
  driving engagement 36
  improving customer services 36
  increasing brand visibility 36
  knowledge sharing 37
  promoting products or services 36
  recruitment 37
social risk and compliance tools 17, 21, 31–32, 33, 77, 78–80, 79, 166, 192
stakeholder engagement 48–50
  and budget 50
  communications 49
  customer services 49
  HR 49
  IT 49
  marketing 49
stock markets, social media impact on 30
strategy (and) 35–64 *see also* strategy design
  advocates and mentors/reverse-mentors 50–55 *see also subject entry*
  aligning governance to 62–63
  crowdsourcing 56–62 *see also subject entry*
  designing 35–48
  stakeholder engagement 48–50 *see also subject entry*
strategy design (and) 35–48 *see also* case studies
  content 38–42, *41*
    blogs 39
    infographics 39
    pictures/photos 40
    video 40
  listening 37–38
  mobile vs desktop 42–44, *44*
  purpose of 35–37 *see also* social media: use-cases

targeting networks 45, *46*
time and persistence 45–46, 48, *47*
surveys (on)
  cost of average cyber attacks against large companies in UK in 2014 (PwC) 160
  'Millennials at work: Reshaping the workplace (PwC, 2011) 26
  'NextGen: A global generational survey (PwC, 2013) 26
Sweden (and)
  BioNyfiken and Sjoblad, H 209–10
  trials with biochips for biometric authentication 209

table: KPIs for social networks *110*
The Onion Router (TOR) 11, 207
training and awareness 135–39
  awareness campaigns and ideas 137–39, *138*
  training 135–36, *136 see also* case studies
Twitter (and) 1, 5, 31, 35, 39, 78
  Application Program Interfaces (APIs) 107
  blocked in Turkey 206
  Firehose 107
  Question and Answer (Q&A) events 144–45
  Tweets 192

United States (US)
  Airways 141 *see also* case studies: policy, training and awareness
  Federal Financial Institutions Examination Council 191
  US–EU Safe Harbor 72

voice over IP (VOIP) services 1–2
  Skype 2
  Viber 2

website(s)
  on privacy impact assessments 67
  and responsive web design 44

YouTube 30, 35, 39, 93, 204